D0894319

C153602776

War Child

CHILDREN CAUGHT IN CONFLICT

War Child

Children Caught in Conflict

MARTIN PARSONS

TEMPUS

This book is dedicated to:

*My wife Josephine who has had to put up with my research
into War Children for many years now, and who has often
taken on the role of counsellor to ex-war children who
have phoned at odd times.*
*My close friends the Revd Hugh Ellis, who has not only been
the Chaplain (unpaid) to the Evacuees Reunion Association, but
has always been there when I have needed advice and support,
(usually over a glass of wine or a malt), and his wife Jenny for her
hospitality when I have needed sanctuary and a refuge.*

I am forever grateful.

Cover images: A warden rescues a young boy (Imperial War Museum, D 7895); basic shelter, Hamburg, 1946 (Gollancz Archive, University of Warwick); a child soldier (Reuters).

First published 2008

Tempus Publishing
Cirencester Road, Chalford
Stroud, Gloucestershire, GL6 8PE
www.tempus-publishing.com

Tempus Publishing is an imprint of NPI Media Group

British Library Cataloguing in Publication Data.
A catalogue record for this book is available from the British Library.

ISBN 978 0 7524 4293 8

Typesetting and origination by NPI Media Group
Printed and bound in Great Britain

Contents

List of Illustrations

Preface

In 2003, I was invited to give a key-note address at a War Child conference in Oulu, Northern Finland. I had just got out of my car when a stranger came up to me and introduced herself. She then said, 'I have come a day early to meet you, because if you don't want me here I will go home to Germany.'

I asked, 'Why should I not want you here?'

'Because', she said, 'My father was in the German Army and I am a German war child'.

This comment was made by a very highly intelligent woman who holds two doctorates and who has been instrumental in getting the plight of German War Children recognised. We have since become good friends and often share our knowledge and research. So why have I referred to the occasion? Quite simply it sums up the problems that many war children across Europe have had since 1945, problems which can also be observed in children in modern-day war zones.

Many have taken on the sins of their fathers, many have witnessed scenes and suffered trauma that young children should never encounter. The vast majority experienced the sadness of separation, first from their own parents and relatives and second from the hosts who had looked after them. In many instances they have failed to come to terms with the short- and long-term effects of war-child separation and have passed their concerns and anxieties onto subsequent generations within their families.

This encounter was just one example. Other war children have problems which are very complex … few escaped. Manifestations can be as simple as not wishing to say goodbye, to the other extreme of being unable to form long-term relationships, having a long history of alcohol addiction, and reclusive behaviour. And let us not forget those children in present-day war zones who are separated from families, ostracised from their communities and have little hope for the future.

I often get asked why I research into War Children. The reasons given by my interrogators as to why I shouldn't are usually the same. One ex-government minister asked me, 'Why waste your time researching into war children? You won't get compensation for them you know. I don't consider it to be a waste of time. For too long the effects of war on children have been neglected and I am not seeking compensation for their trauma, nor would the war children I have interviewed over the years expect me to do so.

Many times I have been told, 'But they were only children and there were more important things going on at the time,' forgetting of course that these children were to be the next generation.

Another: 'They were only children, they'll grow out of it!' Sorry to disappoint … but they don't.

There is enough interdisciplinary evidence to suggest that War Trauma goes through three generations. So my grandchildren will be the last generation affected by the war. That's fine if the Second World War was the last war to take place. But as you are reading this there are thirty-one major conflicts going on in the world. All of these war zones contain children and if they are passing on the effects for three generations then that will take us into the twenty-second century.

As with my other works on war children, I could not have done this without the help and co-operation of ex-war children and researchers around the world, some of whom have become good friends: James Roffey in England, Pertti Kaven in Finland, Dr Helga Spranger in Germany, Gonda Scheffel-Baars in the Netherlands, Prof. Baard Borge in Norway, Kai Rosnell in Sweden, Prof. Steven Trout and Prof. Sue Saffle in the USA and Prof. Marina Gulina in Russia. It has not only been a privilege to work with them over the years and be able to contribute to each other's research, but also to share some of their experiences, both as war children and in their ensuing years as adults. I would also like to thank my daughter Hannah, Jan Hamblin and Steve Haley for proof-reading the original draft.

If they forgive me I must single out two people who have influenced my work over the past few years.

The first was the late Prof. Singa Sandelin-Benko, herself a war child, who, having heard me give a key-note address in Mikkelli in Finland in 2000, persuaded me to work with her and widen my personal research brief by incorporating children in other European war zones. As a result, we collaborated on a pilot study and were about to develop a very detailed comparative research programme on the long-term effects of Finnish and British war children, when her untimely death in 2006 halted proceedings, temporarily I hope.

The second is Dr Peter Heinl. As one of the few historians working in this field, it soon became apparent that in order to fully understand the problems that war children have gone through, and are indeed going through, I needed a better understanding of the psychological effects of their experience. Therefore, I am truly indebted to Peter, who as the world's leading expert on war-related trauma in children, has guided me through the complexities of psychotherapy techniques, not only through his groundbreaking book *Splintered Innocence*, which is a 'must' read for anyone attempting to understand what war children went through, but also in observing his practical support sessions with ex-war children. It is really awe inspiring to see a 'master' at work. Many war children owe their present peace of mind to his ministrations. For me it has been a tremendous, but nonetheless enjoyable, learning curve!

You will notice that within the book I have not looked at the Jewish children of the Second World War. This is a huge topic in its own right and it has been ably covered by eminent historians, Sir Martin Gilbert, Dan Bar-On, Nicholas Stargardt and Lynn Nicholas to name just a few. It would therefore be very difficult for me to add to the debate in just one chapter.

Remember when reading this book that the main characters were, at the time, children, and in those chapters dealing with modern war zones … the victims *still are* children.

Introduction

Adults go to war, but they don't realise what they are doing to the children.[1]

There are people who cannot look forward until they have looked back, and that's very important. Having a wife, children and grandchildren may be wonderful, but it does not take away the pain, it does not fill that enormous loss and void in one's life.[2]

In 1900, Ellen Kay, a Swedish educationalist and author, declared that the twentieth century would be the 'Century of the Child'.[3] In reality it was to be a century in which children all over the world would be drawn into two world wars, civil unrest, sectarian violence and acts of terrorism. In some cases, as in some countries in Africa, they would become pawns of both local war lords and national armies. In others, like Spain (1936-39) and Argentina (1976-83), they simply vanished because of the political persuasion of their parents. In Argentina, an estimated 20,000-30,000 people were imprisoned, tortured, killed or disappeared. A policy best summarised by General Saint Jean, military commander of Buenos Aires who stated that, '… First we kill all the subversives, then we will kill their collaborators, then their sympathisers, then those who remain indifferent and finally the indecisive'.[4] Victims included suspected terrorists or dissidents including Marxists, Communists, and those who held liberal views on theology. The scope of those caught up in the atrocities was all-encompassing, and included others who worked with the poor, those who were members of trades unions, students who belonged to political organisations, as well as journalists, lawyers, academics, doctors and psychiatrists. Among them were pregnant women and small children, many of whom were given to other families to raise. Those babies born to women in captivity were handed over to men with links to the military.[5]

In post-Tito Yugoslavia, those with few humanitarian principles took the opportunity to gain control of the country and children, trained to use knives and guns, were used as innocent killers, after all who would notice a child. According to Boro Pandurevic, '... after a while, if a Muslim wanted to kill a Serb, or a Serb wanted to kill a Muslim, no one cared. So it came about that people of other ethnicities were not considered human, even when they had once been personal friends'.[6] As a result of what many people experienced, there will be evidence of psychological trauma among the population of Sarajevo for years to come. The Head of Psychiatry at Sarajevo Hospital, Dr Ismet Ceric, was quoted as saying:

> ... You can see many pathologically disturbed people on the streets, lots of full-blown psychosis and depression. Almost everyone is suffering from stress-related disorders, including the professionals, including myself ... people have shattered identities ... it is hard to explain what happened to people's minds during this trauma when there was no real or emotional protection for an exceptionally long period of time.[7]

There seems to be no break in a circle of violence and war-related trauma, which research reveals spans three generations.[8]

Post-Second World War children across Europe became 'invisible' and a veil was drawn over war child issues, sometimes, as in the UK, where the words Civilian Evacuation were removed from common parlance in March 1946, as part of a national strategy. In others it was simply a question of burying heads in the sand and apportioning blame elsewhere. And after all they were only children who would grow out of it ... wouldn't they? Unfortunately this is still an opinion held by many who question, sometimes very vehemently, why academics continue with the research into war children and not just leave it all alone.

At the end of the Seond World War, an estimated 13 million European children were facing severe poverty, malnutrition and destitution. Children were homeless and stateless. Some were kidnapped or deported, identities were changed. But none of this was new. The case of the disappearing Spanish children has only recently become an important issue as the grandchildren of the victims have begun to ask questions about the Civil War.

And it was only in 2000, when the Catalan government agreed to compensate those who had been imprisoned or had been deprived of their civil liberties during the Franco regime, that the treatment and institutionalised brutality that went on at the time, often with the blessing of the Catholic Church, came into the public domain.[9] In post-Civil War Spain the policy of 'Hispanisation' centred on the names of the children of Republican prisoners being changed to popular invocations of the Virgin Mary in order to eradicate their previous existence.[10]

In immediate post-war Berlin, an estimated 53,000 children were considered 'lost'. There were 49,000 orphaned children in Czechoslovakia, 60,000 in the Netherlands, 200,000 in Poland and nearer 300,000 in Yugoslavia. In Rome, the Quirinale gardens became the known gathering place for Italian children who were homeless, parentless and suffering from the physical and mental consequences of their war-time experiences.[11]

Some children were psychologically, physically and sexually abused. Many lived off their wits by scavenging, prostitution or taking an active role in the post-war black market. As late as 1950, UNESCO[12] used the term 'War-Handicapped Children'[13] to describe this vast horde of children who were not only seen as requiring help, but also as a possible threat to the future stability of a peaceful post-war world. This was very apparent in some countries, especially those territories previously held under the Reich, who continued to view the war children with suspicion and subjected them to abuse and harassment into the twenty-first century.

So what have we learned over the intervening years about war children?

Firstly it is very difficult to define what a war child actually is … is it one who is directly involved in the fighting, one who is affected by the loss of home, family, culture etc. or one who is exposed to the ravages of war or civil unrest? In Norway and Denmark the word 'war child' means a child who has a German father, in Finland a child evacuated to Sweden, in parts of Africa, a child who is affected by war and those recruited as active participants. Whatever the definition is, one thing that can be said for certain is that whatever the circumstance, the child is the innocent and invisible victim. To paraphrase a statement made by Dr Peter Heinl in his book *Splintered Innocence*, it does not matter whether the children were on the side of the victors or the losers (and one could debate whether anyone ever wins a war), they were, are, and sometimes *remain* the sufferers.

Wars have been going on in history forever, and little attention has been paid to the suffering of children caught up in conflicts until the latter part of the twentieth century, and one could suggest that it is not insignificant that many of the eminent researchers in this field were war children themselves who witnessed and experienced first-hand conflict-related trauma.

Independent research would indicate that war children suffer from long-term effects related to their experience. However, this is often shrouded in media generalisations and it is important to remember that the actual effect depends very much on the individual themselves. For example, what was considered to be a traumatic experience by one would not necessarily be defined that way by another. Some evacuees in the UK were treated in a much more loving and caring way by their hosts than they were by their own families, and at the end of the war some did not want to go *home* to possibly abusive situations. Whereas Ann Parkinson (pseudonym) personalises the evacuation issue and describes the whole process as one of internal guilt: 'What you hope for is not to be treated cruelly and beaten, and made to feel even worse about yourself. Your "circumstances" are already a deep dark, mystery and there is a tremendous guilt that you have done something dreadful to have been rejected by your parents.'[14]

Many of the children have suffered from guilt, and they have found their lives debilitated by experiences they witnessed or even participated in at the time. Recent research into war babies has shown that many are very insecure, resulting in multi-marriages or multi-relationships from which, when it comes to making a commitment, they shy away. Some like Dorothy Cherniko found it difficult to make friends and she described her problems as '... Far worse than evacuation was the terrible longing to just belong to somebody'.[15]

Others cannot relate to their own children. A post-war child migrant to Australia under the Jesuit Scheme who later became a mother described her feelings for her son:

> I found it very hard to put my arms around him. If I give myself, I think, what is going to happen? Will he be taken away from me? I can love my dog and show him affection, but with a human being it is different. Even today, when I see my son ... I don't hug him.[16]

She went on to explain that this was because of the brutality she had suffered as a child.

Raelene Houlihan describes a situation which is often forgotten about, but one which must have affected, and still affects many war children, and another which spans the generations: 'I found I had to teach myself mothering, because you didn't have any mother roles in the orphanage; you had no one to demonstrate love, or to teach you the basics about loving someone without placing yourself in a dangerous situation ...'

Some who have married and have had families of their own have passed on their personal anxieties to their children and in some cases their grandchildren. This three-generational phase had also been noted in the work done by the late Professor Singa Sandelin-Benko with Finnish war children. There are war children in Finland whose mothers suffer from untreated traumas based on brutalities towards their family during the civil war in Finland in 1918.

What is also apparent is the position of the child within the family. In many cases where they were the only sibling evacuated, they had nothing in common with the rest of their family when they returned from the reception areas. This was noticeable in Finland where many of those who had gone to Sweden had lost their native language. Veikko Olkinuora from Finland says that 'my childhood ended when coming back to Finland as a 7-year old boy'. Veikko was sent to Sweden at the age of two. Similar problems occurred with some of the 40,000 Spanish children who had been sent to France and were unable to communicate with their family on their return. Where the former was the case, many resorted to what would be regarded today as simple attention-seeking behaviour to gain favour again within the family unit. Many ex-war children have recalled how their stories about their war-time experiences (either good or bad) were largely ignored by family and friends. They were often told, 'While you were away we had to suffer the bombing', or similar accounts. Some were introduced to their neighbours as 'S/he is my evacuee ... just come back', rather than 'this is my daughter/son who has just returned ... isn't it good to see him/her again', or some such encouraging phrase.

Some found it so difficult to settle, that on leaving school they returned to their reception areas where they felt more at home.

Many war children in Finland returned to their foster homes in Sweden immediately it became possible. For some, the last sixty years has been a time of searching ... either for a home, an education or a childhood. One woman told me that she seems to have been locked into the mind-set of a seven-year-old because she has been unable to cope with the pressures of adulthood. For her, it has been a source of escapism from the stresses of what she defines as the real world.

In Britain, class issues underpinned the government planning of the Evacuation Scheme and it was seen by some in authority as a way of controlling the expected panic of the 'working classes'.[17] Even today, textbooks still talk about the working-class children from the deprived areas of the cities being taken in by middle-class families in the countryside, when we now know that the major responsibility for billeting evacuees fell on the working and labouring classes. We still read about the verminous condition of the evacuees, the fact that they were all bed-wetters, that they did not know what a knife and fork was used for, and were generally ungrateful. Most of which is untrue … but it makes a good story. What is missing in these accounts, usually limited in the textbooks to two sides of A4, are the effects that the scheme had on the children at the time and since. And not only on the evacuees, one must also remember that the children within the reception areas also suffered because of shared schooling and overcrowding. It is also easy to forget the effect that the return of the evacuees had on the foster parents, some of whom were childless, who after many years had to give up the children they had lovingly cared for as their own.[18] Little is said about the breakdown of family relationships, sibling rivalry both during and after the war, or the possible return from a loving, caring foster home to a domestic situation where abuse was the norm. And there is the problem of those children who spent their formative years overseas in a different culture, to return to post-war austerity Britain.

What about children in other war zones? Few textbooks in British schools mention war children in other countries or describe their plight as often innocent bystanders caught up in regimes they had no control over, or situations not of their making. Too little is known and written about the terrible sufferings of Russian children in the besieged city of Leningrad during 1941–43, the effects on the children of collaborators, on those who defied the Nazis, and those who became stateless. One also needs to consider the children on mainland Europe who grew up among the bomb sites of towns and cities razed to the ground by bombing, the cities that were 'torched' during the Soviet advance westwards and the streams of refugees and destitute seeking shelter, and those who witnessed the atrocities.[19] Unfortunately it is the willingness to largely disregard this research that means that the problems of children in present war zones are largely ignored by those who find it convenient to do so.

The purpose of this book is to bring the information and up-to-date research of the study of war children into the public domain.

Martin Parsons, 2008

1

Myth Making

Memory is a vast hall in which the whole treasure of our perception and experiences is laid up.[1]

When studying the topic of war children it is important to remember that, setting aside the written documentary evidence available to the academic student, a great deal of what is known about the Second World War experiences, and to some extent those in present-day war zones, has been handed down through the generations as oral testimony. As such, there is a temptation that some of this testimony, together with gaps of knowledge and selective reporting, eventually creates a 'myth'.

Both the terms 'History' and 'Myth' share at least one common meaning in ancient Greek, the sense of discourse or narration, with significantly different implications; 'Mythos' that of 'project, plot and tale' and 'Isortia' that of 'search, interrogation and examination'.[2] This reliance on oral testimony is still very evident today. Over the past decade it has been 'open season' on 'Veterans', in all the countries that took an active part in the Second World War, who have been asked by many people, especially the media, to relate their memories about Dunkirk, the Battle of Britain, evacuation and homecoming, among many others. This in turn has led to further interest in the audio and visual media, book publications and commemorative ephemera. Dealing in war reminiscences has been so commercially productive that some of the events have been celebrated every year, rather than on the major, significant anniversaries. For example, having previously had a day dedicated to the sixtieth anniversary of the Dunkirk evacuations in 2000, a local

BBC radio station had another one four years later simply because of the rise in listener numbers during the VE anniversary broadcasts in the previous month. The producers of many adult television documentaries and schools' broadcasts, both in the UK and in Germany, place a heavy reliance on oral evidence, often using unsubstantiated testimony of ex-evacuees and war children interspersed within the programmes to either give them credibility or purely for illustrative purposes. If one accepts that much of the accessible history of this period is reliant on first-hand accounts and reporting, should the time in which the material was, or is gathered, affect our understanding or use of it? When using and analysing oral history one needs to ask a very simple question: Are memories collected today from ex-evacuees and war children talking about events which happened almost seventy years ago, more, or less, valid than the information collected at the time? Generally speaking, why do historians give more weight to the collection of data by, for instance, Mass Observation, than to a book written in 1990 by A.N. Other who was a billeting officer in the Welsh valleys? It comes down to a very simple answer. Many people would consider that the interviews of Mass Observation, ostensibly dealing with social realism, were carried out at the time of, or immediately after, the events were taking place, by people paid to do the job. They were not affected by personal ideals or philosophies, and they recorded the information verbatim, whereas, on the other hand, individual remembrances can be affected by many external factors. These can include: how good a memory the person has; whether or not they had positive or negative personal experiences; particular personal axes to grind; a perception of what could have happened rather than what actually happened; and the influence of indoctrination and authoritarian regimes. Many would argue that although the former may be considered more useful, the latter's account can still be used because it can be refuted or substantiated by access to other sources. Surely, the same can apply to both. One cannot consider that the Mass Observation material related to evacuation is any better than the ex-billeting officer. The whole project, and his role within it, had to be influenced by what was going on at the time. Another valid reason is that a lot of the Mass Observation work can now also be viewed from a different perspective in the light of new evidence gathered since their interviews first took place. The lifting of restrictions on Government papers allows us to relate the personal information to the wider picture. To take either example at face value would be equally problematical. This is where the difficulty lies in reporting the facts of this period, especially in the perpetuation of the same facts and stories in school textbooks and novels. Despite access to new evidence, the substantiation of information and data is often overlooked purely because of space restrictions within the text.

The recent resurrection of this aspect of historical evidence has led to a certain amount of obsession with the minutiae of everyday life of the period(s) in question, being described and expressed by the interviewees. According to Samuel and Thompson, in the introduction to a series of essays on Oral History, by doing this 'we reintroduce the emotionality, the fears and fantasies carried by the metaphors of memory which historians have been so anxious to write out of formal accounts'.[3] They go on to suggest that the individuality of each life becomes a vital document of the construction of consciousness, and emphasises both the variety of experience in any social group, and how each individual draws on the experience of a common culture. There is enough data to suggest that despite what Samuel and Thompson say, historians have not been anxious to write out 'oral experiences'. In fact, as evidence from the textbooks used in schools would indicate, where there is a definite policy of using oral material, the opposite would seem to be the truth. The problem remains however, that the discussion of the finer points is often being done without any recourse to any substantive supporting evidence.

Another potential problem that historians have to deal with when working with people who are retelling their personal experiences, is the *reliance* one can place on memory. If one takes it as read that memories play an important part in history of any kind, especially the last seventy years,[4] and whatever one tries to do, or how objective one tries to be, we cannot escape from them, we at least need to consider the differences between 'History' and 'Memories'. According to Samuel, memory and history are often placed in opposite camps. The first comes naturally to mind and the second is the product of analysis and reflection. Memory tends to be subjective and relies on concrete images whereas History is objective and has the power of abstraction.[5] Le Goff states, 'just as the past is not history but the object of history, so memory is not history, but one of its objects and an elementary level of its development'.[6]

Memories are fundamental to all individuals and need to be recognised as such if we are to put them in their proper place within any historical study. One thing we need to consider is that memory is very selective in what it retains and discards. This selective amnesia, as Freud would put it, can be just as important to historians using oral history as a means of gathering evidence, as that which is gleaned from what has been said. However, it is only really useful if the historian in question is able to see the omissions for what they are. Perhaps we need to take on the role of psychoanalysts. This is not to suggest that historians become psychotherapists, but that they learn to listen more effectively and become able to contextualise the thoughts, opinions and memories of individuals and interpret their value and work accordingly. This is difficult enough for some historians to come to terms with, therefore it stands to reason that in the hands of non-specialists, including history teachers who do not have the skill or knowledge to con-textualise oral testimony used in the classrooms or reproduced in books and other resources, the validity of this information is open to question and can become very confusing and misleading to pupils and students.

There is another aspect that one also needs to consider. Samuel suggests that history itself involves a series of erasures, emendations and amalgamations where the unconscious mind, splitting, telescoping, displacing and project-ing, transposes incidents from one time register to another and materialises thoughts into imagery.[7] As individuals one remembers the good things and the bad things and those which in some way have had a profound effect on one's life. Therefore, a simple basic requirement of anybody engaging in this form of evidence gathering is to remember that generalised memories can become over-inflated in their perceived importance. For example, as children the school holidays seemed to be endless, the summers were warmer, the winters were colder and the houses we lived in and the schools we attended were bigger. Also, the juxtaposition of personal and national histories are often displaced, and together with event sequences often being telescoped into moments of personal experience, lead, not necessarily to false account-ing, but more of a misconstruction of time, place and event. By their very nature and selectivity these memories can soon become part of an individu-al's or nation's biographical psyche and develop into 'Myths'. According to Jean Peneff, the mythical element in people's reminiscences and life stories is the 'pre-established framework within which the individuals explain their personal history; the mental construct which, starting from memory of indi-vidual facts, would otherwise appear incoherent and arbitrary, goes on to arrange and interpret them and turn them into biographical events'.[8]

Without necessarily realising it, myths are used to great effect today by: advertisers when implying that a certain commodity is not as it should be but is better and more effective than anything equivalent on the market; the tab-loid press which will criticise, praise or denigrate individuals or government policies etc.; and other media readily available to the mass of the population. Therefore, if, in these so-called enlightened times, one is still swayed and influenced by such propaganda statements, it is little wonder that in the age of limited mass media and a certain amount of government control of information relating to the Second World War, myths based on distorted memories, ignorance, hearsay and rumour abounded. Serious concern was expressed by A.J. Cummings in an article entitled simply 'Propaganda'. His views, written in 1937, were very much ahead of their time and he saw it as a 'nascent evil'. He wrote:

> ... this branch of public service has become so much a common-place of civilised society that it has intruded itself upon every form of human activity ... Probably we are only seeing the beginnings of organised propaganda. One can only speculate uneasily about its future. It may yet rule the world with a rod of iron ... Government inspired propaganda will be a major horror of the next war ... Even in peacetime it behoves those of us who care about democratic freedom to be vigilant.[9]

However, myths and memories, if explored objectively, can be potentially useful to historians. They can raise important and hitherto unforeseen questions that may in turn lead to further detailed study of an historical event or perspective. If we concur that in this field of study many of the myths have been based on oral or propaganda material, historians need to be aware of under what circumstances the original myths have been constructed and transmitted and how they might have been adapted and changed to suit the individual, group or nation.

In order to use them effectively as a basis for further study, one should assume that myths are not necessarily false, but based upon an experience of some kind which may underpin them. One also needs to remember that myths and memories can be historically conditioned and in some cases 'establishment induced' in the same way as history can be revised to suit the spirit of the age and subsequent generations. Examples would include 'The Dunkirk Spirit', originally related to the role of the little boats, but which, sixty-seven years on, is still a label attached to any event which demands stoicism from the population, be it local or national, floods, fire, bombs etc. To overcome this, students studying the topic of war and war children, at whatever level, need access to resources which can either refute or substantiate the myths or at least explain the rationale behind them.

Mythological details can be confusing when they have not been contextualised, and many myths related to the British and German home fronts in the Second World War were instigated either deliberately to confuse the enemy, as well as the resident population in some cases, or to keep up morale and explain away any negativity. In Britain, some propaganda developed as a result of a government fear that 'the lower classes would be unreliable and defeatist', and in Germany as a result of maintaining the pretence that the country was winning the war, despite heavy bombing and civilian losses.

It is too easy to take the study of war children at face value simply because the negative aspects are often 'removed' as a result of the victors writing the subsequent history. When new information becomes available that questions the original theories and understanding, those who have either lived through the experience, or have been subjected to the propaganda, are often greatly affected by the situation and can go into 'denial'. What they have believed in and hung onto for individual security and justification has now been removed and to some extent they no longer have the foundation on which they have created their lives. How they react depends very much on the strength of the person concerned and is very much a part of the long-term effects surrounding the war-child experience.

2

British Evacuation:
The Reality

To be torn up from the roots of home life, to be sent away from the family circle, in most instances for the first time in a child's life, was a painful event.

This was no social experiment; it was a surgical rent only to be contemplated as a last resort. ... From the first day of September 1939 evacuation ceased to be a problem of administrative planning. It became instead a multitude of problems in human relationships.[1]

It is worth pointing out at the very beginning that the Evacuation Scheme in the UK was not a question of moving people from areas of danger to areas of safety, but more of a plan to remove people from areas of 'perceived danger' to areas of 'relative safety'. In fact, as we shall see, some people were moved to areas that were more likely to be hit by enemy bombing than where they lived in the first place.

The Evacuation Scheme of 1939-45 was not the first civilian evacuation to be planned. In fact it was the third. The first had taken place at Wareham in Dorset in 1803, when the threat of a French invasion was at its greatest. A scheme was created to ensure the safe removal of population, livestock, food, vehicles and anything likely to be of use in a national emergency.[2] A document issued in Dorchester on 17 August 1803 by the Lord Lieutenant of Dorset, extended the plans to a wider area.[3] The second came in 1938 during the Munich Crisis when 30,000 people were moved out of south London. The Evacuation Scheme implemented in September 1939 had been planned by an Evacuation sub-committee of the Imperial Defence Committee as early as 16 February 1931. It was given the remit to introduce a scheme which would 'prevent panic flight and create an orderly exodus from London in the event of war'. According to Titmuss, it was designed as 'A military expedient, a counter move to the enemy's objective of attacking and demoralising the civilian population'.[4]

However, these hypothetical plans were pure conjecture and not based on any concrete research, but on assumptions of how any future war might be conducted.

On 10 November 1932, in a speech to the House of Commons, Stanley Baldwin stated:

> I will not pretend that we are not taking precautions in this country. We have done it. We have made our investigations much more quietly and hitherto without any publicity, but considering the years that are required to make our preparations, any government of this country in the present circumstances of the world would have been guilty of criminal negligence had they neglected to make their preparations.[5]

A statement made by Winston Churchill in the Commons on 28 November 1934 provides us with an indication of the numbers expected to be caught up in any future evacuations from London. Although the final figures were nothing like the ones projected here, they were used to underpin the planning of future committees. It is also worth bearing in mind that these did not include evacuations from any other city or area of danger.

> … We must expect that under pressure of continuous air attack upon London, at least 3,000,000 or 4,000,000 people will be driven out into the open country around the metropolis. This vast amount of human beings, numerically far larger than any armies which have been fed and moved in war, without shelter and without food, without sanitation and without special provision for the maintenance of order would confront the government of the day with an administrative problem of the first magnitude, and would certainly absorb the energies of our small army and our territorial force. Problems of this kind have never been faced before, and although there is no need to exaggerate them, neither, on the other hand, is there any need to shrink from facing the immense, unprecedented difficulties which they involve.[6]

In fact we can now see, with the benefit of hindsight, that the first evacuation scheme initiated in September 1939 turned out to be a mass exodus before the event!

The planning and implementation of the evacuation programme was made the responsibility of the Anderson Committee, named after its chairman Sir John Anderson,[7] which was established after continued interest by MPs demanding an explanation about any proposed evacuation scheme. The Air Raid Precaution Bill of November 1937 had made no mention of evacuation, although after pressure from some MPs for the inclusion of a clause dealing with the matter, an amendment was tabled to make local authorities responsible for dealing with questions of evacuation. However, this was resisted by the Home Secretary who said: 'The Committee for Imperial Defence is actively engaged upon this problem. We already have certain plans in existence. We intend to make them more comprehensive and we shall have them ready for the emergency ... we have the question of evacuation firmly in our minds'.[8]

By the time the Bill had reached the committee stages the Home Secretary had already made a concession and introduced a new clause which made it the duty of all local authorities to provide information to the Government for the purpose of assisting the preparation of any evacuation scheme. However, he maintained that the Government should remain as the co-ordinating body.

This policy was reinforced in the Board of Education Circular 1461 issued in January 1938 which stated that: '... in areas which were so exposed to danger that it would be decided to close schools during the whole period in which raids might be expected, the ideal solution would be evacuation and the difficulties of such a scheme should not prevent its consideration'.[9]

Initially, Local Authorities were advised to contact the Home Office for help in preparing schemes, but it soon became clear that this lack of direction in shifting responsibility to Local Authorities was creating a great deal of confusion, and a later Circular, No.701262/8, issued by the Home Office on 28 March 1938, instructed them not to prepare any plans at all until told to do so by the Home Secretary.[10]

On 12 May 1938 the Government refused to initiate a billeting survey stating that the problem of evacuation was being studied. Later in the same month, in defiance of Government advice and having received a number of requests to act, the London County Council approved the principle of evacuating school children.

The Anderson Committee first met in Committee Room 13 of the House of Commons on Friday 27 May 1938. Its terms of reference were: '... to examine the problem of the transfer of persons from areas which might be exposed to continuous air attack and to recommend plans for the purpose'.[11]

Among its first responsibilities was the need to divide the country into three categories: Evacuation Areas (from where it would be necessary to move the population), Reception Areas (thought to be safer areas where people could be moved to), and Neutral Zones (areas of no strategic importance, and not considered to be in danger, where people would not be evacuated to or from). According to Titmuss over 200 Local Authorities in England and Wales designated as Reception Areas asked for their classification to be changed to Neutral and a further sixty Authorities, above those already listed, wanted to be classified as Evacuation Areas.[12] No Authority on the Evacuation list argued with the Ministry of Health's decision and no Authority asked to be a reception area.[13] The final register was not completed until January 1939, by which time the Government had decided to transfer all responsibility for the implementation of any evacuation scheme to the Health Departments. They had taken over officially on 14 November 1938, and Sir John Anderson was given a new role of co-ordinating the whole area of Civil Defence.

The Anderson Committee made sure that priority was immediately given to London, thought to be a prime target, and elements of specific detailed planning were also considered.

a. To what extent were there vital activities which must be kept going.
b. The conditions under which public order could be controlled.
c. Transportation.
d. The necessity to feed and house those evacuated so Government departments concerned, i.e. Food, Health, the Board of Trade etc. could be consulted.

The Committee felt that it might be necessary to work out two schemes, one for an orderly evacuation and the other for a sudden emergency. Under the former, known as plan 2, 13 million people were in designated Evacuation Areas, 14 million in Neutral Zones and 18 million in Reception Areas. The Committee also suggested that they should investigate how the French proposed to evacuate Paris should the need arise.[14]

Alarmingly, by January 1939, a report to the Home Defence sub-committee of the Committee of Imperial Defence on 'The State of Readiness of the Civil Defence' concluded that 'Evacuation plans are, at present, very backward'.[15]

3

The Anderson
Committee Discussions

You must have been a very naughty boy. My Mum and Dad would never
send me away to live with strangers.[1]

Whatever historians and ex-evacuees say about the Evacuation Scheme
in the UK, it has to be recognised as one of the most intense logistical
exercises ever seen in this country. Not only did it involve Government
ministers and departments, but it also required the co-operation of legislative groups down to Parish Council level, the takeover of the transport
networks, and the compliance of all those taking part in the Scheme in both
the Evacuation and Reception Areas.

On 30 May 1938, at the second meeting of the Anderson Committee,
members had to consider two basic yet important details regarding the
evacuation, which now tend to be forgotten as most people consider evacuation to be just the movement of the children and non-combatants:

What were considered to be the danger zones in London?

What essential industries would have to continue during a time of war?

There is a tendency to ignore the fact that life within the country had
to go on despite the possibility of war. Although the UK was put on war-
footing, industries providing essential 'home-front' materials, such as power,
needed to be kept going. The committee decided to put their energies into
planning for London, being the prime target, and then replicating their
plans to other cities within the country. As a result, the Greater London area
was divided into three distinct areas:

1. Evacuation, if possible, from an area encompassing Hammersmith to Dagenham and Holloway to Dulwich.
2. A wider area of restricted movement.
3. An outer ring which would receive hospital patients.

The main concerns underlying this plan were as follows.

There was an expectation within some government departments that the *working classes* would lose their nerve and stream out of London. Newsreels showing the Spanish Civil War and the raids on Madrid and Guernica had provided evidence, it was thought, that a similar situation would arise in the UK if and when bombs started falling. As a consequence the plans were designed to facilitate an exodus which, to some extent, the Committee felt would take place anyway and therefore ought to be regulated and controlled. The hidden agenda with regards the evacuation could therefore be seen as simply controlling the panic. It has to be noted that in the event there was little evidence of panic, in fact quite the opposite. It was also important that some men who were essential to vital industries would not be lost to the national effort but would be able to continue to work in the safer zones.[2] The Committee worked on the basis that between 3 and 4 million people would have to be moved out of the city within seventy-two hours, and in order for this to work, they would have to rely heavily on the efficiency and co-operation of the Railway Network.[3]

There was a need for the Government to implement this plan as soon as tension began rather than wait until war was declared.[4]

It was not until the third meeting that the Committee concentrated on the specific evacuation of children. Although they, and representatives from the London County Council Education Committee, felt that the overall responsibility for this lay with the Government, they did agree that many teachers already had experience of moving large numbers of pupils from their schools to major events.[5] In order for the Scheme to be effective it was felt necessary for the Committee to liaise closely with the teachers and their professional bodies. The National Union of Teachers had already been approached in January 1938 when Circular 12461 'ARP in Schools' was being drawn up, so a degree of co-operation had already been established.

On 4 June 1938, the National Union of Teachers executive passed a resolution stating:

> That the executive of the NUT, while not subscribing to any suggestion that war is inevitable,[6] is prepared to co-operate with the Government and Local

Authorities in making plans for the safety of school children as effective as possible, and to recommend its members in the local areas to consider the desirability of co-operating on a voluntary basis.

The NUT regarded themselves as duty-bound to co-operate with the Government, even though some of the decision-making was beyond their control. Any discussion relating to the movement of children inevitably included the question of the evacuation of teachers.[7] On a number of occasions, members of the NUT were asked if they felt that teachers would leave their own families. If not, the Committee asked whether it could be organised so that teachers with family commitments were not employed in the Scheme. As it turned out, most teachers from the Evacuation Areas, with families or not, *were* involved in the evacuation, including those who were recalled from the profession either because they had retired, or in the case of some women, those who had to leave their jobs when they got married.[8]

The discussions at this point centred on those which were similar to the concerns within the German evacuation scheme, the role of the parents and how to convince them that evacuation was the best option. Even members of the same Union had differing opinions. Sir Fred Mander, General Secretary of the NUT, said that it would be impossible to launch a scheme of compulsory evacuation of school children because it would not be practical to override parental responsibility, while in contrast, Mrs Parker, president of the NUT, thought that although the first reaction of parents would be to refuse, if the programme was properly explained to them they would agree. It was left to J. Brown, chairman of the ARP Committee, to suggest a compromise. He stated that in his opinion any scheme had to be 'elastic', allowing parents, previously against evacuation, to change their minds and send their children with the others.

Sir John Anderson argued that parents would be inclined to ask a lot of questions about any evacuation scheme. Therefore they would need to be assured that adequate attention would be given to the welfare of their children.

Teachers were strongly in favour of billeting children in private houses rather than in hostels, camps,[9] or boarding accommodation. As billeting was represented as a 'dispersal of the children' it was considered that in theory, some of the responsibility for looking after the children would be borne by the host, so taking some of the daily care away from the teachers. Under the Scheme, foster parents and other hosts were to be given the authority to act in *loco parentis*. A Government Memo issued in 1939 stated:

In circumstances in which evacuation would take place, householders in the receiving areas could be relied upon to do everything possible to lighten the lot of the children and mothers compelled suddenly to leave their homes and families and finding themselves in strange surroundings. So far as unaccompanied school children are concerned, the householder will be in loco parentis, and should have no great difficulty in controlling the children and preserving reasonable discipline. The children will be accompanied by their teachers, who will know them and will be able to assist in their control.[10]

In the event, some hosts in their new role as foster parents proved to be very effective in taking full responsibility for their charges. However, in many areas, teachers found themselves coping with virtually twenty-four-hours, seven-days a week supervision of their pupils who were, in some cases, to be spread over hundreds of square miles.[11]

Nevertheless, even for those hosts who took their role seriously, it was not always possible for them to control 'difficult' children and some were not prepared to impose any discipline because of the possible consequences from the child's family and the authorities.

In some areas the situation became one of serious concern and in May 1941 the Rural District Councils Association forced questions about it in Parliament.[12] There are also examples of local initiatives. On 12 July 1941, the Chief Billeting Officer in Dorset wrote the following letter to the Clerk of the County Council expressing his unease and offering some suggestions:

12 July 1941
From: Dorchester RDC.
Ref. Government Evacuation Scheme. Difficult Children

1. Cases arise from time to time of children of both sexes who are unruly and with whom the average householder is unable and willing to deal.
2. It can be understood that where stern measures are indicated, any householder applying them may be proceeded against by parents and guardians in the courts and that is a risk most people will not willingly incur.
3. The only possible solution is for these children to be placed in Institutions, under competent supervision, where they can be brought under proper discipline until in the opinion of the person in charge, they can be safely sent back to private billets.
4. The Southampton Authority already run such a home for difficult children, for boys only, evacuated from their area, at Wiverley Park, Lyndhurst. It is

always full and additional accommodation is needed. So far as is known, no provision is made for London children or for girls of any evacuated area.

5. I am unable to give figures for the total number of school children billeted in the County, but in this area the figures are Boys 317 and Girls 279.

6. I suggest provision should be made for 1% of the total number in the County in assessing the size of the accommodation required.

7. I therefore recommend:-

   a. The County Council be asked to set up two such homes in the County, one for each sex, in suitable houses not in towns, the co-operation of the Evacuation Authorities being asked in provision of higher staff.

   b. The administration of each Home to be in the hands of the Local Authority in whose area it is situated.

   c. Administer to the Homes through the Director of Education of the County Council and all applications for the admission of a child be backed by the Head Teachers of the Parish in which the child is billeted.

Signed W. de. M. Egerton.[13]

Having sorted out the basic evacuation provision, the Committee now had to decide on the best way of transporting them out of the city. This was discussed on 16 June 1938.

They needed to plan how to evacuate an estimated several million adults and 750,000 children from the Metropolitan Police district. In the event 827,000 primary-school children, 524,000 young children and mothers, and 12,000 expectant women were the ones eligible. Also evacuated were 103,000 teachers and helpers, a pupil-teacher ratio of 8:1.[14] The unpaid helpers were women who had been appointed by the evacuation authorities to accompany the children to their destination where they were usually billeted by the host authority. During the first evacuation of 1939 around 40,000 had taken part but some of them were totally unsuitable and by the middle of 1941 32,000 had been dismissed, reducing the pupil:helper ratio to 100:1.[15]

The Committee realised that any plan had to be simple, flexible and allow for immediate adjustment to meet any conditions which might not have been foreseen. Nonetheless, this was to be a major undertaking and far greater than those seen within the other countries in mainland Europe. They also recognised that the proportion of inhabitants being evacuated would differ from area to area because of the density of population and their potential vulnerability. Frank Pick, the vice-chairman of London Passenger

Transport suggested to the Committee that the eastern area of the zone should be considered to be the highest priority (especially the Southwark area, south of the Thames, which was very densely populated). The western area had less population, and in his opinion there was no risk to the north. His definition of a congested area was one of more than 150 people per acre where bombs could cause great havoc.

Although the final figure would very much depend on the amount of permissible luggage, it was estimated that a total of 110,000 people could be taken by bus.[16] This meant that, allowing for a three-hour return journey to railway stations, 330,000 could be moved per day and this could be increased to 500,000 per day if the number of buses withheld from the scheme was reduced to below 50 per cent. Many of the Committee had felt that the purpose of the buses would be to transport evacuees to mainline stations but Pick had been adamant that it would be far more prudent to take them out of the city to entrain at smaller stations such as Harrow.[17]

The question of use of the London Underground System was also discussed at some length as the carrying capacity of the buses was well below that of the tube. Although the Tube system had a greater passenger capacity, and it was estimated that 100,000 people per hour could be moved if two trains were full, there were serious drawbacks.[18]

The two serious disadvantages of the Tube were the ventilation system, which would have given no protection at all in the event of a gas attack, and the risk of flooding from both water and sewage, especially if evacuation was taking place during a raid. Interestingly enough, they never considered the potential physical and psychological problems which would have been caused had a tube train full of evacuees been trapped in a tunnel because of bomb damage. Even as early as June 1938, a serious debate was taking place within the Anderson Committee as to the actual use of the whole underground transport system. The question of whether or not it should be used as shelters, closed down altogether for safety reasons or kept going, was discussed at length but no decision was made. It was not until 1940 that Londoners made the decision to use the Tubes as shelter themselves.[19] Angus Calder refers to this move as: '… an heroic assertion of popular rights against a legacy of inept bureaucracy and Tory rule'.[20] Ultimately eighty stations became shelters for 177,000 people.

The actual transportation of so many evacuees was seen as having massive inherent problems. However, the Transport Board worked out a scheme which, under Bank-holiday conditions, would evacuate 100,000 persons per hour by underground, 500,000 per day by bus, or 330,000–350,000 under normal conditions. Their target was 1 million per day for the first two days and then 500,000 thereafter.[21]

All the Committee proposals on transportation were sent to the major railway companies and on 21 June 1938 the Committee invited all the General Managers to give their opinions.[22] The Committee needed some reassurance on the actual carrying capacity of the trains. The railway companies calculated that they could move 3,600,000 persons in seventy-two hours if they just ran a skeleton regular service. This was a much higher estimate than the one sent to the Ministry of Transport when the companies said that 60,000 could be moved to a 20–25 mile radius per hour if a skeleton service was used or 115,000 per hour if all trains were utilised.[23] The companies reassured the Committee that the same capacity could be carried even if main-line stations were damaged.

In consultation with the rail companies it was decided that trains actually running during a raid should continue their journey but other activities in the station area would stop, thus allowing station workers and others to take shelter. The biggest problem would be the transfer of evacuees from the underground system. Quite naturally they would be unwilling to come to the surface and it was estimated that a tube train that would normally take five minutes to empty, might be delayed considerably longer, thus causing problems both in the stations and in the tunnels where trains would be backing up. It was suggested that instead of transferring passengers, an alternative would be to take the tubes to the termini. At least in this way the passengers would be taken out of the city and the evacuees could be distributed by the local buses from these points. In the event, many evacuees were transported from their home areas using a combination of transport networks and systems. In fact many of them did not travel on the tube because of the fear of a potential gas attack and the lines' proximity to adjacent underground rivers and sewers.

In the first four days of September 1939, 164 trains carrying evacuees west from London ran from three stations – Ealing, Acton and Paddington. The first train, numbered 101, left Ealing at 8.30 a.m. on 1 September and went to Maidenhead, arriving at 9 a.m. Others, of course, went further distances. The trains, made up of twelve carriages and capable of carrying 800 people per journey, were marshalled at Acton and Old Oak Common.[24] On the first day fifty-eight Great Western Railway trains, rather than the originally allocated sixty-four, ran from these stations carrying a total of

44,032 evacuees, reducing by the fourth and final day to twenty-eight trains carrying 17,796 evacuees.[25]

London County Council staff assisted railway personnel in organising the children and adults at the stations. Tickets had already been issued at the schools where the children had assembled: Yellow tickets to children with teachers and Pink tickets to children accompanied by their mothers,[26] and to avoid congestions they had been told to arrive fifteen minutes before the departure of the train. The 166-page timetable for evacuation had been printed in early August but because there was still Government concern that evacuation might cause panic, a note on the front cover of the time-table warned: 'The Evacuation Train arrangements shewn in this Notice must not be circulated to more members of staff than is necessary for the smooth working of the Programme and information must not be circulated to the General Public'.[27]

As well as the London evacuation, on 1 and 2 September the GWR moved 22,739 evacuees from the Birmingham area in sixty-four trains. These travelled to South Wales and Gloucester. The company also moved 35,606 evacuees from Liverpool and Birkenhead.[28]

Of course other railway companies were involved. James Roffey recalls travelling from Queens Road Station to Pulborough in Sussex on the Southern Railway. This embarkation point created its own problems. The station had always been a make-shift building. The railway line itself was high on an embankment and to reach the platform children had to climb up a very steep flight of wooden steps with their bags and cases. Gas masks were also a problem as the sharp-cornered boxes banged against knees and the string cut into the owners' necks. A serious situation almost occurred when a girl tripped over on the stairs causing many others to fall with her. When the train, made up of old fashioned carriages with a door to every compartment, eventually came into the platform a melee ensued. Everyone surged forward, brothers and sisters and friends struggled to keep together and everyone wanted a window seat.[29] A scene far removed from the orderly entraining shown in the propaganda films such as the Ministry of Information's *Westward Ho!* made in 1940.

Some evacuees have stated that they travelled by an alternative method of transportation not mentioned at all in the Anderson Committee minutes. They did not use trains, buses or the tube but were taken directly to their Reception Areas by boat from the Ford Motor Company jetties at Dagenham. Paddle steamers such as the *Golden Eagle* owned by the General

Steam Navigation Company, normally seen on cross-Channel routes, had been brought in to pick up evacuees at Dagenham and take them to the east-coast ports of Felixstowe, Lowestoft and Great Yarmouth. These steamers were given a destroyer escort.[30] Unfortunately, these children were not expected and many evacuees spent a few nights sleeping on the floors of schools and church halls in straw-filled sacks before billets could be found.[31] In total 16,984 children had registered for evacuation in this manner, but not all turned up. Other boats used in the scheme included *The Royal Eagle*, *The Crested Eagle*, *The Royal Sovereign*, *The Royal Daffodil*, *Queen Charlotte*, *The Medway Queen*[32] and *The City of Rochester*.[33] Many of these ships were involved a few months later in the evacuation of soldiers from Dunkirk.[34]

Having sorted out the transport problems the Anderson Committee was then faced with the problem of how to decide on reception areas and how many billets would be required: '… the general public hardly realises how arduous and how important a service is being rendered by this great army of volunteers. The finding of a billet is only the beginning. The real work starts later.'[35]

On 23 June 1938, J.C. Wrigley, director of Housing and Town Planning at the Ministry of Health, attended the meeting to give advice on evacuation accommodation and the provision of water supplies in the Reception Areas. His own information came from two sources, both of which were incomplete for the purpose intended. One was the 1931 Census, which gave the numbers of persons living per room, and the numbers of houses erected by local authorities and private companies. It was also necessary at this stage to have some standard on which calculations of how many people could be billeted were made. They therefore adopted the standard of overcrowding contained in the Housing Act of 1935 and the Consolidating Act of 1936. In 1938 the average percentage of houses in the country below the required overcrowding standard of the 1936 Act was 1 per cent. Using the calculations based on this information it was reckoned that a lower-middle-class house, comprising two reception rooms and four bedrooms and with an average residency of four persons, could take in an extra ten to twelve people as evacuees! If children were involved the figure could be higher because those under twelve months did not figure in the equation and those under ten counted as 0.5. These figures were amended drastically and the billeting standard used on all accommodation surveys in England and Wales during the war was one person per habitable room.[36]

As early as 1938, social problems relating to evacuation were on the agenda, and in the light of what was to transpire, discussions were very cursory and measures were ineffective. Wrigley believed that there would be different problems inherent in housing adults and children. In his view, bearing in mind 'normal' domestic arrangements, the latter could easily be fitted in, albeit at some inconvenience to the householder, but adults were a different matter. He envisaged family members being divided up among a number of reception households, thereby creating problems of transport, communication and mutual family support, and he was also concerned about men being taken from their work in London and having nothing to do in the Reception Areas. This was not to become a problem as these men, not called up for military service, tended to stay in the target areas to continue their jobs and in reality few men were actually evacuated.

Members of the Welsh Nationalist Party complained strongly that Wales should not have been involved in the Scheme at all on cultural and social grounds. On 13 January 1939, J.E. Jones, the Organising Secretary of the WNP, said in an article to the *North Wales Chronicle*:

> The indiscriminate transfer of English people into Wales will place the Welsh Language and even the very existence of the Welsh nation, in jeopardy. The national welfare of the Welsh people should be a matter of first consideration by the authorities who are planning evacuation into the countryside. We, as Nationalists, demand that there should be no transfer of population into Wales that would endanger Welsh nationality. If England cannot make its emergency plans without imperilling the life of our little nation, let England renounce war and grant us self-government. [37]

The billeting survey to ascertain how much space was available in the Reception Areas was a massive undertaking and Government Memo EV1 outlined the need for the careful selection of volunteer interviewers who would take on the role with administrative efficiency. [38] These were to be called 'Visitors' and, according to the Government Memo EV2. Part IV, their task was to:

> … enlist goodwill in time of peace, forming a register of assistance which every humane person would hasten to offer if war came … The compilation of the register of accommodation is therefore in the interest of the householders, as it is only in this way that difficulties and misfits can be avoided.

How these words would come back to haunt those who sent children to very poor and sometimes dangerous billets!

There were, of course, those persons who, although willing to take in evacuees, were incapable of doing so. These would include the aged and infirm living on their own, who were barely able to look after themselves; houses where there was a confirmed invalid; and persons living alone whose employment required them to be absent all day.

In such cases the Visitors were asked to explore the possibility of the householder taking in children if they were accompanied by an adult or some arrangement could be made for the child outside school hours. The Government also wanted to ensure that evacuees were not isolated and Visitors were asked to indicate if a billet was more than 2 miles away from a school.[39] Although these concerns were laudable, in practice many children were billeted on isolated hill and moorland farms in Wales and in the West Country, and many teachers had problems keeping in contact with their charges.

When all the returns were collated and analysed, the results showed that on a basis of one person per habitable room, there was enough space for 6,050,000 people.[40] However, not all this space could be used. Some had been requisitioned by Government departments, empty houses had already been earmarked for use by companies leaving London, in some areas there were lack of water supplies and sewage disposal and also close proximity to target areas and military installations.[41]

Taking all the various reasons for not having evacuees into consideration, the final billeting figure was reduced to 4,800,000,[42] but this still remains a remarkable figure and shows a generally favourable response from house-holders to the Government's request for billets.

After all the surveys and meetings, the Anderson Committee produced its report and on 26 July 1938 presented its recommendations to Parliament:

a. That, except in so far as it may be necessary for military or other special reasons to require persons to leave some limited area, evacuation should not be compulsory.
b. That, for the purpose of supporting the national war effort and supplying essential civilian needs, production in the large industrial towns must be maintained, but it is desirable to provide organised facilities for the evacuation of substantial numbers of people from certain industrial areas.
c. That arrangements for the reception of persons who become refugees should be mainly on the basis of accommodation in private houses under powers of compulsory billeting. These arrangements will require very

    detailed preparation in order to avoid unnecessary hardship either to the refugees or to the persons who receive them.

d. That the initial cost of evacuation arrangements should be borne by the Government, but that refugees who can afford to contribute towards the cost of their maintenance should be expected to do so.

e. That, to meet the needs of the parents who wish to send their children away, but cannot make their own arrangements, special arrangements should be made for school-children to move out in groups from their schools in the charge of their teachers.[43]

Despite reaching this report stage very quickly, the Committee for Imperial Defence did not even consider it until 15 September, and in so doing wasted almost two months of precious time. Sir Samuel Hoare, while agreeing that a detailed evacuation plan should be drawn up, suggested that 'in existing conditions it was not desirable to publish the Anderson Report'.[44] It was eventually released on 27 October 1938, ten months before the outbreak of war.

    In the light of some of the problems which were to occur, one wonders why the general plans and views were not amended during this period of time, to take into account the more social and human side of the evacuation scheme. It is very apparent that little, if any, notice was taken of the views and opinions of those who were to take part in the process, basically because of the desire to keep the planning and implementation 'secret'. There was a certain dehumanising element inherent in the organisation. These recommendations came from a bureaucratic procedure which ostensibly ignored the feelings of the individuals concerned both in the designated Reception and Evacuation Areas, relied on the unquestioning co-operation of teachers, without whom the Scheme would have collapsed before it was instigated, and thought fit to create a billeting scheme which required no expert supervision and monitoring from outside agencies both before and during the whole evacuation process[45]. The latter responsibility was very much left to the teachers.

    It is interesting to note that throughout all its deliberations the Anderson Committee made no reference to, or sought the advice from, members of a community who had actually been involved in an evacuation scheme in Cambridge. In 1936, a group of 3,826 Basque children, refugees from the Spanish Civil War, had arrived in England. Twenty-nine of these were housed in a hostel and then billeted in private houses around the Cambridge area.

In many ways this scheme provides an interesting comparison not least the way in which local people raised money to support the hostel in Pampisford Vicarage, and the general supportive attitude they had towards their charges, at least in the beginning, a trait which is not so evident in the Government Scheme from 1939. Members of the local community got together to decorate the Vicarage before the arrival of the children. Jessie Stewart makes reference in her article 'Recuerdos' in the *Cambridge Daily News* in 1938, to the work done by the secretaries in the hostel and the fact that '… they had the support of a large committee including representatives of Societies, Clubs, Laboratories, Syndicates, Schools and Villages which had "adopted", i.e. made themselves responsible for, the weekly payments for individual children'.

Although this type of benevolence would not have been possible on the large scale of the Government scheme, there were other community led events which could have been replicated. Businesses within the area provided funds and there were entertainments which included 'sports, recreation and asking the children away for holidays, and fund raising events such as fêtes and house to house collections'. Had the Committee investigated this in more detail they may have gained some very useful pointers for dealing with the evacuation of children.

However, the group were not to escape the anti-evacuee campaigns that future migrants were to suffer in 1939. The national press criticised the presence of the children and although this was countered by letters from those involved with the Basques, it did have the unfortunate result of putting landlords off having evacuees in their houses, with excuses such as 'the property will deteriorate' and 'the neighbourhood will object' being common.[46]

4

The British Evacuation

It was a problem for me to move from a working class school into an upper class one … In Battersea there was no awareness that there was something on the other side of the fence because all the London children were the same. I had to have elocution lessons when I went to Bromley because I was South London … 'ain't ya' and all that. [1]

In the months leading up to the war, councils at county, district and rural levels within the designated Reception Areas were planning what to do. As an example, an official memorandum relating to the billeting of children was submitted to the Dorchester Rural District Council. It stated that there would be no Evacuation rehearsal and that the railway company would make the entire arrangements for the transport of evacuees from London to the local detraining stations, in this case Dorchester. The council's responsibility would be to undertake the reception and it was expected that:

… children would be marched as quickly as possible to a central place where sanitation, first aid facilities and rough sleeping accommodation, in case trains were delayed, would be available. From here they would be dispersed to outlying villages. The Ministry of Transport would provide sufficient vehicles to transport the children to a central 'de-bussing' station in each village. The Rural District Council would take charge of the children at each of these points. [2]

During the week immediately before the Evacuation Scheme was implemented, hosts in some of the Reception Areas were given an indication of their responsibilities and the amount of money they would receive in billeting allowances, as well as how they could claim it. In some areas they resorted to interesting methods to get the message across. In Weymouth a loudspeaker van was organised to tour the streets telling hosts of the time their charges were arriving and also any other important details they should know![3] They were expected to 'control and care for evacuees as if they were their own children and should any difficulty arise they were to inform the Billeting Officer'.[4]

As in the German scheme, where it was also considered unlikely that people would take in evacuees at their own expense, a billeting payment of 10s 6d per week for the first child and 8s 6d for any other children was made to cover 'full board and all the care that would be given to a child in their own home', but it was not meant to cover the cost of clothes or medical expenses, which hosts were under no obligation to meet. The parents of the evacuees were expected to contribute 6s towards the weekly payment, but the collection of this was not always efficient and some paid nothing at all. Also, despite what the officials said, some of the hosts paid extra out of their own pockets to ensure that their evacuees were suitably clothed and 'shod'. It will never be known what personal sacrifices were made by some of the hosts in the Reception Areas. Payments were to be made weekly, in advance, at the local Post Office on a form issued by the billeting officer. These payments were subject to review throughout the war and were increased in 1940 and 1944. There was also an additional payment of 2s 6d (and a rubber sheet) available to hosts who had a 'bed-wetter' in the house. In some areas, where proof of bed-wetting was not required, this became a way of getting a little extra money. However, the need to eventually account for this expenditure led to the often inflated numbers of evacuees said to be suffering from enuresis. The hosts were also asked to look out for those children suffering from homesickness and to report serious cases to the billeting officers. In addition, although hosts were informed that the children would arrive with rations to supplement their own for forty-eight hours, they were advised to buy and store an additional week's requirements of staple foods.[5] In reality many of these ration bags did not get to the hosts as the contents were often consumed by the evacuees on the journey!

When all the plans had been made and the necessary advice given, 'Operation Pied Piper', the code name given to the implementation of the September evacuation, became active.[6]

By Friday 1 September 1939, all the transport arrangements required to move an estimated 4 million evacuees from vulnerable areas were in place.

On the same day thousands of hospital patients were moved to safer areas or sent home to make space for hospital beds; 2,200 doctors and 15,000 nurses were posted to casualty hospitals. Private vehicles, coaches and trucks were sent as auxiliary ambulances to various areas of the country and thirty civilian casualty trains were sent to specific locations.[7]

Some newspaper headlines described the extent of the organisation and planning in biblical terms:

GREATEST EVACUATION IN HISTORY HAS BEGUN
EXODUS OF THE BIBLE DWARFED; THREE MILLION PEOPLE
ON THE MOVE[8]

By mid-September 1939, the plans made specifically for London were adapted and extended beyond the capital to other areas regarded as potential targets. By the end of the month a total of 1,500,000 people were officially evacuated, 35 per cent of those eligible from the London County Council area, 66 per cent of those from Merseyside, 33 per cent from Portsmouth and Southampton and 20 per cent from Coventry.[9]

These variations may be explained by the amount and intensity of poverty or hardship within particular evacuated areas. In addition, some parents may have been more easily persuaded by the official policy and by the implication that all the needs of their children would be met in the Reception Areas; a situation not unlike that of the Finnish children from poor backgrounds going to wealthier homes in Sweden. Parents also had to have confidence in the Scheme. Asking them to send their children away for an indefinite period, to an unknown destination and to the care of total strangers was not a decision that would be taken lightly. Even so, within the first few days of the Scheme, it was evident that some parents thought they had made a mistake and brought their children home. Some of this came about by a degree of fatalism. 'If one of us is going to die, it would be better if we all died together', heard throughout the war, was not an uncommon sentiment.[10]

Like their German counterparts, the parents of the British evacuees were very concerned about the education of their children. However, unlike the totalitarian control of the National Socialist State, the schooling of British evacuees was still very much under the supervision of their teachers, none of whom were threatened with dismissal or the 'Eastern Front' for not towing a party line. Neither was there any Hitler-Youth-type organisation influencing the political 'development' of the children.

However, providing education was not without its problems. Often two schools had to share facilities, which not only resulted in half-day schooling but also put a great deal of pressure on resources and the local infrastructure. Some evacuated schools were divided and found themselves miles from each other.

> Not the least of the problems placed on the shoulders of the education authorities is the provision of accommodation for children in rural areas. In one case there is a complete school divided among four villages, while in another only half the school came to the Dorset area and the other half went to Somerset.[11]

Entries written in the school logbook of Bradfield Primary School, situated in a small rural village in Berkshire, which usually had a constant 110 pupils on the school roll, provide a fair indication of the difficulties faced by Headteachers:

> Oct. 4th 1939. On instructions from the LEA the children evacuated from the LCC were admitted to school this morning. 57 children were admitted bringing the number on roll up to 206. There is insufficient seating for all the children and some are sitting three to a dual desk …[12]

This had been the second group of evacuees to arrive at the school. The first children had been privately evacuated. At least this village school had sufficient, albeit cramped, accommodation. In other areas the lack of communication between central and local government caused a great deal of confusion over suitable education facilities within the Reception Areas. Evidence would suggest that some Local Education Authorities were not entirely blameless and a lack of local knowledge on the part of those responsible for distributing evacuees did not help the situation.[13] It is worth remembering that, at a time when travelling was not as easy as today, many of the bureaucrats in charge of the Scheme had no physical knowledge of the geographical area where they were sending the children to. For example the West Sussex authority allocated fifty evacuated children to the village of Nutborne which had school facilities for only the twenty children already taught there by one teacher. Thakeham received 140 children in a school which had a resident school population of only twenty, and ninety were allocated to Coldwaltham which had a tiny two-room school with a staff of two who taught everyone between the ages of five and fourteen.[14] These teachers would have been overwhelmed had not two staff come with the evacuees. There were also difficulties in some parts of North Wales where children from Liverpool were sent to schools that had their lessons in Welsh.[15] Despite the fears of the Welsh National Party that situations such as this would harm Welsh nationalism, many Liverpool children learnt Welsh very quickly and some even competed successfully in local Eisteddfods.[16]

Finding suitable buildings to maintain a semblance of education was an ongoing problem throughout the war. Mr Giles, president of the National Union of Teachers, visited Dorset as part of a fact-finding tour and visited about forty schools in the county. He had seen some of the new senior council schools, which he admired, but of the remainder, he described school buildings as being '... now only fit for the scrap heap'. Some schools had no water and no water closets. 'Here is picturesque poverty. Dorset has the children and the teachers but money is not being spent on the buildings.'[17]

Other evacuees tell of similar situations. For example, the Peckham Central Girls School, which had strict rules about the wearing of uniforms, turned up for their first day of schooling in the old Corn Exchange in Pulborough to find that everything was covered in dust, the floor was rotting and there was little furniture suitable for a temporary school. It was not long before the impeccable uniforms became dusty and dirty as the girls were expected to sort out the furniture and clean up the building.[18]

Many evacuated schools were simply imposed on existing classes and classrooms in the Reception Areas, and even LEAs complained that they received no information directly from the Boards of Education either as to the numbers of teachers and pupils expected or the particular schools where they were coming from. This lack of information led to some evacuated schools and existing classes being 'farmed out' to other establishments in order to find space in which to work.

Some evacuees were not afforded the luxury of remaining in one building. Sylvia Rose, (née Eden) recalls that as a member of the Walworth Central Girls School evacuated to Sturminster Newton, Dorset she had her lessons all over the town:

> ... We used to go to the Senior School for our cookery lessons where there was a domestic science room. Other lessons were in the school room of the Wesleyan Chapel ... and the Bridge Chapel room. Games lessons were on the

recreation ground and there were other lessons in the Royal British Legion Comrades Hut. This is also where we had our communal dinners.[19]

Even some London schools that had previously been evacuated in 1939 to their own premises, found they were imposed upon by newly evacuated schools without notice.

In one example, the pressure on accommodation in Didcot was so great that there was nowhere for the children to go at all, and their classroom during the day became their sleeping quarters at night.[20]

In some areas the actual school accommodation was poor, especially where the village schools relied entirely on open fires or small enclosed stoves for their heat. During January 1940, one school in North Wales registered temperatures of *minus* 30 degrees Fahrenheit in the classroom, yet despite the lack of heating lessons continued![21] One teacher described his experiences in a small school near Newbury, in Berkshire:

> … The school had no water supply and every morning the bigger boys fetched buckets of water from a horse trough outside the church … The winter practice had been to gather the nineteen village children around the stoves, sending boys out 'sticking' to keep up the blaze, but with 50 children now in the school the outer rings were fated to shiver, though they sat in overcoats and gloves. Early in the new year an extended cold spell cut off the village for ten days. Every pump and many of the wells froze and food had to be brought from Newbury by sledge. School was impossible; the boys could find no wood for the fires and even the ink froze in the inkwells. We gave up and took the children out for snow fights and sledging.[22]

In some cases, teachers' personal accommodation was little better. Although they were always concerned for the billeting of their pupils there is evidence to suggest that in some areas, after all the children had been housed, teachers were responsible for finding their own accommodation. A suggestion had been made in January 1939 that empty school houses could be used for evacuated teachers, but this did not always happen and in many instances teachers found themselves homeless. Three arrived at Aldeburgh on 1 September 1939 and had housed all the children by 10 p.m. They then found no billets had been allocated to them. Consequently, the billeting officer duly employed the Town Crier, who had to be raised from his bed, to progress through the town shouting out 'Anyone take in a teacher!' By 11.30 they were given lodgings.[23]

Others were placed in buildings which could only be described as sub-standard. One teacher remembered her plight vividly:

> Two of us were dumped at 6.30pm at an ancient cottage; its condition and contents shouted of extreme poverty … We were greeted by our hostess who told us that, the house being near a river and mouldy all through, she had done her best to ensure well-aired beds by keeping them in the garden all day, it had been raining since 11am! …[24]

Others were not even afforded the luxury of a house, finding themselves sleeping on straw in a barn for three nights until accommodation could be sorted out for them.

Bearing in mind that parents had been persuaded to send their children away to safety, the provision of air-raid shelters, especially in schools, became an important issue and in some cases it was the geographical location of a school which determined whether or not it would be entitled to shelters. In May 1940, the Board of Education sent out a circular which advised that not all schools in rural areas 'need be provided with shelters in the same way as urban schools'. Instead, the pupils were to be instructed on how to take shelter within the school if bombs were falling in the area. They were to practise lying on the floor and keeping away from windows and they were to be told that under no circumstances should they leave the school buildings and go into the open![25]

The situation in Manchester provides an interesting insight into shelter provision, and even raises the question of whether or not schools needed to be evacuated at all. On 10 October 1939, the Manchester District Women's Co-operative Guild expressed concern about the lack of educational and welfare facilities for those children who had returned to Manchester during the Phoney War period:

> This conference representing 2561 working class Mothers protest strongly about the lack of educational and welfare facilities for the 50,000 children of school age, who remain in, or have returned to Manchester owing to the partial failure of the evacuation scheme. It suggests that a more acceptable scheme might be evolved, if the cooperation of representatives of both parents and teachers was involved.

There was an equivalent objection from the parents of children at the Burnage High School for Boys who not only complained about the lack of education being provided within the Reception Areas, but also recommended ways in which this could be dealt with. As a *very rare* indication of parent power and evidence that not all parents were compliant, it is worth quoting the petition in full:

Sir

We, the 306 persons named on the attached sheets being parents of pupils of the Burnage High School for Boys, present this, our petition, to urge, as strongly as we can, that the said school should be reopened for our boys for full time educational facilities as quickly as possible.

Our grounds for urging this step are:- That none of our boys who have been evacuated are at present receiving a standard of education comparable to that prior to the War even though this is classified as full-time education. Some, in fact are receiving only part-time education. They do not appear likely to receive their normal standard of education in the reception areas or at home, in the near future – the school is split into three districts and this must of necessity, cause lack of cohesion – there are some Masters at home to run the tutorial scheme for those not evacuated.

That a large number of we parents allowed our boys to be evacuated only because we understood that full time educational facilities would be given to them in the reception areas.

That if our boys do not get full time educational facilities by the re-opening of the School at an early date, the Manchester Grammar School boys and boys of other secondary schools which we understand are shortly to reopen, will have an unfair advantage over our boys, many of whom are in their final years before taking the School Certificate examination. We feel that school staff would support this view.

That homework can be done by the boys much better in their home surroundings than in billets away from home.

That these boys, who are the rising generation, constitute the potential leaders of the future and we should be lacking in our duty if we did not ensure for them an immediate resumption of the education facilities which they formerly enjoyed in their own environment, and which will fit them for the life ahead.

That, as we understand it, the evacuation scheme was evolved to provide greater safety for our boys – we would however, point out that in the event of Air Raids no shelters have been provided at either Ashbourne or Wirksworth

That the Burnage High School is within a quarter of a mile of the Stockport boundary, which is a non-evacuation area.

That the Manchester Grammar School has been reopened upon conditions which apply more particularly to this school:-

Firstly. It's proximity to a non-evacuation area. The Burnage High School for Boys is nearer to the Stockport boundary than the MGS and should therefore be considered a safer area.

Secondly. The Manchester Grammar School has grounds sufficiently large enough for the erection of A.R Shelters. The Burnage High School for Boys has a large area of its grounds which if necessary could be utilised for the provision of Air Raid Shelters. In addition the school has certain basements.

That Burnage High School is a new modern building.

That from the moral standpoint, it is our opinion the boys are being exposed to serious dangers at a time of their life when they require the care and guidance of their own parents but which, under present conditions, they have little chance of escaping – we would however like to say that we appreciate the efforts of the billetees.

That family life is being seriously and unduly interfered with.

That in many cases the boys have to travel from their billets to the School distances up six miles – this, it is obvious, will entail hardship to the boys and girls and a constant source of worry to many parents during the winter months – their health may be affected by this.

That in numerous cases the cost to parents is too great for their resources – some parents having to pay, in addition to the 6/- or 9/- per week billeting charge, travelling expenses, dinners at school if a distance away, washing, extra footwear owing to the different types of roads in the country reception areas etc. School fees are still being demanded.

That ultimately it would be far cheaper, both to the Education Authorities and to the parents, and also more satisfactory for all concerned, that the School should be reopened with proper Air Raid Shelters. Than to keep the boys in what can only be described as unsatisfactory and unsuitable reception areas.

That approx. 200 of the boys have not been evacuated owing to various causes, but mainly that the parents do not believe in the evacuation scheme, and these boys are receiving little education at the present time – in fact, in many cases, the boys are being placed in employment, in numerous instances unsuitable to their education standards, owing to the lack of full time educational facilities.

That there are inadequate facilities in the reception areas for the boys leisure time – at Leek, a club has only recently been opened for a couple of hours twice a week in the evenings – they can be more usefully and profitably employed to their own advantage at home.

That the ages of the boys range from 11-18.

That the Burnage High School is not being used for National Service except, we understand, a small portion for ARP and for which, we suggest there are plenty of empty properties in the district that could be taken over for this purpose if necessary.

That as stated above, 306 parents have signed the form supporting this petition – of this number 70% are parents of boys who are, or have been evacuated but would add that, owing to our not having had access to the School registers, we have been unable to get in touch with all parents with the result, we believe, that there are many more parents in support of this petition than have actually signed same. It is submitted, that in addition to the above we have the entire support of those parents whose boys have not been evacuated.

We therefore desire and request that you and your committee consider the above grounds for this our Petition, in all its aspects – that our request should be granted – that the boys be brought home with the minimum delay to their own school and that the reopening be arranged for the New Year Term.

In response to this petition the Education Committee simply resolved: 'That this communication be dealt with in pursuance of the conditions contained in the approved report on the reopening of evacuated schools'.

However, the school did open again in January 1940, with adequate shelters and provision made for air-raid practices to be allocated on the timetable, usually on a Monday and a Friday. Other schools soon followed the same procedures, to the extent that in July 1940 there were only 7,548 evacuees remaining in the Reception Areas, whereas 67,956 children were in full-time education in Manchester.[26]

Financial constraints rather than safety seemed to be the prime concern of some Councils. Complaints were made at the Dorchester Town Council meeting on 13 February 1940, that there were no air-raid shelters in the town and that something should be done about it. Alderman, Mr Rossiter, asked that as there was nowhere that the town's children or evacuees could go in the event of a raid, was it possible to bring pressure on the County Council to provide shelters. The answer, from the Town Clerk was: '… It is not part of the County Council measures. This sort of thing costs money'.[27]

There were often failings in the provision of protection. A search through school logbooks for village schools in North Wales suggests that air-raid shelters were not provided until September 1940, by which time the area had received numerous air-raid warnings. This oversight created serious problems for some of the teachers. On 17 November 1939, the head teacher of St Matthew's Infants School, Buckley, North Wales, had to send children home during a potential raid:

> An air raid warning was given this morning about 11.15. As we have no shelters and deployment into wet fields is not conducive to good health, I dispersed them to their homes. The school was evacuated in a very short time. Some of the children live 20 minutes walk away. Long distance children are a problem in this respect and something must be done to cater for them.

This action did initiate some response: 'Monday 20th September. There have been several complaints over Friday's dispersal of the children. A manager's meeting is to be held tonight.' There is no further indication of when, or if, shelters were provided.[28]

Unlike the German evacuation scheme where education was determined by an adherence to National Socialism and was influenced by the political agenda of the Hitler Youth and the teachers, the evacuation in the UK has been seen by some educationalists as preparing the way for education reform.[29] Although, there was obviously a shift in teacher responsibilities towards the pastoral side of education, it is now debatable as to what extent pedagogic practices changed beyond those enforced on the teachers by circumstance. Comments such as: 'Evacuation gave schools a chance for personal initiatives and resourcefulness by challenging them to jettison unreal teaching to look outside at real things rather than at apparatus indoors',[30] were really a justification for the sharing of indoor facilities.

Although there was a firm belief that city children could be introduced to new experiences such as *real* nature study and first-hand history and geography, new methods presupposed that teachers were well-equipped to take advantage of the situation. As many were married women and retired teachers recalled back to the profession during the emergency, one would suggest that neither group would necessarily have made curriculum development their highest priority, especially during the evacuation of September 1939. A view supported by the Director of Education in Anglesey who wrote:

> ... the educational needs of the evacuated children had certainly not been the first concern of either the Evacuation or Billeting Authorities, or indeed the Government departments concerned. For not only were large schools evacuated into rural districts and the pupils scattered over a wide area, but also the

billeting arrangements had been more concerned with family units than with school units.[31]

Two teachers, Win Elliott and Sylvia Lewis, described their teaching methods in their diary:

> At Leiston School, for one session each day, we had the use of one small room which we and our evacuees shared with a Dagenham Headmistress. We had no apparatus, no guidance as to what to do or teach … we gradually acquired a small collection of reading books, paper, pencils and crayons etc. No high-faluting syllabus, or structured curriculum, but the children learned to read and write and calculate with enjoyment … The rest of the school day we had to play in the park, or walk the children around the lanes and go to the woods.[32]

Entries in school logbooks of the time reveal little evidence of curriculum reforms except references to Nature Study, Nature Talks and Nature Walks, all designed to take the children out of the classroom. Some teachers did take this a little further and introduced Horticulture and Agricultural Studies which allowed the children to grow vegetables and keep pigs and bees. While some local education authorities, notably Caernarvonshire in Wales, established training courses for the evacuated teachers on Nature Study and Local History so that they could get the most out of the local surroundings.[33]

However, it needs to be remembered that opportunities for change in curriculum areas such as Science and Nature Study, were already predetermined by the local environment and as such in many rural areas Science would have been agriculturally biased. Some schools actually encouraged pupils to work on farms in the local area but not necessarily from an academic or educational motive, but more one of economics and giving the pupils something to do. Some of this extra work was 'suggested' by local authorities:

19th June 1940.   Following instructions, enquiries were made at the farms in the neighbourhood, whether children can help with the work in the fields. One farmer accepted and a dozen older children went this morning to weed.

20th June 1940.   10 children worked in the garden of Buckland Vicarage weeding.[34]

6th June 1941.	The senior children spent all week on the local farm planting potatoes.[35]
30th September 1941.	The senior children spent a lot of time this month on the local farm picking and bagging potatoes.[36]
18th June 1942.	The First team of 6 children over the age of 12 began work in agriculture. 3 hours per day every four days.[37]

In districts where the number of evacuees was substantial, the head teachers of the reception schools were asked to get in touch with their evacuated colleagues and arrange for the reopening of schools on a double-shift system.[38]

The following timetable was drawn up by staff at the Aston Clinton School just a few days after the evacuees' arrival in Buckinghamshire. They were to have the afternoon shift, with the host school having a very similar morning timetable from 9 a.m-12.30 p.m.

It is interesting to note that despite their new countryside environment there is little evidence here of the pedagogic enlightenment suggested by educationalists at the time. Certainly not until 4 p.m.

1.00-1.05	Registration
1.05-1.35	Scripture or Religious Instruction
1.35-2.15	Arithmetic
2.15-2.45	Geography or History or English
2.45-3.00	Recreation
3.00-3.30	English or History or Geography
3.30-4.00	Physical Training
4.00-4.30	English or Nature Study or Art

In some areas, provision was made for the individualised religious education of the evacuees. There were a number of Jewish children in this party to Aston Clinton, so later in the term permission was sought from the Governors to provide Hebrew lessons during the day instead of Scripture.[39] It also meant that some of their school holidays were different in order to take account of the Feast of the Weeks and Feast of the Passover. This was acceptable in London but caused some administrative problems in the Reception Areas.

Day-to-day organisation was also affected by other religious denominations. The logbook for Idbury and Fifield C. of E. School in Oxfordshire, indicates that on a number of occasions Roman Catholic children did not attend assembly and the children from St Anthony's School, Forest Gate, were not allowed to attend. This does beg the question … why evacuate a Roman Catholic school to a small Church of England village school?[40] During the second evacuation in 1940, slightly more care was taken to place Roman Catholics in areas where facilities were available for them. But, in truth, the situation should not have arisen during the first scheme. On 2 May 1939, four months before the evacuee scheme was implemented, a representative from Liverpool Council, H.W. Lowe, addressed a conference at Caernarfon where he had told the evacuating authorities in the Reception Areas to expect 30 per cent Catholics in the total of 24,000 evacuees allocated to the area.[41]

The issue of Protestantism versus Roman Catholicism seems to have been a thorny one. In some areas of Wales, Protestant hosts were chastised by Catholic priests from the evacuees' home area if their charges did not attend Mass. This in itself created problems as there were few Catholic churches and, where there were any, they were usually many miles away in the nearest town or city. If hosts complied with the Priest's requests this often meant them foregoing their own chapel attendance on a Sunday. In April 1940, the Clerk of the Nant Conway RDC reported: '… during the last evacuation, children were made to walk as much as eight miles to attend Mass on Sunday mornings and I consider this a hardship on the younger children to have to do this in all weathers'.[42]

The classroom role of the teachers remained an important one, after all this was their job and what they had been trained for. However, little account was taken of the other duties which were now put on staff in the Reception Areas, as well as those who had been evacuated with their schools. Some of these were to be more of a social service rather than of an educational nature.

Some teachers, having taken on the role of billeting officer, took their duties very seriously and one in particular, Mr M.T. Perks, the head teacher of The Dorset Grammar School, Gillingham, Dorset, organised a full evacuation rehearsal in meticulous detail. He used pupils and staff from his own school, in order that all people involved in the reception process could evaluate and amend procedures they were to use when evacuation became official.

Even after 'practices' and detailed local planning there were still problems and many mistakes were made. In Berkshire, almost twice as many evacuees turned up than were expected, putting a tremendous strain on the organising authorities and the provision of material requirements such as blankets, pillows and so on. It also made the billeting of individuals difficult as in some cases the 'wrong' evacuees arrived. The small village of Bradfield in Berkshire had made provision for 300 evacuees in two groups. The group, when it finally turned up, consisted of thirty-five unaccompanied children and 220 mothers and infants … the latter were totally unexpected. As a result all the billeting arrangements had to be reorganised.[43]

This seeming lack of organisation was not the fault of either the evacuees or the reception authorities, but nonetheless both sides tended to level the blame at each other.

Rather than being members of the 'Party' as in Germany, or the Finnish Aid Committee in Sweden, the billeting officers in Britain were volunteers and often teachers or recognised pillars of the community. As they were usually the point of contact between the evacuee and the host, their job could be particularly onerous, especially when rumours about the physical state of the evacuees were rife.

Although there may have been little curriculum change, what the war did bring about was a shift in the relationship between the teacher and pupil. There was a significant move towards a more pastoral role which was to become a significant part of a teacher's job after the war, and has been ever since. One major reason for this was that both teachers and pupils were experiencing the evacuation process together, and as a result had a common bond. Some teachers were dealing with social problems way above their call of duty, and in some cases way beyond their expertise. The following entry in the logbook of the 'Boys Evacuated School', Aston Clinton, Buckinghamshire, is significant in two respects. First, it shows that some of the problems dealt with in *loco parentis* were very serious. Second, some of the fears parents have today regarding child safety were just as apparent in the 1940s. It is often overlooked that crime still existed despite the war, and within the Evacuation Scheme children could be easy 'targets'.

> … I have today received official information from the Aston Clinton Police Officer, in relation to the indecent assault of J.M., aged 8 years, on Saturday afternoon … at 3pm in a wood beside the main road in Aston Clinton. The matter came to Police notice about 14 days after the event and within two days an Aylesbury man named ★★★★★★ was arrested in Aston Clinton and has since been identified by the children concerned. Children have been repeatedly

warned about walking about singly in lonely places at anytime, though of course no details of what to fear have been given.[44]

Evidence would suggest that in some cases evacuees felt it easier to keep silent about such abuse, especially where the abuser was a well-respected figure in the area. However, in order to put this into context one has to realise that some evacuees, many of whom were now being well cared for in their billets, had come from abusive families. This often resulted in serious emotional and moral dilemmas for the hosts who, at the end of the war, were knowingly sending children back to difficult domestic situations.

Teachers were also responsible for those pupils who, for any reason, decided to run away or return home without notifying anyone, a reasonably common occurrence during the Phoney War period. This pastoral work put an additional physical and emotional strain onto an already overworked profession. In January 1941, the Executive of the National Union of Teachers issued a manifesto which stated that they had under review the impact of the existing war conditions on the educational system within the country. They were particularly concerned with the wide-ranging demands being made:

> … upon the public spirit and voluntary services of the teachers. The care of the children outside school, and the delicate work of billeting, the rest centre and registration office, the National Savings Movement and the ARP and Auxiliary Fire Service and the special police, the Home Guard and the nursing services and many other forms of national effort have already filled the daily programme of the teacher to overflowing.[45]

Almost all the Reception Areas took their 'evacuee' responsibilities seriously, but in some cases the welfare of the teachers accompanying them was forgotten. In some areas there was evidence of discrimination, with the evacuee teachers being treated as second-class citizens, whereas in others, such as Buckinghamshire, head teachers from evacuated schools were invited to regular meetings to discuss evacuation issues. The general lack of cohesiveness between school establishments was seen as a problem in Berkshire as early as October 1939, and the County Council issued the following statement about their education policy and billeting of evacuated schools:

> Various adjustments have been made since the schools were originally reopened and efforts are now being made to arrange for full-time instruction

wherever possible. For this system to work effectively, there must be a willingness on the part of the Berkshire and evacuated teachers to work together and so bring about the ultimate absorption of the London school children within our own school organisation. In this way, identity of the evacuated schools must disappear and this will be the logical outcome of the impossibility of retaining these schools as separate units.[46]

The authorities in Buckinghamshire took this one stage further and actually appointed evacuated teachers to their own county schools. The Authority's own girls' school in Aston Clinton lost a teacher, Mrs Staples, in November 1939. It was suggested that because the evacuated boys' school had fewer numbers they could ask one of their staff to apply for the vacancy. This was agreed and a Mrs Webb joined the staff of the girls' school on 11 December 1939, though, technically, she remained a member of the LCC Evacuee Party.[47]

By 1942, the same concerns about the overburdening of teachers were being expressed at local level, and there were specific worries about the additional tasks having to be carried out by them, to the detriment of their actual roles within the classroom. At a meeting of the Dorset Education Committee on Monday 26 January 1942, the teachers' representative, Mr J.M. Warren, was reported as being very outspoken on his views regarding the role of teachers within the county. He asserted that they were becoming 'Honorary Clerks to the Treasury, Assistants to Milk Purveyors, Housemaids, Cooks and Bottle Washers'.[48]

While many city school children and teachers were being sent to the country, the school buildings they left behind were closed, and remained so until November 1939. Even then, 50 per cent of the children in London were not to receive full-time education until mid-1940. In the designated Evacuation and Neutral Areas of England and Wales approximately 2,000 schools were either requisitioned totally or used by various organisations at different times of the day: 1,692 were used by the Civil Defence, 250 had been taken over the Auxiliary Fire Service, 213 by the military authorities and 100 were designated as Wardens' posts. The remaining seventy were taken over by groups such as the Red Cross, for first-aid posts, decontamination centres, or in some cases, allocated as temporary mortuaries.[49]

In April 1941, it was estimated that 290,000 children in England and Wales were not receiving full-time education. There had been a great deal of confusion over how many children attended school during the winter of 1940/41, and according to Titmuss, the Ministry of Health, the Board of Education and the LCC could not agree a figure. The LCC put the number at 81,000 which was considered too low by the Minister of Health.[50] It is also important to note that because of the general dislocation of the educational structures and practices, it was generally the less able pupils who suffered most. This was due in no small measure to the fact that the 320 special classes in London County Council schools, which had been established to deal with those pupils with special needs, were abandoned during the war years.[51] The more able pupils suffered as well, as they often failed their examinations for the grammar schools because they were so far behind in their studies. Little concession was made for the fact that pupils' education had been disrupted not only by the evacuation, but also by lack of facilities and equipment. As the children gradually returned from the Reception Areas, teachers had to confront the task of bringing children from various ranges of experience up to a common level. No concessions were made to the pre-war examination system and pupils who had been away for some years now found themselves having to sit the examinations for the 'Central' school where they could stay until sixteen, or if they failed, leave school at fourteen. Unsurprisingly, for many, the examination was a waste of time and in most cases the authorities refused to agree to the re-examination of those who had failed. Consequently the children were forced to leave school and find work. This had a very serious effect on the future lives of many evacuees and still remains a source of bitterness. These children had been uprooted from their homes and schools, had had their education disrupted through no fault of their own, yet were expected to compete on equal terms with those who had not had their education interrupted and be tested against examination criteria which had been established pre-war.

Despite the obvious problems of maintaining continuity in education, the BBC tried as much as possible to keep broadcasting programmes specifically for schools, but with a similar scheduling to that of the pre-war service. During the early months of 1940, programmes covered a wide variety of subjects which included *Singing Together*, *Music Making*, world history, British history, senior geography, book talks for senior English courses, as well as senior playwriting and drama productions, the practice and science of gardening, English for the under-nines, physical education exercises, science and the community, and a programme called *The River* especially designed for rural schools. Children also heard about current affairs from 'Alf', a fictional lorry driver. Significantly, there was also a programme called

Home Listening, which was designed specifically for those children who, because of the war conditions, were either working at home alone, or 'in groups of not more than ten with or without the supervision of a teacher'. These programmes centred on the exploits of a milkman from northern Canada, who told stories about his life with the Indians, the lumberjacks of Canada and trappers. There were also broadcasts in the Welsh language for juniors and seniors.[52] For some reason, programmes and material for radio courses in modern languages, which had been established before the war, were abandoned.[53]

In contrast to the German scheme, which favoured physical exercise as a form of healthy living, much more emphasis was placed on the health and *general* welfare of evacuees, both in the Reception Areas and in the cities that children were gradually returning to during the Phoney War period. Initially, the social welfare services attached to schools in effect ceased to exist once the Evacuation Scheme started. One serious casualty was the lack of school meals for the poorer children remaining in or returning to London. In early 1939, the London County Council had been providing 6,000 school meals to those considered in need and who were genuinely undernourished. After the first evacuation, during which they had provided those evacuees without food with packed lunches for the journey, the main school meals' kitchens closed until January 1940. As this service was no longer available, domestic science classes in schools were used to prepare and provide meals for the children. In response to the need, four kitchens were reopened and by June, 2,000 school meals were being supplied in seventy centres at schools. Also, by September 1940, 1,700 daily meals were being delivered from central kitchens to those schools remaining open. Every child was now entitled to a school meal and, if parents were unable to pay, the whole, or part of the cost was returned to them.[54] By 1944, almost 66,000 children were having school meals and the role of the teachers became a supervisory one, a role which incidentally was not relinquished until the change of teachers' pay and conditions in the 1990s. The pressure on working mothers to be out of the house during the school holidays resulted in a limited school meals' service in the London area during the vacation. However, there were serious anomalies, especially in the Reception Areas where unaccompanied children were not entitled to free meals and the burden of payment fell on the hosts who were often financially poor themselves. Whereas children evacuated with parents, who could not afford to pay, not only got free meals but also free school milk. Under the headline 'End this Anomaly of Evacuee Payments', a

correspondent to the *Dorset County Chronicle* and *Swanage Times*, Frank
Lloyd, questioned the scheme and added:

> We are thus left with the astonishing Government attitude that a child who is
> supposed to be fed on as little as 5s 6d a week must not receive free meals and
> school milk, however poor they might be. The Government order says it is
> assumed that the householder who takes in such a child can afford to provide
> it with midday meals and milk. Why? The assumption in many cases is false
> and the 8s 6d child is a burden to many homes. … Surely all Government-
> evacuated children should be entitled to free midday meals at a time when it
> is declared policy to augment the rations of the poorer people by community
> feeding. At least if some of the poor are entitled to free food, all should be.
> Free meals and milk would bring that miserly 8s 6d to a more reasonable
> figure. It is well known to billeting officers that evacuees tend to congregate
> in poor homes. Many well to do people are able to evade their obligations,
> others deliberately make the evacuees so uncomfortable that they leave. I can
> quote cases of both. The evacuee child is therefore often in a home where it
> was difficult to make ends meet before he came. And such a child, with no
> one to stand up for him, is supposed to be fed on 5s 6d a week …[55]

Officials in some areas took their responsibility for providing meals for evacuees
very seriously. As early as November 1939, the Dorset Education Committee
established communal feeding centres in Dorchester and other villages within
the county. The planning and implementation was the responsibility of the
County's Canteen organiser Miss A.M. Anderson. The idea behind the scheme
was that those children whose foster parents were out at work all day, or had
other reasons for being unable to provide a midday meal during the week,
should be able to have a lunch at a communal dining room. By November,
approximately 200 evacuees living locally had used the centres. The cost per
child was 4d a day or 1s 8d a week, which came out of the allowance paid to
hosts. For their money each child could receive two helpings of each course
which included at least 4oz of meat per helping and, because the meals were
done on a three-week rota basis, there was not much chance of them getting
tired of the same meals. A similar communal meal scheme was established in
January 1940 at Bridport, where 100 children ate their midday meal at the
Technical Institute in Chancery Lane, again at 4d a meal. The school milk
requirement also changed over the period of the war. Like school dinners, milk
had been provided pre-war to those children who would benefit from it, but

after the war started there was an aim to prevent infant undernourishment by making it available to all. So from 1941, those children whose parents could not afford the cost got it free. The distribution of school milk was problematic during the initial stages of evacuation, but throughout 1940 there was a gradual improvement until every elementary school in London still open was having milk delivered. In addition the Government decided in July 1940 to give free or cheap milk to mothers and small children. Though, the provision of free milk was not always available in all Reception Areas. The following announcement appeared in the *Isle of Ely and Wisbech Advertiser* in September 1939:

NO FREE MEALS FOR EVACUATED CHILDREN
The Board of Education consider that the payment of 10/6 or 8/6 to the billeting householder sufficient to provide adequate food. Also no free milk will be available except for special dietary cases.[56]

When the allocation of milk to the general public was rationed in 1943, the provision of school milk was cut to one-third of a pint, except for pupils getting free milk. They received two-thirds of a pint a day, whereas normal householders received two pints per week in winter and three to four pints per week in the summer. This was supplemented by National Dried Milk.

Another initiative was the Vitamin Welfare Scheme, which was introduced in 1941 to provide both free orange juice and cod-liver oil to expectant mothers and young children, or Vitamins A and D as alternatives. Additional advertisements on the radio and in newspapers explained the benefits:

FOOD FACTS
MUM! MY ORANGE JUICE. MY COD LIVER OIL.
MEMO FOR MUM!
You can buy continued health for your child at any welfare centre or distributing centre. In exchange for a few pence and the coupons in your child's ration book you can get his orange juice and cod liver oil. Don't get just the orange juice and forget about the cod liver oil – one is just as necessary as the other. Think of Orange Juice and Cod Liver Oil together as you think of pepper and salt, oil and vinegar, mustard and cress. Think of them as the two-part health scheme which your baby needs.[57]

Another adverse spin off from the Evacuation Scheme was the decline in school medical services which, for some pupils, was the only form of treatment they received, as this was well before the introduction of the National Health Service in 1948. In October 1939, the Ministry of Health issued a statement that all categories of evacuees were to have access to local medical services within the Reception Area. However, this immediately raised two specific questions: Who pays? And which doctors were to be called if evacuees became ill? Also, the influx of evacuees was to put a great deal of pressure on the already overstretched medical provision, especially within the rural areas. This was particularly problematic when pregnant mothers were evacuated into the country, as maternity facilities were not always available. In some areas empty private houses were requisitioned to cope with the immediate need, but the attendant costs for rates, rent and staff, were high. Eventually the Ministry of Health agreed to pay and another 1,000 maternity beds were found by the second day of the September 1939 evacuation. Once the babies were born, of course, both the mother and child needed extra social care, particularly important as the mothers were away from their extended families, which would normally have been available to look after other dependant siblings. It also needs to be remembered that Britain in the 1940s was not very liberal when it came to illegitimacy. Illegitimate births rose by 300 per cent and many people refused to house unmarried mothers and their children on moral grounds. As a result many of them were sent to local workhouses. In Somerset, two unmarried mothers were put back on the train and sent back to London. Some areas were a little more sympathetic and, realising that the workhouse was not always the best place, appointed social workers to help in such situations. This created a worthwhile service which had not been readily available before the war, and is one of the more positive 'spin-offs' of the Evacuation Scheme.

There had been problems in Germany where women were called Bomb Wenches and also in the Finnish/Swedish scheme where the latter considered themselves to be superior in social and economic terms, but there was a similar, and to some extent more sinister, aspect of social class in Britain, an issue that was even apparent during the planning of the Evacuation Scheme. When asked to appear before the Anderson Committee on 21 July 1938 to give her opinion on evacuation planning, Lady Reading, head of the Women's Voluntary Service, stated: 'Evacuees would be quite happy to live in barns or garages in the countryside, especially if they were next door to a middle class house'.[58] A note below this comment in the minutes says: '… this view was fully endorsed by the Chairman of the Women's Institute, Lady Denman'. To her credit, Lady Reading did change her opinion and told Mass Observation in 1940, that 'Evacuation had been a terrible fiasco … not nearly enough use had been made of the big houses of England'.[59] In 1940s' Britain everyone knew their place, respected their elders and children spoke when they were spoken to. Many evacuees from working-class backgrounds were treated with a certain amount of contempt and were subject to stereotyping. Comments in newspapers, public information films and even feature films perpetuated the class system and portrayed many evacuees as being uncouth, ill-kempt, disease ridden, verminous and in some cases heathen. This is evident in the film *Cottage To Let*, made in 1941 and distributed by Gainsborough Pictures, where one of the central characters, 'Lady Barrington', when informed by a billeting officer that she was to have evacuees, told her Butler to 'get the spare blankets and eiderdown from the attic … you know, the one with the holes in it', implying that this was good enough for an evacuee. In February 1942, the vicar of St Mary's church, Dorchester, commented on the 'heathen' upbringing of many evacuated children: 'Many of them have been brought up in a manner one could call anything but only heathen. They had never been to any place of worship or Sunday School and had never been taught to say their prayers …'[60]

This propaganda also maintained the image of middle-class families taking in working-class evacuees, whereas, in reality, it was the labouring and agricultural workers in the Reception Areas who bore the brunt of billeting. As Titmuss remarked, '… all too often it was the poor and underprivileged housing the same from the cities' and went on to say that 'the wealthier classes evaded their responsibilities quite effectively'.[61] In 1939, one clergyman in a small country parish who offered to find billets for evacuees in the local village 'tramped many weary miles over muddy field, getting refusal after refusal, especially from many of the richer people'.[62] In some parts of the country the situation was not helped by local legislation, which took away the responsibility for having evacuees from the upper classes. Some residents in a part of Wiltshire were not expected to take in evacuees because '… the servant problem in the large houses is so acute that it would be unfair to billet children on the owners'.[63] It would have been interesting to see the 'class' divisions on the council making this decision! James Roffey recalls that some evacuees were not even allowed in the house. A visit by a host and her evacuees to a friend resulted in the following situation:

> We had been shown the grounds by a girl of 15. Then we were taken to the house, but before we went in we met the girl's mother who asked.

'Where are you taking them?'

'To meet Daddy,' was the reply.

'Oh darling! I don't think that is a good idea. I'm sure your little friends are very nice but we do not want them in the house do we? I'll have the buns and barley-water sent out'.[64]

However, this was not always the case, and others took their responsibilities more seriously and either made over their whole house to the evacuees, or made their stay as comfortable as possible. The family in Parham House, West Sussex accommodated over twenty evacuees and looked after them extremely well ... with the help of the servants.

If anyone refused to have an evacuee they could be fined 15*s*, which to a labourer was a great deal of money, but to anyone in the middle and upper classes would not necessarily have been sufficient enough to make them change their mind. Although there is evidence that the fines could be cumulative as one man in Dorset was fined £5 for persistent refusal.

It would be wrong to assume that although in some areas the responsibility for housing evacuees fell on the poorer classes, they would offer a more caring environment for evacuees from similarly deprived backgrounds. There is plenty of evidence to the contrary, especially where anti-evacuee propaganda and rumour preceded the arrival of the children. In one example, children from a Liverpool school who were billeted in North Wales had their heads shaved, were washed in disinfectant and had their clothes burned, simply because someone had told them that children from Liverpool 'brought head lice, scabies and sores'.[65] In fairness, it has to be said that despite this initial treatment a number of this group of evacuees were then well looked after in their billets and did enjoy the remainder of their stay. But this anti-evacuee sentiment was not an isolated incident. In October 1940, an anonymous correspondent to the *Windsor Express* seriously suggested the building of concentration camps to house evacuees. In addition some councils even discussed the possibility of putting evacuees into segregated communities![66] The use of the words 'concentration camp' could have been forgiven as merely identifying some sort of holding area for evacuees, similar to those used by the British forces to house prisoners in the Boer War. There are many examples from around the country of local communities objecting to having evacuees billeted on them. Some people were not as willing to help, or sympathetic towards the plight of the children, as the propaganda at the time, and even today, would have one believe.

There is evidence of medical certificates being 'purchased' to show that the holder was not medically fit to look after children, although, in some cases, the ploy backfired when people were asked to name their doctor so that their 'illness' could be checked. Letters were sent by people of influence asking not to have to take in evacuees. Favours were 'called in'. In some areas of the country such practices were not tolerated and local newspaper articles of the time were often very critical of such behaviour. A journalist on the *St Ives Times* in Cornwall wrote in June 1940 during the second evacuation:

> I gather that those who have had the task of finding volunteers to house these children have had no light job. A number of people who a short while ago were moaning that they had no seasonal bookings this year were apparently full up immediately the question of evacuees arose. Perhaps we are to have a season after all. I hear that the number of people who have developed heart trouble and kindred ailments this week is staggering. I suppose we must expect to see these poor souls wheeled along the Wharf Road in bath chairs.
>
> One man is alleged to have said he would as soon house Hitler as evacuee children. If this attitude was general he would probably have Hitler and the Gestapo with him sooner than he expected. Perhaps he anticipates becoming a local dictator under the Nazi regime.

Even when they were willing to take in evacuees some hosts, even those in authority, were able to use their influence to manipulate the procedures. A teacher interviewee recalled that, 'The billeting officer drew me to one side and asked if I could recommend one nice, clean little girl as his wife would be pleased to take one evacuee ... I selected a victim ... the "market" was then declared open ...'

It is worth commenting that this intolerance was not altogether one-sided. Some children, and in some cases their accompanying mothers, who had been evacuated from more middle-class areas, objected to having to live in labourers' cottage or a working-class home. One interviewee from a reasonably well-off family was indignant that she was billeted with a very poor couple who had no bathroom and she had to wash in a tin bath in the kitchen. In some areas, this host-evacuee conflict became a serious problem. Had there not been a 'Phoney War' period perhaps the evacuees would have been tolerated in the spirit of 'doing one's bit'; however, as this period of relative 'inaction' continued, tolerance was replaced by intolerance, resentment and ill-feeling in many of the Reception Areas. This resulted in many requests, from both sides, guests and hosts, for evacuees to be moved. Some parents demanded that their children should be moved. The town clerk in Chipping Norton, Oxfordshire, was sent the following letter by a Mrs Reading from Plaistow, after she had visited her children in their new foster homes during the first weekend of the war:

> I went to see my two children today, (Sunday September 10th), and I found Ethel very comfortable and happy with Mrs Webb at No 3 Spring Place, but I am sorry to say I could not say the same for Johnny, he did not complain but I cannot leave him where he is, so I am asking you if you could find some-where else for him. I know Mrs Pickett of No.4 Spring Place would have him and he would have better care taken of him … if he isn't found somewhere better I shall have to bring him back to London …[67]

Some evacuee mothers with children also deliberately moved from place to place and chose the areas they wished to go to. These were called 'twicers' and were in effect getting a guided tour of the best Reception Areas in the country before then returning home. Many local hosts considered this to be an abuse of the system and on 18 September 1939, the *Dorset Echo* reported this under the banner headline:

> EVACUATED WOMEN GOING HOME.
> A CHEAP FORTNIGHT'S HOLIDAY.
> Women evacuated from London appear to be returning home in increasing numbers from the south coast although they are not being encouraged to do so by local authorities. Many of the women were in excellent billets and expressed themselves well satisfied with their reception but stated that they were returning home with the consent of their husbands. It appears that a number of them have treated the evacuation scheme as an opportunity for obtaining a fortnight's holiday at very little expense.

In order to stop some of this *ad hoc* movement, Mr Warren, the Chief Billeting Officer in Weymouth, officially announced on 26 September that all billeted persons within his jurisdiction had to remain in their present bil-lets without exception until 7 October. He stated that:

> The authorities have been very tolerant and have made great efforts to assist the evacuees to settle down. A tremendous amount of work has been done

to try and correct the more obvious misfits. But there must be a limit to the unrestricted movement which appears at present to be taken for granted. Billeting cannot be changed at will by people who profess to be satisfied with what has been provided for them at the Government's expense. Cases of real necessity will still be dealt with by me, but I am determined to put a stop to unnecessary movement amongst the evacuated population and for that reason 'standstill' must be maintained. People who, after this warning, take the responsibility of leaving the billets which have been allocated to them and seek accommodation elsewhere without the consent of the Chief Billeting Officer, run the risk of having to pay for their lodgings from their own resources.

Unlike their peers in Germany, who were trying to get home amid the devastation of post-war Europe, and Finland where in some cases the process took many years, the return of evacuees from the Reception Areas in Britain should have been much easier to control. Yet this was not always the case, as there had been a steady, unofficial drift back home throughout the war, punctuated by re-evacuation in 1940 and 1944. By December 1939, 30 per cent of evacuated unaccompanied children and 49 per cent of accompanied children, together with 50 per cent of the mothers, had returned to London.[68]

There were a number of reasons for this. Most important was the fact that there was nothing happening on the war front, so many hosts and evacuees became very frustrated about staying in the Reception Areas. Also, many of the billeting authorities were making the evacuees feel very unwelcome as they were thought to be needlessly putting a great deal of pressure on the local social, medical and economic services. Some parents took, or collected, their children from the Reception Areas because of the lack of suitable billets, especially when evidence of ill-treatment or inadequacy on the part of the host required more than one move.

Teachers were very concerned that some of these children who returned early in the war were simply walking the streets of their home cities. As a result, some schools were reopened and made available to anyone over the age of eleven who lived within a mile of the buildings, and where this could not happen some of the returning teachers started 'homework' clubs in their own homes in order to provide some semblance of education. This presupposed of course that the pupils had the self-discipline to do independent work. Despite attempts to get them into schools, only 2 per cent of children attended. During the Blitz it soon became apparent that the pupils were not only in danger from the bombs, but also from the structural damage in some of their school buildings.

The evacuation authorities and the Government were so concerned that children were returning that they adopted measures to tempt them to stay. This included money being sent into the host villages and towns to pay for parties and concerts over Christmas 1939, and more dramatically, the cessation of transport to some of the Reception Areas to stop parents collecting their children. Of course, this put more pressure on the teachers who had to remain with the children over Christmas, but it was hoped that their leave entitlement could be staggered after the holiday. In reality they had little break, despite some authorities suggesting that they should be relieved of their duties for a few days as some of them had been working for months without any respite. Unlike their contemporaries in Germany and Finland, British parents had the opportunity to visit their children in the Reception Areas, either independently or in arranged coach parties. James Roffey recalled one such visit with mixed emotions:

> After what seemed a lifetime the convoy of Argosy coaches came slowly down Church Hill and stopped outside the Swan Hotel. All the children were cheering and pushing forward, trying to see which coach their parents were on so that they could be at the right doorway. … Our mother could only stay at Pulborough for a few hours before she had to rejoin the coach and go on to Shoreham to visit our brother Ernest … We sadly watched the coach leaving and then wandered off feeling very despondent and homesick.

For many evacuees like James, these visits were a disappointment and an emotional wrench. Parents and children tried to relate to each other, sometimes in very difficult circumstances, and in many ways the situation was false. There was a hope on the part of some evacuees that the relationship between them and their parents would be the same as it had been at home, but of course this was impossible. For some parents the costs were prohibitive, so eventually the Government agreed to limited travel concessions, and in some areas, such as Weymouth, the local population were asked to contribute to a fund to enable parents to visit evacuees in the locality.

To some extent the final return home at the end of the war was just as significant as the outward journey, and just as much a severe test of logistics. It was certainly not an impromptu exercise, and in the main was far better organised than those in Sweden and Germany. It had been planned as early as August 1943, but the attacks on London by the V1 and V2 rockets in 1944 meant that the scheme was implemented in other areas first. The telegram informing Reception Areas to send their children home was sent on 2 May 1945. On receipt of the message, they were to implement the proposals outlined in the arrangements circulated the previous month. The whole plan involving the London district to recover children from around 1,000 different billeting areas, sort them into travelling parties, take them back to London, sort them into the original eighty evacuation districts and accompany the individuals back to their homes, was to be co-ordinated by the London County Council working with the senior regional officers in the Ministry of Health. They in turn appointed an officer in the Reception Area to take charge of the assembly, entraining and departure of the evacuees in their area. The LCC also appointed a 'train-marshal' for each train with the responsibility for the actual journey. Both of these people were additionally responsible for making sure that the arrangements for overnight stays of evacuees and escorts, luggage and feeding were in hand, although technically it was a 'Food Executive Officer' who was in charge of the feeding of evacuees. Food and luggage were very important considerations. On arrival in London all evacuees were to be given a meal, but for the trip, they and their escorts were provided with packed lunches. As in the original journey in September 1939, drinks were to be provided at stopping points along the route by members of the WVS and other voluntary organisations. Food and drink for unaccompanied children was loaded onto the relevant trains and handed out during the journey. Adult evacuees had been given notices about the movement of their luggage during the time leading up to the actual journey, and they were asked to complete the registration cards. After these cards had been returned to the Senior Regional Officer they were collated, and specially coloured labels representing the first dispersal centres in London to which the evacuees were to be taken, were returned to the evacuees' billets to be attached to their luggage. It was very important that the correct colour corresponded with the addresses on the evacuees' home address.

As far as possible, the plan was to move the evacuees in organised parties travelling by special trains or alternatively in reserved seats on regular trains. Free travel vouchers were to be given to those who wished to travel independently, but only when they could not be included in an organised group, or where insufficient numbers in a specific area warranted an official party. Evacuees whose return had to be delayed were eligible for free travel. The vouchers could only be used on weekdays as the railway companies were not prepared to allow their use at the weekends. The parents or designated guardians of unaccompanied children, who could not be included in the organised travel, could also apply for free vouchers in order to collect their children. This too applied to people acting as escorts to the blind, disabled and elderly. Alternative arrangements were made for those who, for various reasons, were unable to travel by rail. In March 1945, a count of the evacuees remaining in the Reception Areas showed that during the previous six months an estimated 600,000 had returned home independently. This was out of a known total of 1,040,200. As most of these returnees were Londoners, the overall plan was scaled down to account for the decline in numbers, which amounted to a total of 453,200, including 134,000 unaccompanied children. The actual scheme, like its predecessors, was bound up in seemingly endless bureaucratic red-tape, but the plans were designed to overcome any disorganised evacuation from the Reception Areas. As it was, when evacuees did eventually arrive at the main-line stations in London, the sheer numbers of people and the luggage they brought with them, caused a great deal of dislocation to the day-to-day running of the stations.

The Evacuation Scheme officially ended on 31 March 1946. However, not all evacuees had returned. There were still 5,200 unaccompanied children left in the Reception Areas, either in their billets, hostels or residential nurseries. The majority of these remained because of the housing problems which still existed in the former target areas. Others had been orphaned, and twenty-nine had been deserted by parents. The long-term effects of the evacuation, the return, and in some cases abandonment, will be dealt with in a later chapter.

5

British Camp Schools

After working at the Education Offices, Ilford, since January 1930 making
the necessary arrangements for the removal of the school to the Camp, I am
going on today to be ready to receive the boys on the 19th. School furniture,
equipment, books etc have been sent on.[1]

Unlike their German *Kinderlandverschikung* counterparts, those British evacuees who were sent to one of the thirty-two camp schools established in the
UK fared generally better in terms of education, care and overall discipline.
When interviewed, many of the ex-camp-school evacuees consider that
they were fortunate in where they were sent. However, for others who not
only had to cope with evacuation but also with an alien boarding school
situation, the experience could be rather traumatic:

> I had one year when I was extremely homesick. There was a terrific pain,
> I had never been away from my people before, although I had stayed with
> several relatives due to my mother's illness, and my father being in the forces.
> But I had never had this experience before, this terrible longing, this gnawing
> feeling inside of me … In fact at one time I was so homesick and so unhappy
> that the dormitory master had special permission for me to be taken into the
> school hospital to be looked after for a week or two to see if they could get
> me over this terrible crying and feeling of being so lonely.[2]

The majority of the schools were built to a similar pattern and although
there were individual idiosyncrasies, the daily routine followed a comparable

schedule. Jim Bartley, a former pupil of a camp school near Hemel Hempstead, described his average daily regimen:

> We were wakened in the morning to walk to the ablution block to wash, return to the dormitory to fold blankets and make bed area tidy, then in dormitory order went to the dining area for breakfast, then morning school, lunch, afternoon school, tea. After tea there was free time but there were many organised activities especially between the hours of 8.00-9.00pm. Each dormitory was looked after by two teachers who took it in turns to read stories to the boys at bedtime which was usually 9.00pm.[3]

The National Camps Corporation Ltd for England and Wales had been established under the Camps Act which came into being on 25 May 1939, and by July 1939 it had considered 155 sites all of which had been personally inspected by the Chairman or Managing Director as to their suitability. Although originally forty-three camps were going to be constructed, only thirty locations were chosen, (this was to rise to thirty-one) and the camps were to be built from Canadian Maple with shingle roofs, to a design developed in collaboration with the Royal Institute of British Architects. At this time the estimated cost was £17,350 per camp, made up from:

> 15 acre site at £40 per acre … £600
> Layout-roads, drains, central buildings, sleeping quarters … £15,000
> Equipment and furniture … £1,750

Later estimates in November 1939 put the cost well above this, in the region of £26,000-£37,000.

The first camp was completed by October 1939, a further nine by January 1940 and all but three of the final thirty-one by March 1940.

Once they were built, the local authorities designated to use them now had to convince parents that this form of evacuation was a suitable one, and bearing in mind the residential nature of the process, for some parents and children this could be more stressful than evacuation to hosts in residential billets. Very few documents survive that indicate this process, however a rare 'guide' from the City of Rochester (Kent) Education Committee does provide an insight into how parents were persuaded to send their children away to the Wrens Warren Residential School, in Sussex.[4] Note this is entirely different from the tone used by the KLV authorities:

The problem of what to do for the best with regard to evacuating their children is ever with parents in these days of stress and anxiety ... The suggestion put before you is easy to carry out into practice. The cost is the same as if your children were evacuated in the usual way, and is paid in exactly the same manner. There are no tiresome conditions, except that the youngsters must be medically fit, and that there is room for them.

The advantages are worth examination. In brief they amount to the following:-

The children, boys and girls, go to a quiet, healthy spot miles from any town or city, but only 40 miles from their homes.

They are educated and cared for by specially selected staff.

They receive full-time education, with the fullest opportunities for outdoor work, in addition to the usual school lessons.

Games, physical training and sports of all kinds are provided in a way which is impossible in towns under war-time conditions.

Regular medical supervision is afforded free of any extra costs to parents, and there need be no cause for worry on the score of health.[5]

Once a month parents are able to visit their children, being conveyed at a reasonable charge, to and from the school, by buses chartered for the purpose.

The extraordinary character of the school itself ...

One proviso and one alone is made when admitting a child to the school, namely, that he or she remains there as long as possible whilst the war lasts, and the assistance of the parents in not changing their minds without real reason must be insisted upon from the onset ...[6]

The camps were not limited to England and Wales. While unveiling a plaque at the inauguration of the first camp school in Scotland, at Bromlee near Edinburgh, the Secretary of State for Scotland, John Colville, explained that it would have six dormitory huts, each with teachers' rooms and a common room for teaching purposes, an administrative building, an assembly hall and hospital and sanitary units. It would accommodate 350 children and teachers.[7] Under the Camps Act, the Scottish Special Housing Association had already chosen sites in Scotland for four additional camps which would serve two purposes; peacetime holiday and school camps for children who would be sent there for periods of up to a fortnight, and in wartime provide suitable accommodation for evacuated children from the cities.

In the late 1930s and early '40s the whole question of camp schools had led to heated debates between the educationalists on the one side and local and national politicians on the other. Many of these arguments took place within the letter pages of the journal *Education*.

This letter was from Charles Robertson of the London Education Committee re: Camp Schools dated 23 January 1940:

Sir,– In the course of an article on Camps in the issue of Education of January 19, Sir Percival Sharp repeats the suggestion made elsewhere in the Press that the 'hold up' in using the Government's evacuation camps has been due to the unwillingness of London teachers to accept the duties associated with camp life in addition to their ordinary duties as teachers. He goes on to say that I have denied the unwillingness of London teachers, but he does not say that at the same time, I have also explained why the LCC was unable to make immediate use of the camps. The fact is that, as at present designed, they are admirably suited for short occupation by parties of school children. For this purpose, with their central heating and electric lighting, their season could be extended somewhat beyond the usual summer months. It is, however, quite a different question to use the camps for permanent and continuous occupation by evacuated schools.

Sir Percival Sharp says that secondary schools are scattered all over the face of the country, working in some case, under almost impossible conditions, and he suggests that we have in the camps the beginning of a residential public school system available for pupils to whom the hope of such experience has been, and in all probability ever will be, denied. It is difficult however, to see how any secondary school could be successfully run in the camps with their present accommodation.

The only classroom facilities consist of a block of four rooms each capable of holding one form, a hall in which another form might be accommodated, together with two small rooms that might be used for sixth form work. One form could be accommodated during the part of the day in the dining hall. That is to say, there is classroom accommodation for six forms, in addition to the 6th Form an insufficient provision even for a small secondary school that admits only two forms a year. Most London secondary schools admit three forms a year so that, even when allowance has been made for amalgamating some forms because only 60% of the children have been evacuated, it is obvious that the school is woefully short of bare class-room accommodation.

We are told that the purpose of the Camps Bill was twofold – evacuation in war-time and education in peace-time. This succinct statement makes no reference to education in war-time. When children have been evacuated it is still necessary to educate them, and camp facilities that are adequate for supplementing peace-time education that is given for the greater part of the year in permanent school buildings, are not adequate for giving war-time education all the year round, with no access to permanent school buildings. It is not enough to say that the Camps Corporation has worked hard and swiftly, and they had a limited job – that of providing accommodation for others to use. A successful businessman must ascertain in advance what are the needs of his customers and plan accordingly.

Signed Charles Robertson

County Hall London.

January. 1940[8]

Sir Percival Sharp replied to Charles Robertson in his weekly column 'Week by Week':

I am not greatly perturbed by criticism as to the unsuitability in limited respects of the camps for any particular purpose proposed by the government. They were provided, according to Mr Lindsay, for evacuation purposes in war-time and for education in peace-time. I am perturbed by the failure of the government to make reasonable and prompt use of the accommodation provided at so great a cost.

Mr Robertson, Chairman of the London Education Committee, in a letter printed on a later page, takes exception to my suggestion that the camps should be used for the purpose of residential secondary schools on the grounds that the camps are not suitable in all respects for the purpose. I take comfort from the fact that in a circular issued by the Board of Education immediately after my notes were in type, the use of these camps for the purposes I indicated is commended to local authorities.

It is true that modifications and additions which can quickly be made may be necessary if conditions approaching the ideal are to be secured, but it is to be remembered that secondary and other schools broken and scattered are now working under conditions far worse than those obtaining in the camps.

In May 1940, J.V. Strudwick, chairman of the National Association of Labour Teachers added his weight to the argument:

… Assuming that private billeting can successfully account for half a million child evacuees and that the occupation of large mansions and other suitable buildings might dispose of another half a million, there would still remain well over a million from the danger zones who should be accommodated in the safer areas. Where are they to be put? The obvious answer is School Camps.

This has been advocated previously in your columns and it is indeed more than five months since the Association of Architects, Surveyors and Technical assistants published their plan for school camps for all evacuable children. Is it not high time that such a plan was being put into execution by the government?[9]

Some had already been completed by the time this article appeared. One camp school, established in Oxfordshire as early as February 1940, was considered at the time to be an educational experiment. On 19 February 1940, The Beal Modern School, from Ley Street, Essex (a Central School), became the first 'camp school' when seven coach loads of boys were taken to Kennylands Camp, Sonning Common near Reading. The school had originally been evacuated to Ipswich but 182 pupils and twelve teachers were transferred to the camp. The school was divided up into five houses; Wolfe, Drake, Clive, Blake and Scott and they competed against each other in all their activities including school work, gardening, games and the cleanliness of their dormitories.[10]

The camp, built at a cost of £20,000, had central heating so it could be used throughout the year, its own hospital and sewage disposal plant, 20 acres of ground, an assembly hall with stage and dressing rooms, a dining hall, shower baths and a tuck shop.

John Gould, an ex-Kennylands pupil, described the camp:

It consisted of a collection of wooden buildings on either side of a drive … with dormitories on one side and administrative buildings on the other. On the left hand side of the drive these administration buildings consisted of a dining room and a kitchen, there was an assembly hall, a hospital, staff quarters, lavatory blocks, a camp manager's house, a boiler house and classrooms. On the right hand side there were 6 dormitories which were 3 one end and 3 the other end of a development with a splendid cricket ground dividing them. My first day memories are of being shown our dormitory with its rows of bunk beds along each side and the whole room housed 36 boys in double bunks. Great store was set about being self-sufficient and it was all a question of making your own bed and darning your socks. Cleaning the dormitory was considered most important and I can remember on Saturdays the floor used to be polished and a boy was pulled up and down on the carpet whilst polishing the floor![11]

The boys received four meals a day prepared by the camp chef described as 'a great big man, very tall, white hair and honey eyes'.[12] As well as a head teacher, Mr W.L. Norman, the school also had a Camp Manager, Captain F. Mee, who had also been a secondary schoolmaster. When interviewed in 1940, Captain Mee explained the ethos behind the school:

> Whatever the boys show a desire to learn we shall be glad to teach them. We are planting an orchard and ploughing up some land for the boys to work ... This kind of school is what I have been urging for years. It will make the boys self reliant and teach them the value of co-operation and the responsibilities of citizenship.[13]

There would also have been a House Matron, and although there are no specific details for Kennylands, an advertisement for a camp school in Cheshire provides an indication of the basic job description and the remuneration:

> Applications are invited for the post of House Matron at Marton Camp. The matron will act as foster mother to the boys at the camp, and will be responsible for the repair of children's clothing etc. Suitable assistance will be provided. The salary for the appointment, which is subject to one month's notice on either side, will be fixed at a figure between £55 and £90 per annum, plus board, lodging and laundry, in accordance with the qualifications of the candidate appointed ...[14]

Many of the boys studied for the School Certificate or the Royal Society of Arts, but their academic studies were balanced by having non-academic interests for part of the day. These included not only sports, but also such pursuits as bee-keeping and pig-rearing.[15] As the first of its kind, the school was visited by the King and Queen on 30 September 1940. They spent some time viewing all areas of the camp including the dormitories, classrooms and other facilities, before going on to look at the piggeries and chicken houses.

> This has been a red-letter day in the history of the school. At short notice their Majesties King George VI and Queen Elizabeth, accompanied by

Commander and Mrs Campbell and Sir Alan Lascelles, arrived on a visit to the camp … A visit was made to the pigsty and poultry enclosures and the boys who are mainly responsible for the care of the livestock were honoured by being conversed with by both the King and Queen …[16]

But there were some sadder moments:

I have to record the distressing fact that Peter Gillingham, aged 12 of Form 1a, has lost his whole family consisting of father and mother and five young children by enemy action on the night of the 10th May.[17]

I regret to have to record that one of our boys, William Gouldstone, who left school on December 15th last (1944), was killed by enemy action in his home in Ilford on the morning of March 6th. His mother, too, was killed.[18]

This area of the country was popular for camp schools because just 2 miles down the road was another one … Bishopswood Farm, situated between the villages of Peppard and Gallowstree Common. It housed the senior boys and girls from Bedford School who moved in on 26 February 1940. Doug Dielhenn, an ex-pupil, remembered the layout of the area vividly:

As one entered the camp by the main gate, on the left was the Headmaster's house and office and on the right a small infirmary run by the school matron. There were 3 boys dormitories, in each 40 boys sleeping on 2-tiered beds. There was a master's room in each dormitory.

On the far side of the camp there were also 3 huts, but only two of them were used as dormitories for about 60 girls. The third hut was used as a classroom for teaching such things as cookery and woodwork. The main assembly hall, complete with stage, also doubled as a classroom for the older boys only. They had no teacher but sat and did revision of past work, liable to be asked for the work to be shown at any time … Back in London boys and girls never mixed. We saw the girls in chapel every morning where they sat at the centre pews and we boys on either side and at the back. We also saw them at meal times where they were the strange creatures who sat on the other side of the central serving table … At the camp things changed and we had mixed classes, a thing unheard of before. We still sat separately 2 rows of 12 boys and 2 rows of girls. At last we began to realise the girls were human as we were, if you could call us human. The fact that woods surrounded the camp also helped some of us understand more about girls! …[19]

There was also an 'ablution' block containing only twelve toilets which served almost 150 boys. Interviewees remember that these facilities were stretched to the limit every other Saturday when the school nurses gave each pupil a dose of laxative. Two showers a week were an important part of the routine as a great deal of emphasis was placed on personal cleanliness. The buildings were arranged into a semi-circle which surrounded a large circular lawn with a flag-pole in the middle. This area was out of bounds except when used for specific events such as Sports Day. As well as the woods described by Doug, there was also an area of cultivated land where the children participated in the national 'Dig for Victory' campaign. As in Kennylands, there were a number of outdoor pursuits and extra-curricular activities which in some cases initiated life-long interests.

Another pupil was allocated to Bishopwood later in the war. Having already been evacuated to a number of billets, Tony Towner, together with his younger sister, arrived at the camp in 1943 and was to stay there until his mother remarried in 1947. When he was there the school housed the Alexandra Orphanage, which was to amalgamate with another one to become the Royal Alexandra and Albert School. He remembers the school having a 'holiday camp' appearance, but for Tony the experience was not always a happy one. Up until his move to the camp, his life as an evacuee had been somewhat liberal. Now he found himself in what he describes as '… a strict regime, rigidly controlled along military lines, with one of the house masters known only as Sergeant'.[20] The system of control, which required a certain amount of self-regulation by a prefect and monitorial system, did lead to some bullying but nothing like the scale of that witnessed in the KLV camps. The inhabitants of the three boys' dormitories were divided up according to age, eight to ten, ten to twelve, twelve to fifteen, and the progression from one to the other depended on the number of boys leaving at fifteen. Although this 'promotion' was seen as necessary, many, including Tony, did not look forward to the initiation ceremonies that went with it. His personal account gives a very detailed picture of what life was like in Bishopswood, and it is interesting to note the similarities between his description and those of pupils in other camps, such as Jim Bartley. Each day followed the same schedule. The pupils got up at 6.30 a.m. and then had to strip their beds completely from the two-tiered bunks. The mattress was folded in half and the folded blankets and sheet, in the form of a sleeping bag, together with a pillow-case, was placed on top.[21] At 6.45 a.m. they were marched to the toilet block in pyjamas and dressing gowns and then returned to the dormitories to change their clothes, clean their shoes and have a kit inspection at 7.30 a.m. This was a competitive process as marks were awarded for neatness and precision. The time before breakfast at 8 a.m. (9 a.m. on Sunday) was spent standing around outside, unless it was raining. Tony recalls breakfast being the highlight of his day. It comprised of porridge, crispy fried bread, baked beans, fried or scrambled powdered egg. But he was not as complimentary about the lunches which he simply describes as 'awful'. Fatty mince, or meat stew with cabbage, turnip, swede and lumpy mashed potato, followed by a milk pudding of some kind. Everything had to be eaten. Tea was simply bread and jam, and supper a slice of bread and Marmite.[22] In addition, once a week they were all given their 2oz of sweet rations, which became the unofficial currency for bartering.

During their spare time they listened to the wireless and worked on their hobbies. Tony remembers the first Sunday in every month as 'visiting day'. Unlike the parents of the German children who were actively discouraged from visiting their children, those with offspring in the British camps kept in close contact. They would normally travel in hired coaches from London, or by train and then the local bus service from Reading, and arrive after the Sunday morning church service, which was usually led by the head teacher. After spending time with the children they would then leave before afternoon tea for the journey home. For some this was always a heart-wrenching experience as homesickness was a problem, especially among the younger and more insecure pupils.

As well as individual reminiscences, which of course can be subjected to memory distortion, some Local Education Administrators and head teachers of schools kept detailed notes about the process of moving children to the camps. The following example relates to Manchester and provides historians with a very rare opportunity to see a case study of how one particular area dealt with the planning and implementation of such an enterprise.

The camp school assigned to the Manchester LEA was Somerford Hall in Congelton. It stood on a large site 2 miles from the town and it had been designed for 350 pupils. It was described as having 'excellent facilities for physical training and games'. As with other camps, the buildings were made of wood, usually Canadian Maple donated by the Canadian government, and in a pattern similar to the others which consisted of an education block of four classrooms, a hall with stage and an ante-room. It also had a residential block containing six dormitories, a large dining room, kitchens, a staff room, two lavatory blocks with WCs, baths and showers and a drying room.

There was also a small hospital block, quarters for eight teachers and separate living quarters for the head teacher and the camp manager. It was much bigger than the camps at Kennylands and Bishopswood, even though it was designed to house almost the same number of pupils. It had been suggested that, if necessary, minor alterations could be made to accommodate extra classes by adapting a dormitory block and using the dining room.

The Board of Education had requested that the number of children transferred to the camp should not be less than 150 and the suggestion was made that the school should be organised to receive senior boys drawn from Manchester schools and other children, either at home or evacuated, whose parents specifically wanted them to move to the camp. The financial liability to parents would be exactly the same as those allocated to billets, i.e. they would make a weekly contribution of 6s.

The head teacher and the male teaching staff were to be recruited from teachers already on the Manchester LEA's payroll. They would live on-site and in return for residential duties would receive free board and lodging. The Education Committee would be responsible for equipping the classrooms, laboratories and workshops with portable equipment, much of which would be provided out of existing stocks, and all the necessary supplies of stationery, books and other school materials. Any other expenditure would be set against the evacuee account and would be met in full by central Government.

Although there was some delay in using the school because of bad weather conditions affecting the progress of the work, by March the Committee reported that all was in hand. A leaflet had been published giving information to parents, and head teachers had been invited to submit lists of senior boys whose parents wished them to transfer to Somerford. Although every effort was being made to get the school open by Easter, the Committee still had to appoint a head teacher and the required staff. The first batch of boys arrived on 23 April with more arriving on the 25th. A total of 163 boys were then in residence and it was expected that admissions would continue until such time as the full complement of 350 was reached. The number of teachers had been raised from the initial six to eight and the head teacher's wife had agreed to take up the role of school matron. Considering the projected number of pupils this is rather a small teaching staff. Had the school reached its full potential the pupil-teacher ratio would have been 46:1, which even in wartime was rather large. This had been noticed by the head teacher who commented on staffing issues on a number of occasions, often to no avail. Fortunately, the numbers on roll were usually around the 160 mark.

From December 1942, the head teacher wrote regular reports for the Education Committee. They provide an interesting indication of what life was like in the camp and the facilities available to the boys. It is worth remembering that this type of education was alien to all those who went to Somerford because until this time they had been used to attending day schools and therefore going home in the evenings. The boarding scenario, and all that entailed, was very new and some of the boys, especially the younger ones, took some time to settle down to the routine.

On 21 December 1942, the head teacher reported that there had been one case of chickenpox but the boy concerned had been isolated. The time-table had been changed to allow the boys the opportunity to go outside in the afternoon and the afternoon lessons had been moved to the evening. Fourteen boys had been confirmed in the Church of England and a Catholic Guild had also been established. The head teacher had introduced a monthly prefects' supper. In order to stimulate interest in the United States, ten boys had joined the American Foster Parents Plan, and were communicating with 'foster parents' in the USA. Almost all the boys over twelve had been out and about for ten days helping local farmers bring in the potato crop and as a result had earned £80, but there was no mention of whether the boys or the school fund received the money! Preparations were being made for the Christmas pantomime.

18 January 1943. The Dick Whittington production was reported as a great success. Two boys were listed as having scabies and another with an abscess in his ear. Two of the dormitories had been painted in house colours. During the Christmas holidays 123 pupils had gone home leaving only forty in the camp. Those who remained had had a good time. For Christmas dinner they had roast beef, baked and mashed potatoes, sprouts, and Christmas pudding. They had seen films on Christmas night, and on the 27th and on Boxing Day they had had a party. On the 28th a local farmer had taken them to the cinema. As the weather had been so mild they spent a lot of time outside.

It is interesting that Christmas was an important time in all the camps, especially for those children who were unable to go home. The school staff made sure that the children had a good a time as possible under the circumstances. Tony Towner described his Christmas at Bishopswood with some fondness. He recalled a large tree without any decorations, but the highlight was the dinner which included a pudding where each portion contained a sixpenny piece. Presents and parcels which had been sent to the children for Christmas had been stored away to be handed out on the day, and those pupils who did not have a parcel, were given one from the school's emergency gifts so that no child missed out.[23]

15 February 1943. The head teacher informed the Committee that there had been no reoccurrence of the serious incidences of chilblains which had been the case the previous year. The main path to the dormitories had been widened and asphalted. In total 123 boys had returned to the school immediately after Christmas although seventy had not attended by 11 January and six by the 31st. He had since been notified that three boys would not be returning. Those members of staff who had left were not being replaced and this was putting a great deal of pressure on those who remained. The school urgently needed a sewing maid (this had been resolved by the March report). A branch of the Young Farmers Club had been established and it was reported that the boys were already keeping bees and rabbits and it was hoped that they would have some geese by the summer.

15 March 1943. The head teacher reported a clean bill of health. Although the play hut had not been completed there was now an oak cabinet to display trophies. Out-of-school clubs now comprised of handicraft, gymnastics, drama, stamps, hiking (with rucksacks), modelling, aeroplane modelling, rabbit and young farmers, art, gardening, debating and the *Somerford Times*, the camp's own newspaper. It was his aim to get each boy interested in at least one extra-curricular activity. Also, as shoes wore out quickly and repairs were very difficult because of lack of local cobblers, he proposed introducing a cobbling club. During the month, Lieutenant Baum from the US Army had visited the school and given a talk and Captain Campbell, the inspector for the National Camps Corporation (NCC), had made a visit and deemed everything to be 'satisfactory'.

Like many other camp schools, Somerford received gifts and grants from various organisations both in the UK and from overseas. It had received £5 from the American Foster Parents Plan, and had been promised clothing which could be used for 'necessitous cases'. In addition, 100 boxes of toffees and games had been sent from the USA under the British War Relief Fund and they had also acquired enough radios for each dormitory to have its own. The school was also maintaining a certain amount of self-sufficiency, motivated to some extent by awards from the National Camps Corporation. As a result, members of the Gardening Club at Somerford constructed a 16ft greenhouse, fourteen garden frames and a set of garden seats to be placed around the quadrangle.

A Mr Body from the Committee had obviously made a visit to the school. Although he said that his general impression was favourable and the members of staff were doing well, he tabled a number of concerns at the Education Committee meeting. The recruitment of teaching staff had always been a problem and it was accentuated both by the shortage of men under thirty-five (because of call-up into the services) and by the fact that the accommodation for residential staff was very restricted. On the day of his visit there were nine assistant teachers with 160 pupils. Although this staff-pupil ratio could be considered generous for a day school it was at least two, if not three, short of the level required for boarding school requirements. There were two vacancies that needed filling urgently and advertisements had been sent out. However, he notified the Committee that the number of assistant staff should not fall below twelve. He spoke of the general complaints about the school dinners. The breakfasts were fine but the Medical Officer had stated that 'the dinner lacks quantity and variety. Boys who ought to be improving in weight were not doing so (though this was directed at only a few individuals). The meals needed more meat'. It was agreed that bread and butter should be available at the evening meal and boys should be encouraged to have seconds if the opportunity arose. He was concerned to point out that Somerford was a 'little community leading a rather limited life and problems are apt to be magnified'.

By 19 April, the head teacher reported that the teacher's cubicles had been enlarged and there was now space for a sitting room as well as a bedroom. Pupil activities included football and gardening and he brought the Committee's attention to the fact that the erection of the greenhouse had involved cross-curricular input from the maths, technical drawing and handicrafts staff. The newspaper, science and boot mending clubs continued to flourish. The 'Wings for Victory' week had raised the sum of £33 8s, well beyond the target of £25.

There was a catastrophe in May when it was reported that the greenhouse had been blown off its base during a gale! However, the school had had a successful Sports Day. Eighty boys had gone home during the holidays leaving fifty on site. In June, this shortfall in numbers had been made up with a new intake of thirty-two boys, although one was immediately taken home because of homesickness. Eleven boys and two teachers had been invested into the Air Scouts and the food was improving!

In July, the school purchased six goslings and there was a promise of a cricket square. In September, it was reported that the boys had enjoyed swimming in the river Dane. Although there were obviously still problems with staffing, especially over the school holidays when there were only three relief teachers available, the Head was able to overcome this to some extent by spreading staff holidays over a longer period of time.

In October, the boys received 20lb of sugar for their beehives. They had also harvested a heavy crop of tomatoes. The junior boys had collected '1 hundred-weight of rose hips' for the Women's Voluntary Service to be made into syrup. They had also raised £1 14s 6d by making and selling coat posies. This money was sent to Captain Pinnell on the school's adopted 'ship', together with a batch of letters and a large parcel of knitted comforts made by the typing department in the Education Office.

During December it was reported that one pupil had scarlet fever and thirty-six others had tonsillitis. As in the previous year, evening school was introduced to make better use of the light afternoons. A weather station had been established and it was hoped that the Young Farmers Club would include poultry among their other interests.

There was no Christmas pantomime in 1943 but a variety show instead. A hundred boys went home and those who stayed had roast goose for Christmas dinner. The school received a large parcel of small gifts from the USA which were given to those boys who had had no letter or parcel from home. Several members of staff volunteered to forego their holiday to remain at the school over the vacation, but unfortunately the boiler burst and there was no heating. Consequently those boys and staff who were going home went a few days earlier than expected.

The reports continued into 1944 with the head teacher commenting on the day-to-day running of the school. There were no great alarms through-out this time although there were intermittent problems with the central heating system and a boiler that seemed to be an ongoing cause for con-cern. The clubs continued to be popular and the staffing issues took up a lot of the head teacher's time. One problem had been the lack of a school matron since August 1943. As the war progressed and evacuation became a less important issue for parents, the number of boys at the school gradually declined until all of them had either left, because of having reached the school-leaving age, or returned to day schools in their own locality.[24]

There are no reports hinting about its success, or lack of it, but personal research into other camp schools would suggest that most of the boys at Somerton would have received a more consistent and wide-ranging edu-cation than their peers in many of the other schools evacuated into areas where facilities were shared.

The differences between the German KLV camps and the British camp schools are vast. There is no mention within the school activities of political indoctrination, nor of any ideological debates. The activities within the British schools combined academic studies with practical and vocational training. Hobbies were encouraged and there was an awareness of the wider implications of the war. They helped with salvage work, they adopted 'ships', made comforts for the troops, dug for victory and established school savings clubs. It is also interesting to note that many of the camps schools introduced a prefectorial system which meant that to some extent the older boys and girls looked after the welfare of the younger pupils. Research would suggest that like any other boarding school institutions of the time, there was an element of bullying but nothing like the physical and psychological harassment meted out by some members of the Hitler Youth who often abused their positions. The biggest difference is of course that the teachers who worked in the British camp schools were themselves not affected by any hidden political agenda or doctrine, or by an overarching organisation similar to that of the Hitler Youth. As such there was no conflict of interest. The welfare and education of the individuals within the schools was paramount.

Despite the obvious initial problems of putting state-school 'day' children into a boarding-school situation, the camps' scheme was reasonably successful. For some pupils the experience has had a long-term effect on the rest of their lives. Many formed friendships that have remained unbroken, one even became the 'Bat-man' for a member of staff when they both joined the Army, and a group of ex-camp-school scholars still meet every year at the Sayers Croft school in Reigate, Surrey to have a reunion weekend.

Others gained a real taste for the countryside through the various agricultural and horticultural activities they had taken part in. Although some of the experiences such as bee-keeping were very much part of a camp school's extra-curricular activities, others such as 'Digging for Victory' were used across the country. Many non-camp schools grew vegetables and other crops, and kept chickens and other small animals in order to supplement the rationing.

This link between the evacuees and the land was an important one and even resulted in a propaganda film called *Spring Offensive*,[25] which although ostensibly focussed on getting redundant farmland into production, also included the bi-line of an evacuee who is shown to take a very serious interest in farming matters. At the beginning of the war even *The Farmer's*

Weekly got involved. In January 1940, it ran a 'Children's Competition' where country children had to describe an evacuee they had got to know, and explain what they thought of the countryside. At the same time 'town' children were asked to describe their country hosts. Some of the replies to a fictitious 'Mrs Day' were interesting and in the February 1940 edition she replied through her regular column in the magazine:

> The descriptions of your city and country friends have almost all been good, some of them have been very lively and entertaining indeed. It has been interesting to discover the way you think about one another, and the sort of things you notice; and it is especially interesting to learn from these competition entries of yours that so many of the children who war has sent into the countryside are liking it so much that they have no wish ever to live in the town again. Most of the country children say that the town visitors are very quick to learn new things such as looking after animals, even how to drive cattle, and milk and feed cows and clean rabbits and so on ...[26]

In many camps, the children were not only working on their own, sometimes extended plots, but also on local estates:

> 3rd-6th October 1941. Boys from the school (Kennylands) went to work on the farm each day.[27]
>
> 15th September 1943. Boys from 3A spent the afternoon picking up potatoes grown in the camp.
>
> October 11th 1943. 24 boys in 4A are potato picking at Harrison's Farm, Peppard today.

Other evacuees were also allowed to work on farms, usually during the harvest period, but sometimes throughout the year: 'The children are helping magnificently with the wartime harvest. The high-school girl on holiday leads the wagon and the evacuee children are all doing their bit; all helping somehow.'[28]

In 1940, because of difficulty in finding people to work on the land, one county council decided to give 'sympathetic consideration' to all reasonable applications for permission to withdraw children from school to undertake agricultural and similar work immediately they reached the age of fourteen.[29] In February 1940, the Westmoreland County Education Committee drew up a register of evacuees who had arrived in the county from Newcastle and South Shields, and had shown such an interest in farming, that they had expressed a wish to remain in the area as farm workers when they reached school-leaving age, rather than return home.[30] A number of the evacuees who went to live on farms actually became very interested in all aspects of agriculture. After they reached school-leaving age some returned to work as paid farm labourers and as a result a few actually inherited the farm from their hosts.[31]

The camp schools were a very important part of the overall Evacuation Scheme in the UK and for some of the children involved their experience was to be a life-changing one. It is apparent that many received a more stable education than some of their peers who attended schools in the Reception Areas and who had to share facilities with local children. Reports from the head teachers at the time suggest that the curriculum was not only designed to meet the academic needs of the pupils, but in addition the useful and important extra-curricular activities, created to occupy as much of the child's time as possible, were wide ranging and encompassed many activities not often available to 'day' schools.

There is a tendency to look at the success of the camp schools from the pupil's perspective and consequently it is easy to forget that the experience could be just as difficult for the members of staff who were not used to a boarding-school environment and were not necessarily trained to look after pupils all day, every day. Pastoral care became an important and serious issue, especially where some of the children were very homesick and where they had lost parents, and it was essential that some form of one-to-one support was provided in such circumstances. It is apparent from oral and written testimonies, that both the teaching and domestic staff became surrogate parents for many of the children and as such the whole situation was a learning curve for all who took part.

Despite considerable financial investment during the war, the school buildings were not used to their full potential once the war had finished and after all of the children had gone home. In 1945, after the return and demobilisation of the armed forces, many of the female staff and domestic personnel in the camps left to spend more time looking after their husbands and families. As the wages were low it was difficult to find suitable replacements for them. Although some camps continued to provide rural accommodation for city children, others changed their roles. Sayers Croft, near Reigate in Surrey, is still owned by Westminster City Council and provides outdoor pursuit experiences for city children; Finnamore Wood

Camp (near Marlow, Buckinghamshire) became a borstal housing 366 youths but is now derelict; Wrens Warren (near Hartfield, Kent) was used to house Dutch children and some displaced French children (it eventually closed in 1953); and Horsleys Green (near Stokenchurch, Buckinghamshire) remains the home of the Wycliffe Bible Translation Society. Some simply disappeared. The Bishopswood Camp is now a playing field, and the only clues to the Kennylands site, are found in the local street names. In March 1946, the 'Beal' boys had left Kennylands and returned to Ilford, but the Education Authority continued to rent the property from the National Camp Corporation and groups of children from all over Essex were sent there for short periods of time. Eventually it became a full-time boarding school until it was closed down in 1980.[32]

Overseas Evacuation

Went along to CORB after getting a certificate of evacuation from Cook's. She fixed everything up for me quickly, including the 66 coupons which I am allowed for clothes for each child and of which I am the first recipient. But total value of all parcels sent during the year, including birthday gifts must not exceed £10 per child.[1]

One section of the UK evacuee community who had a lot in common with both the Finnish children who went to Sweden, and the German children who were sent to areas within the greater Reich, were the 19,000 who were sent overseas, either privately through sponsorship proposals, or under the Children's Overseas Reception Board (CORB) scheme organised by the Government. Many of those who went to the US, certainly at the beginning of the war, could be considered part of an elite group. One needed a reasonable income to take advantage of the proposals as the original cost of £15 for the travel was well beyond the financial means of the majority of residents in the UK. To put it into context £15 was more than an average month's salary for 75 per cent of the population at the beginning of the war.[2] This private exodus was not restricted to children, and according to the 1 September issue of *The Times*, an estimated 5,000 people had left Southampton for the United States in the last two days of August 1939. In the Spring of 1940, Labour MPs, and a few from other parties, were beginning to express their unease at what they described as an elitist programme, and their disquiet eventually led to the Government establishing a plan that would increase the availability of overseas evacuation to other sectors of the population. The idea was not unknown to them. In early 1939, the Government had already received offers from a number of Dominion Governments offering to take in evacuees. These included Southern Rhodesia, Canada, where the Canadian Women's Organisations wanted to host under-sixteens and over-sixties, and Australia which offered refuge to orphans for the duration of the war. However, all these proposals had been rejected on the grounds that the Government did not see evacuation overseas as necessary. One Government spokesman stated '… the idea is good hearted, but impracticable'.[3]

The authorities were also genuinely concerned that this type of evacuation would be seen as a panic measure and defeatist, an opinion that was to affect the planning of overseas evacuation throughout its short existence. It was also apparent that other factors needed to be thought through and resolved before any such plan could be seriously considered. It was recognised that any voluntary evacuation by those who could afford it would create a certain amount of resentment by those who could not. Elspeth Huxley[4] commented on why the Government was anxious that any proposal should be seen to be egalitarian. In June 1940, she wrote,

> In England, as the papers filled with pictures of the children of the well-to-do posing happily on the country estates of Long Island and Quebec, feeling grew that the safety of the nation's children was too vital and too sacred a thing to be bought with gold. Why should the son of a rich man sleep in security in New York's gay lighted towers, the roar of traffic bound on peaceful errands in his ears, while the son of a poor man dozed in the crowded shelters below our dangerous cities, menaced by the bombers drone? It was unfair; and something ought to be done.

It was also recognised that any possible Government scheme could not compete with privately sponsored ones, simply because there would be fewer ships available to transport those supported by the administration. In addition, projecting into the future, what would happen if the allies gained the upper hand in the war, yet were unable to win it outright? Some of the children might never be able to return home.

However, after lengthy discussions at Cabinet level, it was agreed that the threat of invasion outweighed these negative concerns.

Geoffrey Shakespeare, who had been MP for Norwich since 1929 and was Parliamentary Under-Secretary in the Dominions Office, was asked to chair an inter-departmental committee[5] to 'consider offers made from overseas to house and care for children, whether accompanied or unaccompanied, from the European war zone, residing in Great Britain, including those orphaned by the war and to make recommendations thereon'.[6] After consultation with other interested parties such as the Ministry of Health, the Board of Education and the Ministry of Pensions, Shakespeare presented his final report to the War Cabinet on 17 June 1940. His recommendations included:

> Children should be between the ages of five and fifteen.
>
> The children should be attending school.
>
> A minimum of 90 per cent of those selected for evacuation had to be attending grant-aided schools.
>
> Parents of these children would have to pay the normal rate of 6/- per week for maintenance, the same amount applicable to British based evacuees, but the fare for the overseas transportation would be free.
>
> Parents of children from independent schools would be required to pay £1 per week maintenance and £15 towards travel costs.
>
> Preference would be given to children from areas considered to be at most danger from enemy action.
>
> Preference would also be given to children from less affluent families.
>
> Children would be fostered by host families or relatives in the overseas reception areas.
>
> As part of their responsibilities, parents had to accept the warnings that children were to be evacuated for the duration of the war. They would only return to Britain as soon as possible after the cessation of hostilities.[7]

However, while giving this report, Shakespeare was interrupted by a messenger informing Churchill that the French were about to surrender. Although the Cabinet Minutes show that the scheme had been endorsed, Churchill himself was so preoccupied with the situation in France that he had not realised a decision had been taken. Had he done so it would seem from comments he later made in Cabinet meetings and in the Commons, that he would have opposed it.[8] On 21 June 1940, he had told the Cabinet that:

> ... a large movement of this kind encourages a defeatist spirit, which is entirely contrary to the true facts of the position and should be sternly discouraged. It is one thing to allow a limited number of children to be sent to

North America, but the idea of a large scale evacuation stands on a different footing and was attended by grave difficulties[9]

Once he had the go-ahead, albeit somewhat unwittingly, Shakespeare established the Children's Overseas Reception Board (CORB) which was to oversee an evacuation scheme to include participants from all strata of society. This egalitarian aspect won the support of many Labour MPs and the overall scheme was also supported by those with other motives. Some, for example, like Colonel Josiah Wedgewood who wrote to Churchill suggesting that '... He should approach the United States and get them to take our useless mouths. Their conscience would make them consent; at worst the race would survive; they would be by far the best propaganda for armed help.'[10] Others because 'the soldiers would fight more happily if they knew that their wives and children were safe'.[11] One of the hidden agendas of the scheme was that some thought that seeing the children having to leave the UK would persuade hosts countries to join the war on the allied side. On the other side of the Atlantic, Lord Lothian, British Ambassador in Washington, was in favour of the scheme. He felt that the US was out of touch with British war aims and, as a result, reluctant to make contributions of weapons and other material. He hoped that the arrival of the children would help sway United States' public opinion. In April 1940, he commented that 'the United States is 95% anti-Hitler, is 95% determined to keep out of the war if it can, and will only enter the war when its own vital interests are challenged, though these vital interests include its ideals'.[12] Another major player was Eleanor Roosevelt, America's First Lady, who immediately after her election as Chairman of the US Committee for the Care of European Children received more than 2,000 offers from people wishing to adopt children. Others were made directly to the administration in Washington and to other city authorities. Companies like Kodak-Eastman, Hoover and Warner Brothers got involved and offered to take the children of their employees in Britain.

Newspapers in the US also did their bit to generate interest. *The Herald Tribune* referred to inviting evacuees as 'guests of the nation' and the *New York Daily Mirror* wrote a leader under the heading 'This nation's duty to England's future ...' stating that it would be a duty and privilege to give them a home.

Even as late as 1941, Elspeth Huxley wrote, 'All over Canada and the United States, from the bustling seaboard cities to the flat and sun-soaked prairie towns, from the mansions of millionaires to the cramped framed houses of the poor, men and women offered the safety of their homes to children from the battle zones'.[13]

However, the question of elitism remained and undeniably there was a certain amount of substance to the claim. On 1 July 1940, on the same day that the Cabinet had decided to close the overseas lists, Frank Aydelotte, American Secretary of the Rhodes Scholarships, appealed to American Rhodes scholars throughout the US to help house 'one or more children of Oxford and Cambridge dons, or those children of dons from other universities'.[14] A few days later the suggestion that only the titled and wealthy were wanted by American hosts was played down by the American Committee in London for the Evacuation of children, who explained that some sponsors were paying for the transportation costs of the poorer evacuees. However, it needs to be recognised that those children who were being sent to friends in the US were likely to come from families who were well travelled and so had been able to make personal contacts of this nature.

The following week, on 9 July, Eleanor Roosevelt established the 'National Child Refugee Committee' in New York, in order to raise $5 million, (at the time approximately £1 million) to provide homes for 'refugee' children. She addressed a large audience of welfare workers and stated that speed in raising the money was vital. In answer to the question of whether or not the American Red Cross could send ships to collect the children, Mrs Roosevelt stated that: '... it would be a very grave responsibility, and might get us into the war. The US, in all probability, would not feel that they could assume that responsibility'.[15]

The Government recognised the concerns and in a debate in the House of Commons on 3 July, Attlee pointed out that although the overseas evacuation scheme was part of the national defence, there was no intention to clear everybody out from the country except fighting men and those engaged in war-related industries. He went on to stress that there was no class privilege in the scheme, a fact reiterated by Shakespeare in the same debate. He recognised that nothing would undermine public morale more than granting such facilities to the privileged few.[16]

Churchill was also keen to play down the possible perception of exclusivity attached to the overseas evacuation. On 18 July, after the scheme had been 'closed', he felt it necessary to address this question in the House of Commons:

His Majesty's Government has been deeply touched by the kindly offers of hospitality received from the Dominions and the United States. They will

take pains to make sure that in the use that is made of these offers there shall
be no question of rich people having an advantage, if advantage there be, over
poor.[17]

However, because at this time the country was neutral, the only evacuees
who could go to the US were, by necessity, private ones. Despite the wishes
of Shakespeare, an official CORB scheme to the US never materialised.
Although he had had discussions with Joseph Kennedy the US Ambassador,
and details had been worked out in Washington, the rigidity of American
immigration laws threw up many barriers. Primarily, there was a quota system in place for each nationality and the arrival of too many from Britain
would have upset the allocation of numbers. In addition, medical tests for
migrants were very stringent and could never have been applied to children in wartime. Also there was the fundamental problem of guardianship
responsibilities and to what extent hosts could act 'in *loco parentis*'. All these
issues were not insurmountable and were in the process of finally being
resolved when in September 1940, the SS *City of Benares* carrying evacuees
was sunk and the CORB scheme came to an abrupt end.

On 17 June, Circular 1515, outlining the CORB proposals, was sent
secretly to Local Education Authorities with instructions that they had to
be distributed to grant-aided schools attended by the less well-off. The circular was also sent to private schools.

On 19 June, Clement Attlee, as Lord President of the Council, tabled
the CORB recommendations and report in the House of Commons. On
the 20th, the written information reached the relevant parents at the same
time that it was announced on the radio and in the Press. By mid-morning
the response was so great that more than 3,000 people were queuing outside the CORB offices in Berkeley Street, London. On the following day
over 7,000 letters arrived, 94 per cent of them from working-class families.
Despite having done a 'dress rehearsal' on the previous day, and the reception
desk being looked after by two ladies, Thelma Cazalet MP and later Lady
Cheetham, both very capable of dealing with the public, the clerical staff of
thirty were totally overwhelmed.[18] Within a few weeks the staff increased to
500, reaching a peak of 650 by September 1940, and included such names as
Vera Brittain, and the wife of Hugh Dalton, the former Chancellor.

At the end of June 1940, articles appeared in some local newspapers outlining the rationale behind the Overseas Scheme and explaining to parents
what their responsibilities would be should they wish to consider the option.

This one relates to Weymouth in Dorset but they were replicated across the country. It is interesting that the correspondent mentions 'forever contaminated by war'. Of course he was referring to total physical war, he had not considered, along with the vast majority of people at this time that children would be affected by the psychological effects of war and the trauma of being separated from their parents. It is also worth stressing that, with the benefit of hindsight, it is known that the war finished in 1945, but when statements like these were issued, nobody would be aware of this and comments like 'face the pain of not seeing their own children, for perhaps years', would carry a greater poignancy. (In 1940, when asked how long he thought the war would last, Harold MacMillan replied, 'twelve months if they win; five years if we do'.) [19]

PROBLEMS FOR PARENTS

Very soon all Weymouth mothers and fathers will be confronted with perhaps the biggest problem of their lives. Should they keep their youngsters by their sides in Weymouth, a so-called safe area, or send them overseas to a safe land?

They must decide whether they will face the pain of not seeing their own children for perhaps years, when at the most important stage in their young lives, but knowing that they are growing up safe from Nazi bombers, from death, injury, and that the youthful minds will not be forever contaminated by total warfare.

All parents in Weymouth are to be sent two forms, dealing with the evacuation of Weymouth children from 5 to 16 years of age to Canada, USA, Australia, New Zealand and South Africa.

Parents with children attending grant maintained schools should send their replies to the Local Education Authority, Municipal Offices, Weymouth. Those with children attending secondary schools to the Director of Education, Dorchester … and other schools to the Secretary of the Overseas Reception Board c/o Thomas Cook and Sons Ltd., Berkeley St., London W1.

It is explained on the sheets that before going overseas the children will have to pass a medical examination, which will probably be held in Weymouth. They will travel under suitable escorts and, on arrival, be boarded with private families and not institutions. They will receive as good an education as the children in the neighbourhood to which they are sent and their welfare afterwards will be carefully watched.

Extra clothes will be issued to them free, and when the war is won they will return home again.

Travel will be free. Parents will be expected to contribute for the maintenance of each child as much as they would have contributed had the child
merely been evacuated to a receiving area in this country. If they offer to pay
more than 6/- a week or more, no enquiry will be made; if not, they will be
assessed according to their circumstances.[20]

Today the language of these articles would seem to be rather fatalistic so
it is really no wonder that parents were persuaded to apply, and this was
Weymouth, an area unlikely to be attacked, so imagine the effect such
appeals would have had in areas which were known to be in danger.

The huge public response, which perhaps revealed to some extent the depth
of public apprehension for the future state of the nation, was of great concern
to the Government, and the minutes of the Cabinet meeting on 1 July state:

The Prime Minister drew attention to the scheme for evacuating children to
North America. Many people were now expecting the scheme to develop
on a considerable scale. A large movement of this kind encouraged a defeatist
spirit, which was entirely contrary to the true facts of the position and should
be sternly discouraged.[21]

Shakespeare was instructed to issue a statement to calm things down and
'draw attention publicly to the dangers and difficulties involved in sending
children overseas'.[22]

Issued later on the same day it simply said:

The Government has no intention of shipping large numbers of children
overseas. Any idea of mass migration is absolutely contrary to the wishes of
the Government concerned. For scores of thousands of children to be transferred in a few weeks, as suggested in some quarters, is outside the bounds of
any practical scheme and would be an extremely dangerous process.[23]

This message was very similar to the one he had made on the radio some
days earlier:

Any notion of sending hundreds of thousands of children overseas in the
space of a few weeks was both dangerous and stupid ... The scheme could
only operate subject to the limitation of shipping and offers made by each
Dominion.[24]

The statements did little to quell the rush, and by 4 July the total number of applicants was 211,448. Of these 11,702 were from independent schools and 199,746 from grant-aided schools. Almost 50 per cent fulfilled all the criteria.[25] Overwhelmed by the numbers, the Cabinet decided to postpone the scheme, 'without killing it to ensure that it was kept to quite small proportion' and closed the lists stating that they had more names than they could cope with. Again Geoffrey Shakespeare was ordered to diffuse the situation.[26] As a result further proclamations were placed in local and national newspapers.

> It has now been announced that in view of the adequate response already received from parents wishing to send their children overseas, it will be impossible for any more applications to be entertained until further notice. No further applications from parents should therefore be made to either the Local Education Authorities or the Children's Overseas Reception Board. Similarly, no further applications should be made for employment as escorts.[27]

Shakespeare and his team now had to arrange the transport. In collaboration with the Ministry of Shipping and the Admiralty, future dates for sailings were worked out in enough time to allow for the selection of children, the process of informing parents and the signing of the requisite legal documents. Each application was reviewed alongside school and medical reports, and those who were considered to be unfit or unsuitable were rejected. Those who were accepted received standard letters like this one explaining what would happen next:

> … In the accompanying letter you are informed that your child (children) has (have) been accepted for evacuation overseas. This does not necessarily mean that they will be sailing at an early date, but only that they have been placed on a waiting list from which children are selected as and when shipping accommodation becomes available. You should, therefore, make no special preparations until you have had further notification … When you receive notification you may conclude that the ship in which your child (children) is (are) to sail will be convoyed … In the interest of security for your child (children) and others who will accompany them, we ask you to regard this information as confidential …

The accompanying letter referred to above, covered four main points:

For retention by parents.

It is important that you should read the attached letter very carefully.

The main points are

That consent to the sending of the child must be given by persons having proper authority to give it.

That the child will be sent at the risk of the persons making the application.

That the Government will do their best for the child but cannot accept responsibility for him or her.

That the parents or guardians will be liable to make payments mentioned in paragraph 4 of this letter.[28]

It is interesting to note that the Government were not prepared to take responsibility for the children whilst in its care. The parents were asked to respond to this letter within forty-eight hours of receiving it, but it was recognised that there might be problems getting the signatures of fathers in the services.

A few days later, after receiving the letters, families were asked to take their children to a School Clinic for a medical examination. It was pointed out that this inspection was an essential part of the CORB scheme and no child would be considered for acceptance unless it was carried out.

On 2 July, the CORB planning was thrown into disarray when the former Blue Star liner *Arandora Star*, carrying 1,500 Italian and German internees and eighty-six prisoners of war, was sunk off the north coast of Ireland by U-47 while en route to Canada. A total of 714 lives were lost and although no children were involved, it did convince the Government to cancel the CORB scheme, while at the same time allowing private travel to go ahead. This created a great deal of bitterness. The Labour MP for Llanelli, James Griffiths, informed the House of Commons about the resentment in his constituency because children of 'responsible public men' had been sent overseas, while 'poor children' were left behind. He went on to say that '… common people did not ask for anything more than the ordinary protection which everyone else gets, but they resent it and feel indignant if rich people are looking after their own children and allowing the children of the poor to stand all the risks.' His comments were reiterated in a Home Intelligence Report dated 16 July, which said that the postponement of plans for evacuating children to the Dominions was leading to 'sharp recrimination against the rich, whose children were enabled to sail'. Another MP raised the question, 'Was the scheme merely a camouflage to get out the well to do?'[29]

The following day the Government reversed its decision.

However, the question of shipping became a serious issue and of great concern to members of the Admiralty. They stated that there were three factors that would make it impossible to move all but a handful of children:

Few ships were available and capable of carrying large numbers of children.
Most of the available passenger ships were needed to transport enemy aliens to Canada.
U-boats were operating in the Atlantic and the Western Approaches, and the Luftwaffe was also attacking shipping, resulting in a shortage of Convoy escort vessels.

The scheme went ahead despite Churchill's reservations and its detractors, who were concerned that they had got tied up in a scheme driven by crisis and emotion rather than rational thought, having just cause to stop it. However, on 9 July the Admiralty once again warned the War Cabinet that the Navy could no longer provide adequate naval protection, and on 16 and 18 July both Attlee and Churchill told Parliament, in answer to a series of questions, that the scheme had again been suspended.

In the Commons on 18 July 1940, Frederick Cocks, Labour MP for Broxtowe, Nottinghamshire, asked the Prime Minister whether '... in view of the fact that the large scale evacuation of children overseas was an important factor in the military defence of Britain, will he reconsider the decision to postpone the scheme, bearing in mind that children can be evacuated in ships which are already convoyed?'

Churchill replied:

It is most undesirable that anything in the nature of a large scale exodus from this country should take place, and I do not believe that the military situation requires or justifies such a proceeding, having regard to the relative dangers of going and staying. Nor is it physically possible ... The scheme has been postponed, not abandoned, but any further emigration that may be possible, as opportunity serves, will be regulated, with a view to restoring the balance between classes, and not in pursuance of any policy of reducing the number of persons in this well-defended island. Furthermore, the scale of movement must necessarily be small in number and dependent in time upon naval facilities.[30]

The Labour MP Benjamin Smith asked the Prime Minister whether he would, at some later date: '... reconsider the possibility of evacuation of children by neutral and American ships'. Churchill replied: 'Yes, of course; if a movement to send United States ships to these shores were set foot from the other side of the Atlantic, it would immediately engage the most earnest attention of His Majesty's Government'.[31]

Reading through the debates of the time one can sense Churchill's displeasure about the whole scheme. The concerns he expressed in the Press release of 1 July were reiterated in this debate on 18 July:

> I must frankly admit that the full bearings of this question, (Overseas evacuation) were not appreciated by His Majesty's Government at the time when it was first raised. It was not foreseen that the mild countenance given to the plan would lead to a movement of such dimensions, and that a crop of alarmist and depressing rumours would follow at its tail, detrimental to the interests of National Defence ...[32]

Despite the official postponement, the scheme continued, and Churchill must have been aware of this situation when he sent a memo to Sir John Anderson on 18 July 1940, questioning the relevance of Geoffrey Shakespeare leaving his post in London to see off 100 evacuees departing from Liverpool. The latter usually took the opportunity to say a few words to the children before their departure. In his memoirs he recalls:

> I usually told the children that they did not represent themselves when they were sent overseas, and therefore they could not behave as they liked. They were, in fact, like British Ambassadors and consequently must behave even better than they knew how. If they behaved badly people would say 'What frightful children! Their parents in Britain really cannot be worth fighting for' on the other hand, 'What splendid children these are! We must do everything we can to help their parents win'. I said that when things go wrong, as they often will, remember you are British and grin and bear it ... Be truthful, be brave, be kind and be grateful ...[33]

Those selected began to arrive in Liverpool where they were accommodated in schools, hostels and orphanages. The private evacuees were supposed to stay in the relative luxury of the Adelphi Hotel, but in reality spent their nights in the air-raid shelters as Liverpool was being bombed by the Luftwaffe. Margaret Wood, who was to sail on the *Llanstephan Castle* to South Africa on 23 August, stated that the only thing she can remember about her two days in Liverpool with her fellow evacuees was spending the time in a shelter and 'being dosed with Castor Oil ... all 302 of us!'[34] The longer the children waited for embarkation, the greater the danger of homesickness, under the circumstances not an uncommon occurrence. Shakespeare described the problem: '... homesickness is a strange disease; it comes suddenly like a virulent germ, and such is its physical effect on the child that it lowers all power of resistance. But the same child within an hour is laughing and joking again.[35] However, those with extreme homesickness were sent home, together with those children who, despite the initial medical examinations, were not fit to travel. The total rejected at this stage was around 11 per cent.

The remaining evacuees were seen by their ship-board escorts, who took over responsibility from the 'train' escorts, and each child was given a metal identification disc with their CORB number inscribed on it. Those who lacked suitable clothing were kitted out by the WVS, and games and books were made available. Before departure, and on board ship, the children were given lessons in etiquette and provided with information about the country they were going to. In general terms it could be said that these children were facing a far more difficult time than their counterparts who had been evacuated within the country. Many of them were on their own, no siblings, no school friends, no teachers who were known to them. Those from the poorer areas who had probably never been outside their immediate locality before, now found themselves on board a ship destined to take a journey to a country whose culture might be totally alien to them. They really were travelling into the unknown. Those escorting them took on the tremendous responsibility of making sure that the journey and the experience was as good as it could be, given the circumstances. There was one escort for every fifteen children, one doctor and two nurses for every 100 and Ministers of leading denominations in every large group. Many Salvation Army Officers went as escorts with the evacuees and ensured their wellbeing. The Government was anxious to secure the help of the Salvation Army, so an appeal went out in the June 1940 issue of the 'International War Cry' asking for volunteers, but stipulating certain criteria. They had to be:

Experienced in controlling children.

Not more than 55 years of age unless possessed of exceptional health and other qualifications.

Available at short notice.

Good sailors.

Persons with experience as leaders of Young People's Groups such as Life-
saving Guards and Young People's Corps.[36]

The total number of applications to become escorts, from all sources,
reached more than 19,000.

The first evacuees to Canada sailed on 21 July 1940 on the *Anselm* in
convoy OB 189. The convoy was attacked by U-boats on 27 July but, despite
four vessels sinking, the *Anselm* survived.[37] Between July and mid-September
nineteen ships sailed. Of the 3,119 evacuees, 90 per cent left during August,
and by September sixteen ships had reached their destination. It is interesting to note that only eight of the nineteen ships could take more than 100
passengers. This was a calculated decision. Security of the children was a high
priority and CORB had the choice of either sending them in unescorted
fast passenger liners, or slower ships in a convoy. Had they chosen the former,
the number of available ships would have been greater and the evacuation
speeded up, but if torpedoed the casualties could be high. After the sinking
of the *Arandora Star*, it was agreed that a small number of evacuees would
be transported on each ship and these would then travel as part of a convoy.
This would slow down the process, but nonetheless hopefully be safer. Three
ships sailed for Australia. On 5 August the *M.S. Batory*, a 16,000-ton luxury
liner of the Polish Gydnia American Line, sailed with Convoy WS2 with
a complement of 1,340, including 477 children and fifty-one escorts and
medical staff. It had originally been designed to carry only 300. The ship
arrived at its destination on 16 October 1940, and in the New Year Patricia
Johnston's parents received the following letter from the CORB offices:

January 1941

Dear Sir

I am glad to be able to tell you that Patricia is now living with Mrs William
Fisher, ★ ★ ★, Victoria. I hope that you will be receiving letters regularly and
that Patricia is settling down happily.

Yours faithfully

Elspeth Davies.

On 24 August, the *Nestor* of the Alfred Holts Blue Funnel Line, sailed with
Convoy OB203 with eighty-two children and eight escorts and medics. On
17 September the *Diomed* left with eighteen children.[38]

Margaret Wood was to travel from Liverpool to Gibraltar in convoy with some merchant vessels, together with an evacuee ship going to Australia. All the ships steamed east into the Mediterranean whilst the vessel *Llanstephan Castle* struck out alone into the Atlantic, zigzagging its way to Cape Town, hoping to avoid the U-boats. The journey lasted five weeks instead of two weeks because of these evasive measures. In her diary Margaret describes conditions and life on the ship:

> On Friday, 23rd August 1940, we boarded the Llanstephan Castle. We were very well looked after on the ship. Each morning for about an hour and a half, we had lectures on travel, South Africa and divinity. There was a church service every Sunday. There were two concerts, one was given by the escorts and the other by us. I sang duets with Olwyn Gibson, 'The Indian Love Call' and 'Somewhere over the Rainbow'. The voyage was quiet and the only port of call was Freetown in Sierra Leone. We all had to drink quinine, ugh! – and plaster ourselves with ointment if we went out after sunset because we were in a malaria infested area. When we crossed the line, the equator, we had a big party. It was very riotous and ended by putting bread and jam down each other's backs.

The *Llanstephan Castle* had been converted into a troop ship so Margaret and her fellow travellers slept in three-tiered bunks. They bathed in hot sea-water and used a 'rough chunk' of soap which was supposed to lather. The food on board was very good and in marked contrast to the sleeping arrangements. The restaurant was run on pre-war style and they even provided printed menus. Some were devised to make them fun. For example, the tea provided on 3 September 1940 comprised: 'Filleted Fitness, Soused Hasty Words with Toasted Tempers and Bright and Breezy salad'.

What the majority of parents did not know, or realise, was that when these ships and convoys travelled from Britain they only had a naval escort for 300km west of Liverpool. At that point the convoy scattered and the individual ships took their chance against the U-boats. This was because, as the USA had not entered the war and had remained neutral, there was no provision for refuelling in ports on the east coast of America. In addition, the naval escorts were required for coastal protection in the Western Approaches.

In his book *Children of the Benares*, Ralph Barker describes the pattern of the convoys:

They were arrayed on a broad front three miles across in eight columns of two vessels each, with an asymmetrical ninth column of three to vary the pattern, their generous spacing allowed them to zigzag in concert either side of their mean course to a prearranged schedule. This was their only defence, passive and ultimately unpredictable, against the submersible enemy ...[39]

An indication of how dangerous the journey could be can be found in the number of U-boat 'kills' confirmed during the summer of 1940: fifty-eight in June, thirty-eight in July and fifty-six in August, as well as fifteen other vessels sunk by the Luftwaffe.

On 30 August 1940, the liner *Volendam* carrying a total of 606 passengers, including 321 evacuee children, twenty-six escorts, two doctors and three nurses, was torpedoed, together with the *Arandora Star* off the northern coast of Ireland, by U-60. Fortunately a second torpedo did not explode, so she did not sink and was towed back to Scotland by tugs. The news was relayed to Shakespeare, who by good fortune was close to Glasgow where the survivors were to be taken. There were no casualties among the 321, but one evacuee did go missing. Robert, a boy of nine, was asleep in his bunk and among all the confusion had not been seen by the crew. Meanwhile, all the other children had moved into the lifeboats. At around midnight, Robert woke up to find himself alone. He went on deck, saw that the boats had gone and the ropes dangling from the davits, and decided to go back to bed! In the morning Robert, along with a skeleton engineering crew, were taken aboard a destroyer. He arrived in Gourock clutching half the German torpedo. Had the news of this 'loss' got out it could have damaged the whole scheme, but Shakespeare was able to persuade Robert's father, and Robert himself, not to reveal the true story.[40] As a postscript one of the ex-*Volendam* evacuees was to die on the *Benares* just three weeks later.

The escorts on the *Volendam* all received copies of the following letter from the CORB offices. (Note this postdates the sinking of the SS *City of Benares*.)

23rd September 1940

Dear Miss Close

Although our experience in going with a party to Canada was so unfortunate, I am writing to ask whether there is any likelihood of your being able to help us in this way on another occasion. If so, will you please let me know when you will be free and which of the Dominions you would prefer. We will then let you know exactly what is being done with regard to a renewed exit permit ...[41]

Two escorts were reselected and sailed to Canada on the *City of Paris*, and others readily accepted the invitation to reapply. The Press and the Ministry of Information took the opportunity to use this narrow escape as positive propaganda, commenting that, 'the CORB children transferred to other ships in perfect order ... like guardsmen on parade, in high spirits ... with pride in their adventure'.[42]

However, little was learned from the experience. The *Volendam* had been the leading ship in the centre column of the convoy and was therefore visible to other vessels, including the enemy. Also, she was carrying a cargo of wheat to sell in America, thus making it a legitimate target. It is surprising that such a cargo was on an evacuee ship.[43]

Those travelling on the SS *City of Benares* were not so lucky. On 17 September a similar prominent position in Convoy OB213, together with in this case lack of escort protection, possibly contributed to the sinking of the ship. The *Benares*, was torpedoed by U-48 under the command of Heinrich Bleichrodt,[44] with the loss of seventy-seven children, six escorts and 173 adults and crew. The parents of the children lost in the tragedy received a short letter from CORB headquarters simply stating:

> ... I am very distressed to inform you that, in spite of all precautions taken, the ship carrying your child to Canada was torpedoed on Tuesday night, 17 September. I am afraid your child is not amongst those reported as rescued, and I am informed that there is no chance of there being any further list of survivors ...[45]

Twenty sets of parents were to lose more than one child and the Grimond family from South London lost five of their ten children in the disaster.[46]

It is ironic that until 1 a.m. on the morning of the 17th the convoy had been supported by the destroyer HMS *Winchelsea*, which had used her submarine detection echo sounders (ASDIC) to monitor U-boat activity in the vicinity of the convoy. There was such a shortage of naval escort vessels in the Western Approaches, that they were compelled to leave outward-bound convoys 200 miles out from Liverpool, carry out anti-submarine patrols and then wait to escort incoming convoys to either Liverpool or the Clyde. The *Winchelsea* was ordered to leave OB213 and pick up the inward bound HX (*Halifax*) 71 convoy carrying ammunition and other supplies. Before going off station, the commander of the *Winchelsea* warned the commander of the convoy that there was a U-boat operating in the area near to Longitude 20° west. There were other contributory factors. The ships were only making 6.5-7.5 knots into a headwind, and although the *Benares* could go faster she was restricted by the given order of only going as fast as the slowest ship in the convoy. Had she been allowed to travel on at her own speed she may have survived the attack. However, had she been originally permitted to sail on her own she would not have been allowed to carry evacuees in the first place and it later came to light that the owners had requested convoy protection. Thirty evacuees were killed almost immediately by the force of the explosion beneath their cabins. Those who survived did so primarily because they were thrown from their bunks.

There was also a lot of confusion when the lifeboats were launched, one tipped over depositing all the children into the cold sea. To add to the problems, weather conditions were bad, with gale force winds and high waves. Two of the escorts independently described the situation in their boats:

> … the little ones faded out, quite unable to stand up to the awful conditions … All we could do was to hold them above the water till they were gone … we gave them what comfort we could.[47]

> … the children started to go into a coma one by one … We slapped their hands and faces, and then kept their heads above the water until we could tell it was no use.[48]

Miss Day's boat was picked up by the crew of HMS *Hurricane* twenty hours after the event. Forty-six of the survivors, including six children, spent eight days in an open lifeboat before eventually being rescued by HMS *Anthony*. The fact that they survived was very much down to the fortitude of their escort, Miss Mary Cornish, who kept the children amused by telling stories and getting them to sing songs. She later received the British Empire Medal from George VI. Another escort of note was Michael Rennie, who dived into the sea on numerous occasions from the lifeboat to rescue children swimming in the water. Sadly, he was one of the casualties and died as the *Hurricane* came into view.[49]

The fact that some people remained in the sea for so long was partly due to an Admiralty order which forbade the crews on convoy escort duty to pick up survivors if it endangered the safety of their own ships. Any rescue by ships in the rear of the convoy would only be allowed, '... when a local escort vessel was present. If such an escort is not present, a rescue ship should not act as such unless this can be done with undue risk.' In the case of OB213 all the ships were in danger because of the U-boats still in the area, so a later Board of Enquiry concluded that, 'it would not have been proper to depart from these orders on account of the children ... as this would have endangered the ship'.[50] Therefore, as soon as the *Winchelsea* went off to meet the incoming convoy she had in effect neutralised the ability of any other ship to act as a rescue vessel.

At home, the Ministry of Information used the tragedy as anti-German propaganda and referred to it as 'a new Nazi outrage against all the rules of war'. Shakespeare himself was widely quoted as speaking of his 'horror that any German submarine captain could be found to torpedo a ship over six hundred miles from land in a tempestuous sea ... This deed will shock the world.'[51] It was acknowledged later that this tragedy took place in a time of war, and although some authors and contemporary journalists labelled it a war crime, it is now important, almost seventy years on, to look at the event from the U-boat commander's point of view. As far as he was concerned he was torpedoing an unlit ship in a convoy. He had no idea that there were children on board, and as with other vessels carrying overseas evacuees, there were no signs or other recognisable features on the boats to indicate that they were being transported. Therefore, it could be argued that he was simply carrying out his orders. The *Benares* was only one of eight ships he sank on this, his first mission at sea. So he did not pick it out as a specific target. It is perhaps possible that had the British Government declared in some way that the ship was carrying evacuees, the Germans, recognising the potential for anti-German propaganda, would not have sunk it. It also needs to be remembered that the *Benares* was also the flagship of Rear-Admiral Mackinnon, the convoy commander, thereby making her a legitimate target.

Mistakes were obviously made, and after the initial press response on both sides of the Atlantic with banner headlines such as 'Murder at Sea' and 'Loathsome lawlessness of German conduct in war', questions began to be asked. It soon transpired that some of the drain plugs in the lifeboats may not have been in position, that the handles used to propel the lifeboats were too stiff to operate and one lifeboat only had a single oar, which was broken. There were also some serious doubts cast on the Lascar crew's efficiency to perform well in a crisis, as they were ill-equipped to deal with the sea conditions at the time. Marjorie Day, the senior escort, commented that had there been a British crew on board the loss of life might not have been so bad.

At a subsequent enquiry it also transpired that when the *Winchelsea* was told to leave the convoy, the commander-in-chief of Western Approaches had also sent a direct order to Rear Admiral Mackinnon to disperse the convoy ships at noon on the 17th. For some reason Mackinnon did not pass on this order until just after 10 p.m., so until that time all the ships were in convoy formation, not taking zigzagging anti-submarine avoidance measures, and therefore making it an easy target for any U-boat in the area. As the convoy commander did not survive, the answer as to why he ignored the commander-in-chief's order for ten hours, will never be known.

For a number of reasons it was decided not to have a public enquiry into the event, primarily because it would have done little for morale and contributed nothing to the war effort. Also, as most of the proceedings would have had to have been held 'in camera' to avoid the possibility of any information falling into German hands, the enquiry was unlikely to be public in the truest sense. One positive thing to come out of the sinking of the *Benares* was the introduction of small fast vessels for the sole purpose of rescuing people from the sea. There were only twelve, but they rescued over 4,000 seamen. It meant that escort vessels did not have to endanger themselves in a rescue mission but could instead concentrate on engaging the enemy.[52]

Shakespeare now found himself in a quandary. There were 270 evacuees on the *City of Paris* ready to embark. Should they go? The situation was not helped by the news on 21 September, that the *City of Simla* had also been sunk, fortunately only two people had been killed in the explosion, all the lifeboats had been launched, all the survivors rescued, and the Lascar crew proved to be very efficient. However, he felt it only right that the parents of the children on the *Paris* should be given the option of withdrawing them, and so decided to cancel the sailing.

On 22 September, Shakespeare reported to CORB on future policy, while recognising that 'On the one hand is the delightful welcome and home life awaiting the children, free from war atmosphere and particularly the nervous effects of discomfort of air raids.'[53] He accepted that the risks involved were increasing.

On 23 September, Churchill informed the Cabinet, that '... in view of this recent disaster to the ship carrying women and children to Canada, the future evacuation overseas of children must cease'. However, he acknowledged that 'there is strong feeling against a complete discontinuation'.[54] Having discussed the issue at some length with members of CORB, Shakespeare made the following recommendations in a letter sent to the Home Secretary:

> Children should be sent on vessels crewed only by Europeans.
>
> During the winter months, no more children should be sent overseas in a slow convoy.
>
> To continue to send children to the other three Dominions, provided convoys were available.[55]

On 30 September, Sir John Anderson recommended that 'no more CORB children should be evacuated either in slow or fast convoys' and that the Government should announce the suspension of the scheme. He also raised the question of whether or not parents should be allowed to evacuate their children privately. The Cabinet decided that:

> The CORB scheme should be suspended, but it would not be officially announced for two days in order to allow time to inform and discuss the matter with the relevant High Commissioners.
>
> They should not refuse permits to those parents wishing to make private arrangements to evacuate their children overseas.

It is interesting that this latter decision went against all the CORB philosophy in that it reopened the question of elitism, and the fact that money and privilege could still 'purchase' safety overseas. However, there was a hidden political agenda behind this decision as the British Government were still intent on maintaining strong links with the USA in the hope that they would join the Allies.

On 2 October 1940, the scheme was officially abandoned and the four groups of CORB evacuees waiting to embark were sent home. Although there were suggestions up to March 1941 that it should be resurrected, to all intents and purposes it finished on 17 September 1940 with the sinking of the *Benares*.

After the evacuation of 2,671 children, of whom 1,535 went to Canada, 577 to Australia, 355 to South Africa and 204 to New Zealand, the official scheme was now finished.

The Children's Overseas Reception Board itself did remain in existence, albeit with reduced personnel. They now had the responsibility for maintaining contact with those children who had safely been evacuated abroad. The McGintys (Patricia Johnston's parents), amongst others, received somewhat cursory annual school reports as well as other updates via the CORB offices:

12 March 1941
You will be interested to know that we have received a report from Australia about Patricia. She has settled down well in her school and her progress has been good. She is in good health and attending a State School ...

18 March 1942
We have just received reports from Australia on all the children in Victoria, including Patricia. They were of course written a month or two ago.

   She is in very good health, and is happy and contented. She is making good progress in grade 4 at the State School where she is popular with teachers and scholars. You will have heard that she has been appointed a class monitor ...[56]

Not all the communications dealt with domestic issues. Just a couple of days after getting the school report, the McGintys received a further letter. As Japan was now in the war, there were serious concerns about the possibility of Australia being attacked, and as a result CORB was quick to allay any fears that the parents of evacuees in the country might have:

... I should like you to know that the Board is in close touch with its representatives in Australia who reports that arrangements have been made by the authorities to evacuate school children from danger points if this should at any time be considered necessary ... You may rest assured that should it be decided to evacuate the children from any district, the parents will be informed as soon as possible by the Board. In one or two instances private arrangements have been made by individual foster parents or schools, to move children inland, but there has yet been no official evacuation ...[57]

Face to face meetings between CORB representatives and the parents were also held to discuss various issues, such as education, training and employment. They were also given advice on sending parcels, 'airgraph' letters and transferring funds to both the children and in some cases the foster parents.

Another way of keeping in contact with all overseas evacuees was by radio. This need to remain in touch was supported by Princess Elizabeth and Princess Margaret who made their first broadcast to evacuated children at home and overseas on 13 October 1940:

> In wishing you good evening, I feel that I am speaking to friends and companions who have shared with my sister and myself many a happy Children's Hour.
>
> Thousands of you in this country have had to leave your homes and be separated from your fathers and mothers. My sister, Margaret Rose, and I feel so much for you as we know from experience what it means to be away from those we love most of all … All of us children who are still at home think continually of our friends and relatives who have gone overseas, who have travelled thousands of miles to find a wartime home and a kindly welcome in Canada, Australia, New Zealand, South Africa and the United States of America …

Individuals were also able to take advantage of pre-recorded radio broadcasts. Although they were few and far between and parents were only given thirty seconds, about the time for ninety words, they did provide a vital and necessary link between the child and home:

> 15th April 1943
>
> Dear Mr and Mrs McGinty
>
> We should be glad if you could come to The Art Gallery, Mosely Street, Manchester on the 21st April at 4 p.m. to record a short message to your child overseas. It will be included in one of our programmes 'Hello Children' to be broadcast in our Overseas Service within the next few weeks. The children concerned will be cabled about time and wavelength …[58]

There was also an equivalent programme called 'Hello Parents' when the children's recorded messages were broadcast back to the Britain. (Unfortunately the McGintys missed Patricia's from Australia, but luckily, against all the normal procedures, they were given a typescript of what she had said.)

It is interesting to note that by early 1944, CORB was considering the future of some of the children in the Dominions. A letter had been sent to parents in April asking them not to bring their children home without the Board's written consent:

... as in some cases their children have found good openings in the Dominions
and wish to stay there ... I can assure parents who fall into this category that
they will be consulted in writing before any arrangements are made for their
children to return. The Board has always foreseen the possibility that some
of the children evacuated under its auspices would wish to take advantage of
the opportunities open to them in the Dominions, and that neither they nor
their parents would wish them to return to the uncertain conditions which
will, at any rate for a certain time, prevail in post war Europe ...[59]

This was rather against the ideals of CORB as there is little documentary
evidence to suggest that staying in the Dominions was one of the options
available. In fact, in August 1944, CORB officials told parents that all children would be expected to return home with an official party unless they
were remaining overseas to complete an apprenticeship, or course of exams.
Nothing was said about staying overseas because they simply wanted to take
the opportunity to do so. Indeed, CORB would only pay the transport costs
of those coming back on prearranged vessels so any other arrangements
would have been very costly for those parents whose children remained in
the host countries.

In June 1945, after the situation in Europe had become more stable, they
were informed by a general letter that their children would soon be arriving
home. Those with children in Australia, where the Japanese threat of attack
was still perceived to be real, received the same letter but with significant
amendments: '... the passage accommodation for civilians is limited and
there are many calls upon it; also as long as hostilities with Japan continue,
military requirements must come first ...'[60]

The actual date of arrival was unknown until the last minute due to
inconsistencies with the travel arrangements, but, when the details were
available, the parents were sent additional information about the times, and
where they could meet their children. Few of the reunions took place at the
port of entry; most, like Patricia, met their parents at Lime Street station, or,
had they travelled on, in railway stations nearer to their homes.

As with Finnish evacuees in Sweden, some children found the return
home just as traumatic as the journey out, if not more so. Jean Cheyne,
who returned home in April 1945 from Canada on the SS *Cavina* wrote: 'I
had wanted to go home so much. But, when the time came, I really did not
want to go. I am afraid I cried a great deal, but, as so much was happening,
I didn't have time to be sad.'[61] Some of the children, now in their teens

and older, had been away from Britain for a long time and had developed strong relationships with their foster parents, and had boyfriends or girl-friends who they now had to leave behind. It was also a wrench for some of the hosts giving up the children they had lovingly looked after as their own for five or six years. Rita Patterson, who returned from Sydney on the *Andes* commented later that:

> it was one of my saddest memories … my relatives took me onto the ship and insisted on seeing my cabin. I was inspecting everything excitedly, and when I turned round they had gone. I ran after them but wasn't allowed ashore. I know great-uncle had taken my aunt away because she was so distressed, and I think that was the only way he could do it.[62]

Her arrival at home was just as emotional:

> In the dusk we rolled across the Tyne Bridge. Through the window of the train, I saw Mum and Aunts start running alongside the train as they caught sight of me. As we stood there, embracing and crying, I looked over their heads and saw father at the gate. And as I write this, I'm crying again … I will never forget that meeting as long as I live.[63]

For some, the homecoming was not as welcoming. Some found that their parents had separated, that they had new siblings; they were disappointed in their homes and resented returning to a drab, austere country still picking up the pieces of war. It was all too easy to make comparisons between what they had left and what they had returned to, and comments about their lives overseas and the families they lived with often led to resentment within the families. (The effects of this separation will be dealt with in a later chapter.)

Between May 1945 and February 1946, when CORB eventually closed its offices, 2,209 CORB children, had either returned home or were on their journey. Some did not return until 1947.

7

Hitler Youth

[The Hitler Youth] ... was one of the great propaganda achievements of the Nazi Rulers, that they were able to offer a political and ideological world view that granted them status, certainty, and power to young people, so much so that teenagers of both genders could accept and abide by prescribed behaviours without any qualms

Michael Kater[1]

As we will see in the chapter dealing with the evacuation of German children under the KLV, the Hitler Youth played an important role in both the organisation and the implementation of the scheme. However, unlike youth movements in other countries in other European countries during the Second World War, the Hitler Youth, or Hitler Jugend (HJ), was a pervasive organisation that reached all parts of the National Socialist regime.

The age range, 10–18, was similar to that of the Boy Scouts and Girl Guides in the UK, but beyond that the similarity ended. Originally, some children and adolescents joined because of a need to 'belong'; others, in a similar way to youth membership of the NSB in Holland, were forced to join by their National Socialist parents who viewed it as a way of progressing within the State structure. When membership became compulsory in March 1939 this was not seen as so important. It is interesting to note that despite this legislative compulsion, throughout the war the Nazi elite continually stressed that war service was totally voluntary and carried out as a 'service of honour to the German people'.[2]

One has to realise that for some children who were born after 1933, they had had no experience of pre-Nazi Germany, so when the State infrastructure collapsed in 1945, many were at a loss and found it difficult to cope with the consequences. How did this come about and how were the children lured into a system, which for some has had a hold on them ever since?

During the early history of the Nazi party, Hitler had little time for German youth, as he saw them as of little importance, simply because they could not vote and they were not yet old enough to be members of the party. He was far too concerned on winning over the parents. It was not until the 1930s that he realised that in order for the 'Thousand Year Reich' to develop, he would need to initiate the children into the National Socialist philosophy and in so doing create the leaders of the future. (Although, in practice, there was little evidence of younger leaders being given much responsibility or decision making within Hitler's own inner circle, right up to the end in 1945.) In December 1938, Hitler announced publicly his political intentions for the youth of Germany:

> After these youths have entered our organisations at age ten and there experienced, for the first time, some fresh air … we shall under no circumstances return them to the hands of our old champions of class and social standing, but instead place them immediately in the Party of the Labour Front, the SA or the SS. And then the Wehrmacht will take them over for further treatment … And thus they will never be free again, for the rest of their lives.[3]

The history of the organisation can be traced back to a group set up by Kurt Gruber in the mid-1920s which allied itself to the nascent Nazi party. It was not called the Hitler Jugend until 1926 when it became the responsibility of the *Sturm Abteilung* (SA). To begin with it was seen as a working-class, blue-collar organisation, but as its popularity grew it became more encompassing and the middle and upper classes became more interested, especially when it was seen as a way of personal progression. In 1930, a girls' section was introduced called the *Bund Deutscher Madel* (League of German Girls), the BDM.

In October 1931, Baldur von Shirach,[4] who was in his early twenties, was appointed as 'Youth Chief' and in 1932 he arranged a Hitler Youth rally in Potsdam, the first of many such events. Almost 70,000 attended from all parts of Germany at their own expense. Eighteen months later, in June 1933, he was promoted to Youth Leader of the German Reich, a position he held until 1940 when he was replaced by Artur Axmann.[5]

Shirach was determined that all young people in Germany should become aligned to the Party. However, although the rise in membership was impressive, reaching 60 per cent by 1 December 1936 at the implementation of the Hitler Youth Law, which stated that 'the entire German Youth within the territory of the Reich is coordinated in the Hitler Youth', it never did achieve a full 100 per cent. Although, when a decree was issued in March 1939 stating that all young people from ten to eighteen were obliged to join the Hitler Youth, the membership did reach 98 per cent.

In the 1930s there had been alternative youth groups other than the HJ, but over time these were gradually phased out, subjugated, or subsumed within the HJ. They included the communist KJVD (*Kommunistischer Jugenverband Deutschland*), whose members were sent to a concentration camp, the *Wandervogel* and the *Deutsche Freischar*. Their demise was accelerated by the Gestapo using a resurrected Emergency Decree issued in February 1933 which forbade the meeting of proscribed groups. According to Kater, the rise in numbers of the Hitler Youth was 'in large part contingent on the forced incorporations of previously organised leagues and less on voluntary membership'.[6]

However, even after the 1939 compulsion order, youths still had the possibility of opting out, a situation which Shirach found untenable. Some found the meetings boring, some did not like the activities, and others simply did not turn up. As a result, social and political pressures were brought to bear on both the individual and, in some cases, their parents. Some were debarred from apprenticeships or inheriting family farms; students at the gymnasium schools who were not members were not permitted to take the exams required to go on to university, and the final sanction was to be barred politically from the Nazi Party. However, as Kater points out, this was really a meaningless gesture as one would assume that anyone not wishing to join the HJ would not have wanted to hold public office within the Nazi state.[7] Parents of children who missed HJ meetings were often threatened with the removal of social benefits until their offspring took their membership seriously. These sanctions were not universally successful and there are many instances of parents, and indeed whole communities, joining together to stop their children becoming involved in the way in which the hierarchy wanted them to. The State response to this was the introduction of the Youth Service Compulsion Decree in November 1942,[8] when the police were given more powers to imprison and fine both parents and their children for not complying with HJ regulations. However, despite this legislation, evidence would suggest that the total compliance towards the HJ was not as successful as the propaganda machine would have the population believe. Although there were exceptions:

21ˢᵗ September 1941

An 11 year old girl has been noticed in school continually refusing to give the German greeting. She gives her religious convictions as a reason and quotes several passages from the Bible. At school she has a complete lack of interest in matters concerning the Fuhrer.

The parents, who have another daughter of 6, approve of this attitude and stubbornly refuse to influence the child in a contrary direction.

The Youth Department has proposed the removal of the children from their parents.

Case: The Refusal of the German greeting by a child of school age. Guardianship judgement.

Turned down request for removal from parents and ordered supervision. It has not been proved that the parents are opponents to National Socialism.[9]

The Court of Appeal revised this judgement and ordered the removal of both children from their parents, on the grounds that they were unsuitable to bring them up and that the Guardianship Court had displayed a misunderstanding of the principles of National Socialist youth education. Although not everyone agreed with the State's control over its youth and 'dissidence' was the exception rather than the rule, it did take place, much to the annoyance of the regime. This took many forms and even though one is more aware of the major protagonists such as the 'White Rose' and the '*Edelweisspiraten*' groups, there were ordinary people who were prepared to make a stand by doing 'little' things such as continuing to buy goods from Jewish shops. A few of these dissidents were actually members of the HJ who had become disillusioned with the organisation. One example was Sophie Scholl[10] who had been very much in favour of National Socialism but then became a leading member of the White Rose resistance group, based in Munich. However, one has to ask a basic question. Did such groups and individuals oppose the State because they were indeed prone to criminal acts and 'revolution', or were they labelled as such simply because the regime had introduced so many decrees and other pieces of legislation against so-called anti-social and anti-State behaviour that they were entrapped? As well as being ex-members (and in some cases still members) of the HJ, others had belonged to proscribed or religious groups. Their activities ranged from non-violent actions such as handing out scathing anti-Nazi propaganda leaflets[11] (which eventually led to the downfall of Scholl and her friends)[12] and, in the case of the 'Swing' group, demonstrating their non-alliance by what they wore, the unconventional length of their hair and the American 'swing' music they listened to, to more extreme behaviour such as stealing cars, assaulting members of the HJ, and derailing freight trains. It was only a matter of time before the State reacted and introduced further measures to curb what it considered to be immoral behaviour. In March 1940, a Police Decree for the Protection of Youth was issued which basically amounted to a curfew and an 'exclusion' edict. People under eighteen were excluded 'from public streets and squares during the hours of darkness, from public houses, from public cinemas and theatres after 9 p.m., from dance halls after 11.00, and public shooting and gaming premises.' In addition, those under eighteen were banned from drinking spirits and those under sixteen any alcohol at all, and smoking was banned in public for anyone under sixteen. In essence this was a decree against leisure time. Any youths contravening this decree were subject to a maximum of three weeks' imprisonment or a fine of up to RM50 (50 Reichsmarks). Parents and owners of bars, dance halls and cinemas etc., who permitted such contravention could face six weeks in prison or a fine of RM150. There was also a serious hidden agenda within this decree in that it allowed the NSV[13] to intervene in the cases of parents not supervising their children properly and in so doing enforce the ideology of the party. In October 1940, a further decree, the Youth Penal Code, was introduced giving further powers to the regime. Under the terms of 'Youth Arrest', offenders could be imprisoned in solitary confinement for up to four weeks on a diet of bread and water and in total silence. Other measures such as caning and Youth Protection Camps, some of which became race-eugenic experimental establishments, demonstrated the hold that the State now had over the discipline of the German youth. Members of the Swing groups, who were considered to be depraved, were to suffer greatly within these institutions and some of the leaders were sent to already existing concentration camps such as Auschwitz and Bergen-Belsen. In retrospect, this group had not committed any indictable offences. Their main 'crime' was simply that their life-style, which included a great amount of sexual liberalism, was liable to 'taint the racially pure community'.

Although, at least in the beginning, the HJ was 'advertised' as a social organisation with the emphasis on the youths' responsibilities within the

State, the underlying message was militaristic and always linked to ideological and political indoctrination. Goebbels, who was very much aware of the power of propaganda film, allocated what he called 'cinema time' to the HJ on two Sundays in every month for the showing of Youth Films. These included documentaries entitled *Victory in Poland*, *The Luftwaffe's Baptism of Fire*, *The Hitler Jugend at War* and feature films such as *The Daredevils* and *The Young Eagle*. All were laden with ideological rhetoric. In *The Daredevils* an instructor says to an HJ recruit: 'I know it's never been easy for you to obey orders but we pilots are risking our necks all the time. *Schweinhunde* who question the reason for an order are of no use to us.'[14]

In 1937, Rommel, then a lieutenant colonel, was appointed as liaison officer between the HJ and the Wehmarcht. Many of the HJ exercises were often military training under a different guise. Seemingly innocent activities, such as map-reading, hiking and camping, took on a strategic importance.

An article written in the January 1940 edition of the Nazi Party monthly journal, *NS Monatshefte* entitled 'German Youth on the Domestic Front', makes reference to the importance of this 'fieldcraft':

> Fieldcraft lies at the core of military training. There are schools ready to train the necessary instructors and 30,000 pass through each year … By practicing fieldcraft, which represents a kind of pre-infantry training, the boys (between 10 and 18) learn how to master the territory in which they are operating, which involves disguise and camouflage, the use of every hollow in the ground, orientation in darkness and in a strange environment. These exercises, which have the character of military training and, at the same time, satisfy the youthful urge to play games, correspond to the tasks of military reconnaissance units.

So too did sports, which were seen as not only creating competition, but also enhancing bodily and spiritual development.

In the Hitler Youth War Service Plan issued on 4 February 1940, specific mention is made of these pursuits:

> All units, with the exception of the 16-18 Hitler Youth boys and the members of the BDM section 'Faith and Beauty', will take part in a two hour sports session every week involving basic gymnastics. This compulsory sport can be scheduled for weekdays or Sundays depending on the local availability of gymnasia and sports fields …[15]

Yet these were open to abuse and members were forced to participate in actions which under normal circumstances they would find frightening and dangerous. These included non-swimmers being forced to jump into pools, unaided climbing using little or no equipment, and extended route-marches. Other activities were even more life threatening. As young soldiers, some members of the HJ were forced to dig fox-holes in the ground to hide in, minutes before they would be driven over by tanks. If the depressions were not big enough the recruits would be crushed.[16]

To provide a balance, there were more aesthetic pursuits. Academies were established for HJ musicians, and their orchestras and small groups would often play on the radio as well as performing at HJ functions. In fact, music and singing was an important part of the HJ daily regime of marching and drill:

> The cultural activities of the HJ will be continued. In the summer there will again be singing in the town and village squares. The brass and pipe bands will perform in the open air and at the Youth Meetings and Youth Film Hours. The HJ will also continue to sing and play at parents' evenings and in hospitals and factories …[17]

The Service Plan covered other aspects of their training and duties including: leadership, general duties, parades, summer time activities, special actions during wartime, and others.

Most of the HJ experience came via their compulsory, weekly 'hostel evenings'. The leaders were provided with materials from the HJ central office either for specific topics or via the Indoctrination Service Manual. All were highly charged with National Socialist ideology as this example from a meeting in April 1942 demonstrates. To put this into context the HJ had already been told that the Bolshevik armies had been destroyed and that Germany was now safe:

> In two evening sessions we will try to get to grips with this tremendous event in our nation's history. In the first evening session we shall discover that the core of our German history is a movement from West to East, i.e. our nation has always sought to find its living space within the east. The second evening session will show us that the Fuhrer is continuing and completing his historic mission of our nation. It is only in the east that the fate and therefore the future of our people lies.[18]

Other lectures, organised by Alfred Rosenberg,[19] were broadcast over the radio in 1940 and teachers and employers were told that all young people in their charge were to listen to them. All of these sessions were accompanied by relevant slogans which then became the main topic of discussion between teachers and pupils. Although in some quarters, they were not considered to be that successful:

> Ref. Decree of 9th August 1940 on School radio broadcasts.
> We have all become convinced that the intended effect is not always achieved. As is the case with every broadcast listened to en-masse, the same is true on this occasion, namely that even a not particularly good speaker, who appears in person in front of the pupils, sometimes has more impact than the best speaker on the radio. They were held at 8 o'clock in the morning. A large number of pupils fall asleep on such occasions, namely the younger children, particularly when they happen too often. In our view they should be restricted to special occasions.[20]

As war came ever closer, the roles of the HJ changed and the militaristic emphasis was much more apparent. By the end of 1942, 162 camps had been established under the close supervision of both the Wehrmacht (120) and the SS (42), to prepare seventeen-year-old boys for their eventual call up. The courses lasted three weeks and groups either attended with their peers from school, or if in work, had to take their holiday entitlement. Sebastian Haffner describes how youths, including himself, could easily be drawn into the ethos of the Hitler Youth:

> During the daytime you had no time to think, no opportunity just to be yourself. During the daytime comradeship brought contentment. It is indubitable that a certain kind of happiness thrives in such camps, it is the happiness of comradeship. It was a pleasure to go for a cross country run together in the morning, then go naked into the communal hot showers together, to share parcels that one or other received from home, to share the responsibility for misdemeanours that one of your comrades had committed, to help and support one another without reserve in all the actions of the day ... we were all the same ... who could deny that this brings happiness.[21]

Significantly, Haffner was one of the few who could see the invasive power of the Hitler Youth and eventually left Germany in 1938. Written under a pseudonym, his book is a very important treatise on how the German hierarchy were able to exploit the psychological weaknesses of both adults and children. Later in 1939, now in 'exile', he wrote about how the Hitler Youth had won them over by stealth. Referring again to the comradeship and happiness, he stated:

> Who would deny that men yearn for this, a yearning that is rarely satisfied in ordinary peaceful civilian life? ... and yet I know for certain that this very comradeship can become the means of the most terrible dehumanisation, and that it has become just that in the hands of the Nazis. They have drowned the Germans, who thirst after it, in this alcohol to the point of delirium tremens. They have made all Germans everywhere into comrades, and accustomed them to this narcotic from the earliest age ... in so doing this they have driven out something irreplaceable that cannot be compensated for by any amount of happiness ...[22]

Members of the BDM were also involved. They had been primarily responsible for collecting the harvest in 1942, and while the younger ones were employed in collecting medicinal herbs and other recyclable materials (in a similar way to their British counterparts), the older ones were employed in various industries and other duties. During the war, together with the younger members of the HJ, they helped wounded soldiers returning from the front, became air-raid wardens, built street defences and dug people out of bombed buildings. In a speech in October 1940, Artur Axmann, now leader of the HJ, made reference to the necessary change in responsibilities: 'During the next period, the leadership issue is the most important one for the Hitler Youth and, as a result of the big shortage of personnel, it will get even worse during the coming years'.[23]

By 1942, the HJ was also heavily involved in the Reich's colonisation policy and it was then mandatory that all members should at some time work in conquered areas which were being prepared for German settlers.

Recruitment of HJ into the SS was always a problem, despite Axmann's close relationship with Himmler and Heydrich. One has the impression that joining the SS would be seen as a natural 'rite of passage' for HJ members but this was not always the case. Many were put off by the long casualty lists in SS units and preferred the less demanding nature of the Wehrmacht. Those who did join were drawn to it by its uniform, elite status and above all its strong personalisation of National Socialist and racialist ideology and philosophy. All the same, out of the 66 per cent allocation of conscripts and volunteers to the Wehrmarcht, only 3 per cent of all German forces belonged to the SS. As a result, persuading the HJ to join its ranks became somewhat underhand. Some were asked to sign innocuous forms regarding a medical examination for tuberculosis to find that the 'small print' meant that they had joined the SS. Others were recruited by flattery. The problem was however, that many of those introduced to the service in this way did not meet the very high racial and physical membership criteria set by Himmler. The most serious example of this military indoctrination was witnessed in 1943 when a special Hitler Youth Division of the SS was established. The composition of this unit was made up of HJ leaders, some of whom relished the idea of moving from the HJ into the SS, and others who were literally press-ganged into it. One account tells of boys being locked in a room and being harangued by a recruiting officer pointing out the merits to all those present to volunteer for the SS. Some did. Those who were less willing were made to stand to attention for eight hours. They were then interrogated and in some cases denigrated by individual instructors. Some boys continued to maintain their unwillingness to volunteer and were subjected to further bullying until the following morning when they were sent to a recruitment camp, but 90 per cent did succumb to the treatment. Those who were harassed were asked to sign a declaration denying that any coercion had taken place.[24] Those who remained became part of the HJ Panzer Corps. They were trained for months and eventually saw action on 7 June 1944, near Caen. It has been estimated that 20,000 boys took part in the battle but by July more than 3,000 had been killed. The HJ Division was finally defeated in September 1944 when it was surrounded near the town of Falaise. Both events were used by the propaganda machine to recruit more youths to the unit.

> The SS Panzer Division 'Hitlerjugend' which has been sent into action in the west has proved itself heroically and after a brief spell of fighting has already earned the recognition of the Fuhrer. Contrary to the concerns of many, that a division comprised only of young soldiers with no experience of the front line would not be up to the demands placed upon it, the HJ Division has proved that it knows how to fight with heroism.[25]

For the majority of HJ members escape from their responsibilities was unthinkable. It was in fact easier to be on the 'inside' and part of the group identity, rather than on the 'outside' and seen as a deviant, an attitude which continued throughout the war, where service was not necessarily the result of total obedience, but seen by many as the only alternative. On the walls of some HJ hostels the words 'We were born to die for Germany' summed up the indoctrination. After all, this was what they had been trained for, and many had known nothing other than the Reich's tenacious control over most elements of German youth. Artur Axmann made a significant speech to the Wehmarcht High Command which supports this premise:

> We are convinced that our youth will not deteriorate in the war. It is growing more and more to meet the demands of the war. The young will no longer be able to make the comparison with peacetime. They will regard the state of war as normal. They will see this war as their mission.[26]

During the war the age level at which people were called up fell six times. In 1940 the age was nineteen, in 1941–2 it was eighteen, in 1943–4 it fell to seventeen, in 1944 those aged sixteen were asked to volunteer and in February 1945, the remaining sixteen-year-olds were conscripted, and in the following month those who had been born in 1929 were called up, making some of them only fifteen years of age. At the time Axmann commented:

> The enemy stands in our homeland and is directly threatening our lives. Rather than let ourselves be annihilated or enslaved, we will fight hard and doggedly until the final victory. Those born in 1929 will receive long-term, varied and conscientious training. This training will later combine with their courageous conduct to gain superiority over the enemy.[27]

Those who were not fit for military service, either through age, reserved occupation, or disability, were called up into the *Volkssturm* (an equivalent of the Home Guard in the UK), which had been established in September 1944 to provide a defence force on the Home Front.

> Fuhrer Decree: (26th September 1944)
> The Gauleiters should immediately register all compatriots of between 16 and 60 years of age who are capable of bearing arms for the establishment of the German Volkssturm. In recruiting for the German Volkssturm, account should be taken of the need to maintain functions vital to the war effort, namely armaments, food supplies, transport and communications ...[28]

However, these units were ill-equipped and it is significant that a decree issued in October 1944 stated: '... the establishment of the Volkssturm must not cause either weapons, articles of clothing or items of equipment to be withheld from the active Wehmarcht'.[29] which in effect rendered the *Volkssturm* useless. As a result they were forced to rely on home-made weapons, which by their very nature brought them into very close physical contact with the enemy forces.

Despite the general lack of morale within these units, some boys acquitted themselves well and there are famous propaganda pictures and film clips (repeated in the recent feature film *Downfall*)[30] taken in the garden outside Hitler's bunker showing the Führer awarding Iron Crosses and Military medals to boys as young as twelve years old, on what was to be his last birthday, and his final appearance in public.

Memories of such scenes have haunted some people ever since: 'I never want to see those children's faces with steel helmets on their heads. Child labour is bad enough, but making children into heroes is even worse. I never want it to happen again'.[31]

Yet, for others, they were a source of inspiration. In 1945 an officer stated:

> Obedience was the one thing they learned. When they got an order, there were no questions asked. But we had to restrain them, dampen their enthusiasm. They had even been sent wild by pictures in the press of Hitler awarding Iron Crosses to youngsters. We really couldn't make proper use of them. They were just sacrificed. It made no sense, because they achieved nothing.[32]

With the war now entering its final stages the role for some HJ changed yet again. Detachments were rushed to the western front to build fortifications and some, carrying obsolete anti-tank rockets, and rifles which dated back to the nineteenth century, were pitted against advancing allied tanks. One eyewitness recalls:

> Hitlerjungen, just kids, were literally jumping at tanks with their grenade launchers. My God, how they were mown down ... Beside a wrecked tank on the road lay a heap of dead or dying kids in their brown uniforms. One was crawling round in circles. His face was nothing but a mass of blood ...[33]

It was difficult for some older members of the Wehmarcht to remember that they were fighting alongside children until something specific reminded them. One Wehmarcht officer, not much older than the HJ in his command, stated that, 'I found it extraordinarily depressing psychologically to see how these young people broke down emotionally, when the fighting virtually became hand to hand. Many of them were weeping, screaming, running away and something which affected me deeply, crying for their mothers.'[34]

Many of the HJ in the east, spurred on by reports of the rape and killing of local civilians, and fighting to defend their families from the same fate, suffered agonising death at the hands of the advancing Russians, from artillery shells and by tanks being deliberately driven over them. A few of those who were captured were summarily executed.

Some HJ joined the Werewolves, basically small groups of boys and girls who were dropped behind enemy lines, both to the west and the east, to carry out suicide missions in a vain attempt to halt the allied advance. A HJ leaflet, published as late as April 1945, stated:

> Wherever the enemy may break through, he will come up against our home defence front. We will continue our fight until the hour of the German soldier strikes again, until our Wehrmacht finally drives the enemy out of German territory. It is for that hour that we fight. Our struggle is our victory! Werewolves, go get them!

However, the results of some of the HJ fanaticism had devastating effects on some members of the population who wanted to surrender. One example of this happened in the village of Brettheim. As American tanks advanced, a group of HJ arrived to defend the village. A farmer, afraid that the settlement would be devastated, threw his weapons into the pond. In response the HJ complained to the nearest SS commander who sentenced the farmer to death. However, the local mayor and the local head of the Nazi Party refused to sign the death warrant. As a result all three were hanged from trees outside the cemetery. According to Knopp, the people of Brettheim still suffer from this incident, devastated by the fact that even in the face of obvious defeat, the HJ were still prepared to denounce their fellow Germans.[35]

During the last few days of April 1945, the HJ, together with a number of civilians, fought futile last-ditch battles in Berlin against the Russian forces, which were advancing street by street. Against increasing odds they were ordered to secure bridges and strategic sites but many, if not all, died in the process. It was ironic that despite his rhetoric, 'It is up to you, whether you want to bring things to an end, and be the last of a worthless race, despised by posterity, or whether you want to be the beginning of a new age, one more glorious than you can ever imagine …'[36]

Axmann, who had recently been awarded the Gold Cross of the German Order of the Iron Cross by Hitler, used one of these bridges to make his escape out of the city on his way to southern Germany. While he fled, the boys he had been in charge of, some now just eleven or twelve years old, were dying for the cause, or if they ran away, were being hanged from lamp-posts and trees as cowards. Out of the 5,000 HJ who were ordered to defend Berlin, only around 600 survived.

According to Gerhard Hafner, a flak auxiliary, 'the youth were sacrificed, or in their blindness, let themselves be sacrificed, at a time when the war had long been lost, simply to allow their Fuhrer to live a few days longer'.[37]

When the Russians finally took Berlin, many could not believe that the majority of the defenders were just children. A Russian cameraman described them:

> You couldn't call them soldiers. They were boys of fourteen, fifteen, maybe sixteen, little lads who lived at home with their mothers. They may not have been soldiers but they behaved as if they were. They wore army greatcoats which hung loosely on them, because they were much too big, not made for them.[38]

It has been estimated that by the end of the war almost 12 million Germans had been taken prisoner by the allies, 3 million by the Russians, and one could surmise that at least 50 per cent of these had been in the Hitler Youth at some time in their lives. However, one of the Soviet Generals, Gareyev, is quoted as saying: 'There were a lot of terrified lads, who were still just children. One could take pity on them. Many of them we didn't even take prisoner, we sent them straight home'.

Many of those retained by the Russians were to die in the harsh conditions in their camps. As the USSR had never signed either the Hague or Geneva conventions they were not obliged to treat them with any form of humanity. Those taken by the US and British forces fared marginally better.

On 30 April 1945 Hitler, together with his new wife Eva, committed suicide in the bunker. Goebbels announced that he had died defending Germany. One member of the HJ announced: 'Hitler is dead, and that means the Hitler Youth is dead. No Hitler, no Hitler Youth …' Another commented: 'Everything we believed in then turned out to be worthless. We were left with nothing'.[39]

According to German statistics those called up into the army in 1939 had a life expectancy of a further four years. The youths conscripted in 1945 had, on average, one month left to live. Those who survived suffered for many years afterwards, some to the present day.

Kinderlandverschickung

I hereby give my permission for my son/daughter to be sent away on the programme of the Extended Kinderlandverschickung by the NSDAP. I agree to him/her being sent away for a period of at least six months, and appreciate that he/she cannot return before this period has elapsed. I also give my consent for him/her being vaccinated prior to departure …

signed Father or legal guardian.[1]

The official German policy regarding the protection of children, and in some cases non-combatants, was to avoid wholesale evacuation at the outbreak of hostilities. Instead the plan was to implement a gradual dispersal of the population away from the towns and cities in order to cut down the possibility of panic, which could obstruct vital communication networks. The German High Command also felt that the effect of any air attack on civilians might be overestimated and that during the first week or two after the war started, the situation might become clearer.

As early as 1935–6, a series of articles appeared in *Gasschutz & Luftschutz*, (*Gas Protection and Air Protection*) the official magazine of the Reich Air Protection League, discussing the difficulties of evacuation. In October 1936, Colonel Teacher, an official at the Air Protection Department of the German Air Ministry, stated in this publication that the practicality of evacuation would depend on three considerations:

a. The number of people to be moved.
b. The time the movement was to take place.
c. The means of transport involved in the movement.

Teacher went on to suggest that the first consideration was impossible to forecast because those in the military would have left home, the German ARP would absorb the others, as anyone over the age of fifteen was required for ARP duties, and anyone under the age of ten had to stay with their parents wherever they were, even in vulnerable areas.

It was thought that government officials and businessmen would remain, as well as the old and infirm who would be unable to travel. Prisoners should also be evacuated, not for any humanitarian reason but because of the danger they would cause if the prisons were bombed and they escaped. He also recommended that some people should be allowed to find their own accommodation. However, although their departure should not be hindered, they would have to satisfy the police that they had made arrangements for the care of their own homes. They would also need to obtain written permission from the police in order to move, as it was felt that too much voluntary evacuation would develop into panic flight.[2]

Despite these initial suggestions, it was only at the beginning of 1938 that the German government developed concrete plans for the evacuation of children under the age of fifteen to the countryside as a precautionary measure against enemy air attacks.

In a secret directive to the leaders of the local Nazi party branches, Hitler set out their responsibilities during any evacuation:

> As part of the mobilisation, evacuation measures will be carried out in certain parts of Germany. They are designed to secure important materials, objects and equipment; also those men liable to military service living in these districts will be removed to the interior of the country. This evacuation is a precautionary measure which is made necessary due to the proximity of the enemy's frontier. The task of the local branch leader is to convince the population of the necessity of these evacuation measures, to urge them to remain calm and to prevent any movement of refugees.[3]

On 5 September 1939, the federal minister gave instructions to prepare for the evacuation of school-aged children by local 'air-raid protection leaders', in cooperation with local school authorities, so that any such scheme could be implemented as soon as it might become necessary.

As the air war against Germany grew apace so too did the German evacuation scheme, known as *Ewertite Kinderlandverschickung*[4] (KLV), which was organised, at least in the beginning, with typical Aryan efficiency. This was not a new idea.[5] It had first been introduced in the nineteenth century when churches organised country holidays for children from the poorest city areas and again during the Weimar Republic when the same practice was carried out by the Workers' Welfare Organisation. Under this latter scheme children stayed with industrial workers or in KLV Camps. According to Gerhardt Brook, the evacuation measure instigated in 1940 was ordered primarily for psychological reasons and was to be used for the pacification of the population, who were shocked by experiencing the first bombs.[6]

In September 1940, Hitler ordered the voluntary evacuation of all children from those areas that were being targeted by the RAF, and on 26 September gave Baldur von Schirach[7] the responsibility for organising it. Having retained an interest in the Hitler Youth, Schirach took the opportunity to marginalise the education authorities, particularly the *Nationalsozialistische Lehrerbund*[8] (National Socialist Teachers League), and increase the influence of the Hitler Youth. However, Hitler, as in other areas of social and military policy, kept more than a just watching brief on the scheme and insisted that evacuation (*Verschickung*) should be voluntary and, as a consequence, ordered that the number of teachers should be cut by 50 per cent. He was not concerned when Schirach pointed out to him that this policy could have a detrimental effect on the children's education, and he insisted that his directive be carried out:

> In reply to my question whether or not the evacuation of young people should be compulsory or voluntary the Fuhrer replied that the whole action should be on a voluntary basis. The number of teachers should if necessary be halved. I pointed out that in these circumstances regular instruction could not be absolutely guaranteed. The Fuhrer said that one would have to put up with that ...[9]

He also ordered that the label '*Verschickung*' should not be used and the scheme should retain the appearance of simply moving the children into the country.

The next day Martin Boorman issued a circular to members of the party, which included the following statements:

- Young people who live in areas which are subject to repeated air raid warnings should be sent to other areas of the Reich on a voluntary basis.
- This should be aimed particularly at those children who live in areas with inadequate shelter provision.

- Teachers will be involved in the organisation and will make sure that lessons continue in the new locations.
- Accommodation will be organised so that schools and classes can stay together. This will be in youth hostels, inns etc. This will begin on October 4th 1940, and the Hitler Youth will organise the housing of children from the 5th school year and above.
- The NSV (Nationalsozialistische Volkswohlfahrt)[10] were responsible for sending away pre-school children and children in school years 1-4. The NSLB (National-Socialist Teacher Association) were also to be involved in the scheme.
- Young people were to be dispatched in two groups: (1) Ages 6-10 (2) Ages 10-14. Group 1 were to be housed with families and Group 2 in Camps, Youth Hostels and School hostels.
- The reception areas would include: Bavarian Eastern March, Brandenburg, Upper Danube, Saxony, Silesia, Sudetenland, Thuringia, Wartheland and Ostland.
- Gauleiters will be responsible for persuading parents to send their children away.
- Letters will be sent to parents but there will be no propaganda or announcements in the press. However, there can be press releases in local papers in the reception areas.

It is interesting to note that although the numbers of teachers were to be reduced, those remaining in the profession were still expected to take a lot of responsibility for ensuring that some semblance of an education continued.

As with the British scheme, the central government directives were cascaded down to local level via local administrators, as this instruction from a Gau representative of the KLV to district leaders indicates:

> In accordance with the Fuhrer's instructions … Please begin at once with the recruitment of host families, since the children are expected to arrive in January. You should take note of the fact that the number allocated to you by the Gau Headquarters of the NSV in the enclosed letter must be adhered to without fail …

Although the evacuation of German children was voluntary and free (the costs were borne by the NSDAP and partly by central government), like the British scheme a great deal of pressure was applied to parents to send their children away. On a simple level, warnings stating that if they didn't go children would be without their friends and would have to move schools were common: 'While the children who are sent will have the best possible education from their own teachers, those who remain behind will have to expect to be transferred to a class containing a collection of children from other classes or to another school'.[11]

As the intensity of the war on the Home Front increased, so too did the need for removing the children. In 1942, the authorities in Hamburg sent letters to parents explaining the scheme. But in order to maintain the pretence that there was no serious cause for concern on the war front, reasons for going were not given on the grounds of escaping the bombing, but as protecting them against health risks during the winter.

> Hamburg 7th November 1942.
>
> … It is the Gauleiter's strongly held wish that as many Hamburg children as possible should be protected against risks to health this winter. As is well known, up to now over 150,000 boys and girls from our city have spent six months at a time in southern Gaus and have had many happy experiences in the KLV camps. Experience has shown that their education can best be assured if they are sent away together as classmates … Carefully selected efficient Hitler Youth and League of German Girls leaders support the teachers in their work and ensure that Hitler Youth duties are carried out in an exemplary manner …[12]

This latter situation created a great deal of conflict between the teachers, who were responsible for the education of the evacuees, and the Camp Team Leader and his Hitler Youth subordinates, who organised youth activities outside the classroom. Tension was apparent before children even reached the reception areas as this letter from a Hamburg teacher would indicate:

> We have already noticed the opposition of the BDM (Bund Deutscher Mädel)[13] to the teachers at the preliminary meeting before the departure of the transport. In response to a remark made by the district leader concerning our responsibility for the dispatch of the children, one of the BDM leaders declared that they were not teachers' skivvies and that they received their instructions from the BDM alone. This negative attitude led to various tensions during the journey. For example, our instructions were criticised and revoked in front of the children … The BDM girls announced that they had the decisive authority in the KLV programme and the teachers were responsible for the school work …[14]

The first batch of children left Berlin on 3 October 1940 and travelled to Saxony. At first only Berlin and Hamburg were involved,[15] and by the beginning of December 189,543[16] children had been moved to either KLV camps or private homes. Although the reception areas were mainly in the north and east of the Greater German Reich, there were also KLV camps in regions that had been annexed, these included Hungary and Poland.[17] By November 1942, a total of 1,198,377 people would be transported by 1,654 trains and seventy-eight ships on the Rhine and Weser rivers.[18] Of these, 335,409 were to be youths aged between 10–14, who were destined for KLV camps and 862,968 mothers and children who were being cared for by the Nazi Welfare Agency. These 'evacuees' were issued with 127,000 tubes of toothpaste, 7,500 first aid kits, 9,900 musical instruments, 140,000 suits for boys, 130,000 suits for girls and 110,000 pairs of wooden shoes.[19] This was in total contrast to the British scheme where no evacuees were given such official help with clothes and basic necessities. (Although, a series of Ministry of Health circulars that arrived in the reception areas only six days before evacuation took place did give permission to those authorities responsible for evacuating persons from their areas to buy boots, clothing and knapsacks up to the value of £1 for every 200 children, on the strict understanding that no publicity was given to such help.)[20]

Officials were appointed from the Hitler Youth with specific responsibility to ensure that the reception of the children went as smoothly as possible, requiring them to liaise closely with the local administrators. Running parallel to this, Gauleiters looked after the 'party' side. Using a Reich law[21] introduced on 1 September 1939, the KLV representatives were able to start requisitioning hotels, hostels, and other suitable buildings in the reception areas. Initially, an attempt was made to place children of a specific social and economic background with equivalent hosts and, in order to achieve this, the domestic circumstances of the children were listed on their register. However, as more children arrived in the reception areas this became unworkable.

At first, unlike the British evacuation, children were to be boarded free of charge but this proved to be difficult and on 28 March 1941, the following rates were introduced to hotels:

(RM. Reichsmark)

	For mothers … up to	For infants and children … up to
Class 1	5.50 RM	3.00 RM
Class 2	4.50 RM	2.50 RM
Class 3	3.50 RM	2.00 RM

The NSV also paid host families up to a maximum of 3.50 RM for mothers and 2.00 RM for children.[22]

The German equivalent to the British billeting officer had the responsibility of not only visiting the children on a regular basis in order to make sure that all was going well, but also of organising at least two games sessions a week, or excursions, in order to take the pressure of the hosts. For their part, the hosts also had to make sure that the children kept in contact with their own families.

In the 'Guidelines for the Reception of Children in Host Families on the Basis of Special Action', issued on 20 April 1940[23] by the NSV headquarters in Wurttemberg, there was a special section on how to deal with enuresis. Any chronic bed-wetters were not to be sent to host families but to unspecified 'alternative accommodation'. Only those who wet the bed as a result of insecurity and changes in routine, were to be tolerated, and in such cases hosts were to be given help on how to deal with the situation.

Despite the planning there were still problems, especially relating to class divisions. This resulted in some Berliners complaining that there was too much official concern for the welfare and safety of the middle classes. This was evident in the policies whereby those working in offices had evacuation priority over those working in the factories and, if further proof was needed, figures show that more people were moved from the middle-class areas west of Berlin than from the more working-class north.[24] Even when the evacuation went reasonably smoothly, tension remained just below the surface. For example, in the south the name given to women evacuated from the Rhineland was 'bomb wenches'.

After a while there was a drift back of evacuees from the reception areas to their home towns and this caused a great deal of concern, to the extent that the numbers coming back from South Westphalia were so large that the 'home' authorities cancelled the returnees' ration cards, an ill-planned move that resulted in food riots. Movement back was also prompted by the fact that those remaining in the danger areas were given preferential treatment when it came to the allocation of food and scarce consumer products.

In many areas the situation was not helped by the fact that many evacuees were billeted with farmers who, because they were registered as 'self-suppliers', were excluded from any rationing schemes. This meant that in many cases they ate well and when their food was compared with the meagre rations of other evacuees there were some grievances and ill-feeling. From the hosts' point of view there were also complaints that their 'guests' sat around and did nothing except '... while away their time in gossip, pram-pushing and raids on the meagrely stocked shops'.[25] (Very similar to the comments made by residents in some of the reception areas in Britain.) Complaints were also received in some reception areas where hosts were forced to take in people from towns further afield, yet were unable to take in those nearer to them geographically. This was evident in the Allgau district where residents were asked to take in evacuees from the Ruhr instead of Munich, an area where many of them had relatives.

Religion also played a part in the discord within reception areas. In a situation similar to that of the Catholic evacuees from Liverpool being sent to non-conformist 'Chapel' areas of Wales, some evacuees from the Rhineland, who had been used to the National Socialist neo-paganism, were sent to villages in the Alpine regions still practising fundamental Catholicism. Although the Hitler Youth, a fervent anti-religious organisation, was responsible for extra-curricular activities in schools, the KLV were anxious not to alienate parents too much and allowed children to attend church and other religious groups if they wanted to. However, as the evacuee children were the responsibility of their teachers who, as members of the NSLB were discouraged from having anything to do with churches, a lot of pressure was applied to children in some areas making it difficult for them to practice their religion. Although, this did very much depend on where in the country the children had gone and the views of the evacuating authorities. For example, Hamburg separated church from education and issued the following directive to teachers:

> ... The KLV camps should be made to exercise the strictest possible reserve in confessional matters. On no account should there be any instruction by clergy, members of religious orders or church representatives. On the other hand, there should of course be the closest possible cooperation with official agencies of the NSDAP,[26] its formation and organisations in the receiving Gau.[27]

This was a point taken up by some parents. The author of a report on the progress of the KLV, issued in September 1943, commented: 'Churchgoers express the view that the whole point of evacuation is to separate the young people from their parents in order to teach them to become heretics in the camps'.[28]

In February 1939, the Youth Service Day was introduced, and implemented for the first time in 1940. The HJ set out to challenge the role of the Church by creating an elaborate induction ceremony for its fourteen-year-old members. This was deliberately planned to compete with the Confirmation and First Communion services of the Protestant and Catholic Churches. One girl described the event in her diary:[29]

> … The ceremony took place in the market square. A huge platform covered in a shining swastika was erected in the middle and we recruits were lined up in rows of four in front of it. … The swearing-in flag was carried in and then four of us had to step forward in helmets and rifles at the ready … We were then inspected by the Mayor … then came the swearing in. I have sworn loyalty to the German Flag and to Adolf Hitler.[30]

As the allies continued their destruction of German cities in the west, more and more evacuees and refugees were moved from the cities of Essen, Düsseldorf, Dortmund, Cologne and others, to the east into Saxony, on the assumption, to begin with, that they would be beyond the range of the RAF and USAAF bombers. As a result the area became known as the *Reichsluftschultzkeller* (the Reich's air-raid shelter). As many of these evacuees from the west were children, the *Gauleiter* of the area, Martin Mutschmann, a hard-line Nazi official, issued a secret communiqué in July 1943 to Burgomeisters of the major cities in the area, ordering them to organise the enrolment of individual evacuated children and whole schools and their teachers within existing establishments. There were really two reasons for him doing this. Firstly, as the 1940 edict stated, it was easier to assimilate whole schools because they would be with their friends and teachers and secondly, it made the supervision of National Socialist policies, through the auspices of the Hitler Youth and the League of German Girls, easier to control. As in the UK, many school buildings had already been taken over for other purposes so it meant that as schools' populations increased in size,[31] teachers and pupils alike had to cope with extremely difficult and cramped conditions. As a result, again similar to the situation in Britain, the authorities had to resort to double-shift schooling in some areas with the effect that the education of both evacuee and indigenous pupils was affected. There was also an additional problem. As many of the schools had been taken over for industrial and military use, there was little shelter accommodation for the children, or indeed the adults, a situation which was to become very serious in February 1945.

As the number and the intensity of the raids over Germany continued to rise, more evacuees arrived in the area, especially from Hamburg and

Bremen. By the end of 1943 the area was saturated with incomers to such an extent that the authorities could not take any more, a situation not dissimilar to that in Dorset and other reception areas in the UK. In fact, the following comment, made by a local party official in northern Bavaria in April 1944, could also have been said by some billeting officers in the Britain:

> … It is always the people who've been bombed out who are responsible for the general mood. There are always some of them who have something to grumble about and are continually discontented. Big city people and country people simply don't suit each other. One woman says: 'we're left to starve here in the sticks'. Another complains that there's no entertainment here; another says to the shopkeeper: 'I'll buy anything off you but not your Bavarian stupidity'. One often has to step in and sort things out.[32]

During Christmas 1943, the children stayed with their schools and spent the time making decorations and toys, while older pupils took part in Hitler Youth activities and general low-key war work, thus enabling adults to be released for call-up into the military or, alternatively, into industry.

But unbeknown to the evacuees the authorities in this 'safe area' were becoming increasingly concerned about the closer proximity of the allied air raids[33] and during the latter months of 1943 they had been making secret preparations to evacuate the children again, this time into the surrounding countryside. Everything was in place and all the arrangements had been made by November. As in the UK, during the months prior to the war the population was kept in the dark in order to avoid panic[34] but secret documents had been sent out to head teachers outlining the plans for dispersal. A few days later, Leipzig, only 60 miles away from Dresden, was bombed. As a result, on 6 December the head teachers were permitted to inform their staff of the plans but, as in September 1940, they were specifically ordered not to use the word 'Evacuation'; instead they were simply to use the phrase 'Country Vacation'. Three days later the *Gauleiter's* office issued an 'Address to Dresden Parents', which stated: 'The danger exists that after his attack on Leipzig, the enemy will extend his aerial terror to other cities. In order to keep the losses as low as possible, it is planned to transfer school children from the most at risk cities to less threatened places.'[35]

Parents were assured that the 'vacation' would be voluntary and would only take place after the Christmas holidays. Newspapers were forbidden to mention the scheme so as not to incite any panic or unnecessary unease and on 11 and 12 December school meetings were held in order to encourage parents to either send their children to friends or relatives in the country-side, or join the Government Scheme. However, few did either and only 30 per cent of the children in Dresden became involved.

A report from the SD[36] issued on 30 September 1943 had already stated that the success of persuading parents to send their children away depended very much on the skill of the speakers involved. The fact that some of them, especially in Berlin, could not provide specific details about when and where the children would be relocated was having an effect on the numbers signing up for the proposal. Even Goebbels extolled the virtues of the KLV scheme, and in order to allay parental fears his ministry produced propaganda films such as *Hands Up*, which showed a rather romanticised view of camp life.

If one looks at a specific area it is possible to see what effect these plans had on both the local domestic and political infrastructure. The movement of children from the Ruhr started in January 1941, but as in other areas was met with strong parental resistance. According to Gerhard Brock, only 40 per cent of the school children eligible in the industrial city of Bochum were evacuated. In addition, approximately 16,000 school children were moved on their parents' initiative to relatives and friends.[37]

In the summer of 1943, this evacuation measure increased as a direct reaction to the four months' continual bombing of the Ruhr by the Allies. It could also possibly have been in response to the situation where all the schools in areas that were in particular danger had to be closed and eviction orders had already been issued. A circular, sent from the Federal minister for Science and Education on 4 June 1943, stated that school instruction for the establishments affected by such measures would be available in the KLV camps.

Despite the dangers it was obvious that some parents were keeping their children at home and 20 per cent of the total remained in the area through-out the war, even though Bochum was very heavily bombed. The first intensive raid began on 14 May 1943, when 394 houses were destroyed and 302 people killed and the second, more devastating because of the ensuing fire-storm, occurred on 13 June, resulting in widespread destruction and the deaths of 312 inhabitants. Bochum was not the only city to demonstrate parental resistance. In the neighbouring city of Herne, 41 per cent of those eligible for evacuation remained.

Quite simply, some parents did not wish to be separated from their children. In addition, the situation was not helped in the Saxony area by an order forbidding mothers to travel with their offspring. The Gauleiter explained the reasons for this by suggesting that there would not be enough accommodation for the mothers, but his hidden agenda was that as these children were to be the future of the Reich, the Party wanted control of them without undue interference from parents. This had always been the not-so-hidden agenda of German evacuation. As we have seen, even the official policy of evacuating whole schools under the KLV scheme had a dual role – that of removing the children to safer areas and, from the State's point of view, taking the children away from parental and, in some areas, religious influences. However, perversely, for this to work the State still needed support from the parents and there was a genuine concern that some parents did not quite believe the humanitarian intentions of the authorities and were beginning to see that perhaps there could be other motives. This resulted in a directive being issued in 1943 telling parents that what some of them were hearing about the scheme was simply a result of rumour-mongering:

> Rumours have been spread in various Gaus in the Reich that the sending away of young people of school age is not purely a war-time measure but intended to remove from parents the education of their children and to place the boys and girls under the exclusive influence of the State and the Party. These rumours must be vigorously refuted. They are spread by enemy propaganda to disturb parents and are gladly passed on by negative elements among our people. The extended Kinderlandverschickung is of course a measure designed purely for the protection of the lives of German youth as a result of the air war. After the war Kinderlandverschickung will be returned to its original purpose and will have the sole task of providing children with impaired health with the opportunity to recover.[38]

Nevertheless, despite these assurances the desire for State control still resulted in those teachers in the KLV camp schools, who either disagreed with the policies or tried to dilute the National Socialist side of the curriculum being called up into the Wehrmacht and sent to the Eastern Front. This had always been a problem. In April 1933 the Law for the Reconstitution of the Civil Service had been used to dismiss Jews and the 'unreliable', i.e. those who were of a non-National Socialist persuasion, from the profession. Until the end of the war those remaining, including teachers, were subject to regular screening and if necessary 'weeding out'.

By mid-January 1944, the authorities were becoming very concerned with this continued parental indifference and issued a statement through the local press saying that if children remained in the cities they would not be entitled to schooling. The order was sent to parents who had to acknowledge receipt of it and then make a decision to send their children away or not. In Bochum, all children between the ages of nine and thirteen who were still in the city, had to report to the Hitler Youth and then be sent on to a KLV camp. If this did not happen, the parents were informed that they were deemed to have removed their children from compulsory education and would be subjected to the legal consequences. But this action did little to increase the numbers of children sent away. In fact, by February there were many reports of children already in the country now experiencing homesickness and expressing a desire to return to their families. A gradual drift back to the cities began despite the authorities closing down the city schools while keeping the ones in the country open.

On 24 August 1944, the USAAF bombed Freital to the south-west of Dresden. More school meetings were called and the Ministry of Education compiled lists of those children whose parents still refused to move or had returned to the cities. These were to be put to useful work through the Hitler Youth networks. At the same time, teachers were ordered to make home visits to parents to 'persuade' them to send their children away.

However, a few weeks later everything changed. The National Socialist People's Welfare organisation in Berlin sent out a message to Dresden and other areas informing them that the concept of 'Total War' had been redefined and there were no longer any available resources to help in the protection of the civilian population. All financial and human assets were to be redirected towards the military war effort.

As a result, all civilians would have to fend for themselves in a country where civil authority was becoming more disrupted and disorganised as the months went on. Nevertheless, thousands of children still continued to pour into Saxony in search of a safe haven. As a result many were in Dresden on the fateful night of 13/14 February – another story entirely.

During 1945, as the allies drew closer to their goal, the KLV camps in the east were becoming particularly vulnerable. The camp leaders were sent a communiqué by their Hitler Youth superiors stating:

> The enemy threatens your camp. I am compelled by the present situation of the war to put the destiny of the children entrusted to your care into your hands and to leave all responsibility to you. In this hour of need use all your

willpower. The most difficult task of your life is imminent. The existence of our nation through our German children is decidedly in your hands! The youth of Germany has got to exist! The time will come that they will erect the banner and will avenge our dead comrades![39]

They were ordered to think only of the children in their charge and cast aside any personal fears or concerns. Under the title 'In Case of Invasion', they were provided with lists of clothes and food that was to be taken with them and if there were not enough haversacks to carry the articles, they were to make them out of blankets or BDM skirts. They were to move from one KLV camp to another, preferably during the night. If there was no transport they were to march. Before leaving they were to destroy all documents that might give away any information about the KLV. They were also given specific instructions about what to do if confronted by the enemy. If the English/American forces arrived they were to keep the children in the camp, making sure that all Nazi insignia, camp names and personal badges were removed. The camp was to be referred to simply as a residential school. However, if the Russians arrived first they were to remember the motto 'No child in the hands of the barbarous Soviets' and leave quickly.

They were now left to their own devices; the central organisation had cast them adrift and if and how they survived very much depended on their own resilience and adaptability. As a result, many of the children sent to so-called safety now found themselves facing the onslaught of the advancing armies. Many were killed, many were raped and many of those captured were sent back east and never saw their homeland again until the 'Wall' came down in 1989.

Lack of actual numbers makes it difficult to be specific about how many children were involved in the whole process, but according to the estimates of the last leader of the KLV scheme, Gerhard Dabel, 2.8 million girls and boys between the ages of ten and eighteen were sent to 9,000 KLV camps. In addition, around another 3 million toddlers, mothers and children between six and ten were evacuated under the KLV scheme. A most recent study suggests a lower total, but nonetheless the figure is around 2 million.[40]

LIFE IN THE CAMPS

Unlike the British Camp schools, which were all purpose-built to a similar design, the KLV camps took on many guises. Some had been hotels or boarding houses, others had been youth hostels, convents and schools. In some of the country areas the facilities were very primitive whereas in others, especially those that had formally been popular areas for tourists, they could be considered luxurious. However, some hoteliers and resort owners opposed the requisition of their premises because they were concerned about potential damage and whether or not they could be used in their original state in the future. Some boys were sent to work on the local farms, as in the district of Swabia. Conditions in the camps varied. In his autobiography, *A Hitler Youth in Poland*, Jost Hermand described the different camps he was sent to during the war. One was a brick-built school in a small village with no electricity or running water and no access to a shop or post office, one was a luxurious villa in San Remo where they were served by waiters, and the other was a skiing camp where he received winter-war training.

The everyday life in the camps was strictly regulated, even down to the amount of allocated dormitory space for each individual, reckoned to be about three cubic metres per person. Each room had to contain at least three beds. The children were either to swim or have a shower once a week and they were to wash their hair every fortnight. During their stay in the camps they were to receive instruction and take part in recreational facilities. But there were also punishments for those who stepped out of line, usually in the form of beatings or extra drill, even though the former was officially banned within the camps. One boy commented later that '… all four pairs of shoes had erupted insoles, because of the marching and the penalty drill'.[41] In fact, over time many of the punishments on the 'banned' list were used more frequently and it very much depended on the camp ethos as to how the children were dealt with. In some, the teachers and HJ leaders were much more liberal in their approach, whereas others were run by Nazi 'hard-liners' who maintained a harsh regime.

One aspect of the camps that was never discussed was the length of stay. This caused a great deal of anxiety for the parents who wanted to be given some indication of how long their children would be away. Eventually the duration was technically limited to six months, but in practice the KLV authorities could extend the length of time at will by simply saying that 'war conditions' made it necessary.

Although most camps had cooks, housekeepers and medical staff, the management of the school was the responsibility of the teachers who, where possible, would come from the same area as the pupils. Although the teachers were technically in charge of the education, the responsibility for delivering it was that of the Camp Leaders (*Lagerleiter*), who in some cases were teachers themselves. However, the overall coordination of all the other elements of camp life was carried out by a member of the Hitler Youth with the title of *Lagermannschaftesfuhrer*. This boy, or girl, would have been previously trained in a special school where they were prepared to take responsibility for introducing Hitler Youth activities and supervising children during their free time. He, or she, insisted that the qualities of discipline, comradeship, honour and hard work expected from all German boys and girls were maintained. As more and more of the older HJ members were called up, those left in charge of the KLV were now much younger and lacking the maturity and experience not only to organise the activities, but liaise with the teaching staff. As a result, the latter were gradually able to assert their authority. However, teaching staff were also subject to call up, so many of them were replaced by those returning from retirement. Again, a similar situation to that witnessed in the UK.

Von Shirach stated that camp life was the 'ideal form of life for the boys where community was worth everything and the individual nothing'. Hitler himself had introduced the pedagogic strategies of the Hitler Youth stating that: 'I want my youth strong and ready. I want an athletic youth. I don't want any intellectual education. With knowing, I spoil my youth.'[42] In another speech he commented:

> My pedagogy is harsh. Weakness must be chipped away. The youth that will grow up in my fortresses will frighten the world. I want a brutal, authoritarian, fearless, cruel youth. Youth must be all of this. It must be able to bear pain. It must not have anything weak and gentle. The light of the free, marvellous beast of prey must once again shine from their eyes. I want my youth to be strong and beautiful ... then I will be able to create the new.[43]

The life of the girls was determined by his desire to make them good German mothers.

As the philosophy was one of the survival of the fittest, those children who were weaker in terms of sport and physical prowess etc. found the life in the camps very hard. The insistent military drill and 'physical hardening' did not suit all.

The hierarchical 'pecking' order meant that the strong could dominate the weak, often in a brutal way. Everyone knew their place – those who were forced to clean the shoes of their stronger peers, or do the academic work for those who could not be bothered, those who were sexually abused or in some cases forced to be the abusers. For those at the bottom of the pile, life could be intensely hard.[44] According to Hermand, gaining the approval of one's peers governed one's behaviour. He describes an incident in which he was forced to take part:

> Even when the local Party leader, with whom we normally had little to do, ordered us to chop the heads of chickens, twist off the heads of pigeons with our hands or clobber little rabbits behind the ears with a stick and then cut their throats, we did it without the blinking of an eye. After all, none of us wanted to be called a 'sissy'.[45]

Added to all of this pressure was the uncertainty of what was going on at home. Were their relatives safe, what was happening at the front? Despite outwardly displaying confidence, many of them suffered from homesickness, considered to be a sign of weakness, a condition not helped by the irritant diseases such as lice, scabies and impetigo inherent in some of the camps. One of the worst things that could happen to a boy was to have a visit from his mother. Although some women moved to be near their children this was considered to be disruptive and was publicly condemned in a speech by Artur Axmann. In some camps there was no contact with life beyond the gates at all. There were no radios, letters were often censored and few had any idea what was going on in the war. This was particularly the case of those camps situated in Poland.[46]

However, as in any other situation the experiences of the KLV children depended very much on individual circumstances and despite the problems it is apparent that the KLV scheme did save lives. One ex-evacuee, now in her seventies but then aged eleven and the daughter of a merchant, was sent to a KLV camp. She described how life in the camp had been tough but her presence there had possibly saved her life. Her home town had been bombed and she had to wait weeks to get any message from her mother. Her fears for her mother's safety were not helped by the teachers' comments that she was certainly now an orphan. Both the mother and the child survived. Another girl was sent to a camp where the teachers were a little more liberal in their regime. She only had to wear her uniform when she left the camp, her mail remained uncensored and racial/ethnic study was not on the curriculum. Whereas a boy sent to Hungary, initially for six months but extended to a year, describes how he was harassed by the teachers and that little sympathy was given to him when he developed epilepsy.

Some parents were becoming increasingly concerned about their children and despite the moral pressure and the threat of sanctions, such as withdrawal of food cards, some parents tried to get them back, and in some cases even offered money for them to stay at home.

The immediate result of the KLV scheme was that several hundred thousand young children and adolescents were taken out of the cities, considered to be targets for the allied bombers, to areas, at least in the beginning, of perceived safety. It was intended that in the designated reception areas they would live a relatively quiet life away from the psychological and physical impact of the air raids. For some it was an adventure, one that their working-class parents would otherwise not have been able to provide. Though, as in any scheme of this kind, there was a down-side. There was the pain of homesickness, bed-wetting brought on by insecurity, the lack of facilities, the unfriendliness of some hosts, the lack of education, the neglect and the often brutal treatment meted out by the Hitler Youth and BDM leaders in the KLV camps. The same camps would provide the intensive political and ideological education thought necessary to maintain the National Socialist state. Nevertheless, it is impossible to overlook the fact that the war that had been unleashed by the Nazi regime was the very same one it now wanted to protect its children from – a policy which in the end was doomed to fail.

As a result, within all this state planning and control there is a dichotomy that has to be addressed by all historians investigating war children in Germany. As with children in all the other countries at the time, and since, they were at an impressionable age. They had little experience of a pre-Nazi state and therefore, by necessity, were unable to adapt to the changes in their own lives and to those around them caused by the social, ideological, political and geo-political circumstances surrounding them. It is therefore very difficult to generalise about the nature of their experiences, in the same way as it is impossible to do the equivalent with the children in all other Axis and Allied countries. However, what can be said is that all their lives, be they German Nationals, Jews, Sinti, Sudeten or subjugated children within the greater Reich, were intrinsically linked under the overarching power of the totalitarian state. As Stargardt says in *Witnesses of War*:

It was precisely what was irreconcilably different about their individual experiences that linked them together within the same system of rule in which officials badgered some parents to let them be evacuated to the safety of the countryside, while at the same time logging the transports that took others to be killed ...[47]

The Finnish War Children:
The 'Sotalapsi'

> The initial aims had been to save the human resources of Finland during a very difficult time and eventually have the children return in a good physical and mental condition so that they could re-build the country. So was it basically a question of population policy?[1]

In order to look at the practicalities and long-term effects of the Finnish evacuation of children throughout the Second World War, it is necessary to give some brief background details about Finnish history, bearing in mind that it was still a very 'young' country at the time the war took place. Very little is known about Finland's role in the war against the USSR, a war which was to result in the evacuation of more than 80,000 children and have sociological and psychological effects for decades afterwards.

From 1150 until 1809, Sweden and Finland had had a common history. It was then ceded to Russia and became the autonomous Grand Duchy of Finland. As a result of these strong ties, the country had taken the Swedish model of government, the judicial system and religion as its own. When it came under the auspices of the Russians (1809–1917) it maintained these institutions despite an attempt of 'Russification' between 1899–1917.[2] The old four-chamber *Diet* was replaced by a parliament (the *Eduskunta*). For the first time in the world, universal suffrage and eligibility was introduced when, in 1906, Finnish women were the first to gain full voting rights, as membership of an estate, land ownership or inherited titles were no longer required. However, in reality, at the local level things were different, as voting in the municipal elections was tied to the amount of tax paid. This resulted in rich people being able to cast a number of votes and the poor perhaps none at all. The municipal voting system was changed to universal suffrage in 1917 when the left wing gained a majority in Parliament and nineteen of the 200 MPs were women.

In 1917, after the Russian Revolution, the country declared its independence and between January and May 1918, Finland experienced a brief but bitter civil war. On the one side were the 'White' civil guards, who fought for middle and upper classes, and opposing them were the Red Guards, consisting mainly of workers and tenant farmers. The Finnish Socialist Workers' Republic had been proclaimed. The defeat of the Red Guards was achieved with support from Imperial Germany and only Germany's defeat in the First World War saved Finland from perhaps becoming a German satellite state. Lenin had given his support to the Red Guards, so had they won, Finland would probably have become a Soviet satellite state.

During the latter months of 1939, the USSR was worried that Germany was planning to attack them through Finland, and it was suggested through diplomatic channels that should this happen, Finland was to accept military assistance from the Soviets. However, Finland kept to her policy of neutrality and independent sovereignty and replied that she would defend herself against every attacker. Part of this rebuttal was the desire of the Finns not to become part of the USSR sphere of influence.

To everyone's surprise, the USSR then signed a non-aggression pact with Germany in 1939, the Molotov-Ribbentrop Pact and, of significance to the Finns, within the agreement there was a secret protocol which declared that Finland was to belong to the Soviet Union:

Secret Additional Protocol.

Article I. In the event of a territorial and political rearrangement in the areas belonging to the Baltic States (Finland, Estonia, Latvia, Lithuania), the northern boundary of Lithuania shall represent the boundary of the spheres of influence of Germany and the U.S.S.R. In this connection the interest of Lithuania in the Vilna area is recognized by each party.

During the negotiations in Moscow in October 1939, Stalin proposed a pact of mutual assistance, but again this was refused by the Finns. In order to achieve extra security for Leningrad the Russians were interested in the Hanko Peninsular, the western part of the Karelian Isthmus and some of the outer islands in the eastern Gulf of Finland. It was clear that the Finns would get no military support from Sweden, and when Paasikivi[3] started new talks in Moscow in October 1939, no agreement was reached.

Despite official optimism on the part of the government, the Finnish military presence on the Karelian Isthmus was reinforced and the Finnish army was fully mobilised in October 1939.

By 30 November 1939, the USSR had lost patience, cancelled the non-aggression pact, broken off diplomatic negotiations and initiated a broad attack along the whole of the 1,200km of the Finnish eastern border. The attack involved four Soviet armies of twenty-three divisions (460,000 men) and 2,000 tanks, and at the same time bombers attacked Finnish cities, including Helsinki, resulting in the deaths of 161 civilians.[4] The Soviet strategy was to overcome Finland in two weeks, install a 'puppet' government in Helsinki called the 'Terijoki Government' and then establish the 'Democratic Republic of Finland'. The Soviet high command were so confident of success that they issued written guidelines to military commanders instructing them not to cross the Swedish borders to the west of Finland, and within the seventh army they even included a full military band to play at the expected victory parade in Helsinki.

Field Marshal C.G.E. Mannerheim[5] was appointed Commander in Chief of the Finnish Defence Forces at a time when there was a shortage of everything, especially weapons and equipment. Still, this was more than compensated by a strong sense of national unity known in Finland, even today, as 'The Spirit of the Winter War'. The Finnish defence was very successful. Its full field army of 200,000 men up (rising to 340,000 men in February 1940) were deployed eastwards into defensive positions and it soon became clear that the country would not be defeated as quickly as had been believed, so by February 1940 the Russian forces had increased to 1 million men with 3,000 tanks and 2,500 aeroplanes. In December 1939, the Finns destroyed huge Soviet units and captured weapons and other military equipment at the battles of Suomussalmi and Raate.

The USSR started an attack on the Karelian Isthmus in February 1940, where their forces were concentrated on Summa, and they managed to break through the Finnish positions, forcing them to withdraw from the western part of the Isthmus. The situation became more threatening as the Russians attacked over the frozen Bay of Viipuri and advanced as far as the Viipuri-Hamina road, an area around which fierce battles continued until the end of the Winter War.

Between September 1939 and May 1940, during the so-called 'Phoney War' period in Western Europe when little else was happening, the Finnish

Winter War of November 1939 to March 1940 received a lot of attention in the British press, in the newsreels and in the British Parliament. In a speech of January 1940, Winston Churchill, then at the Admiralty, reflected the national mood in suitably dramatic terms:

> Only Finland – superb, nay, sublime – in the jaws of peril – Finland shows what free men can do. The service rendered by Finland to mankind is magnificent … If the light of freedom which still burns so brightly in the frozen North should be finally quenched, it might well herald a return to the Dark Ages, when every vestige of human progress during two thousand years would be engulfed.[6]

He said almost the same thing during a radio broadcast on 20 January 1940, which he finished by saying: 'The service rendered by Finland to mankind is magnificent. They have exposed, for all the world to see, the military incapacity of the Red Army and of the Red Air Force'.[7] (This broadcast resulted in thirteen pages of critical comments from nations that had heard it. On 26 January 1940, Lord Halifax sent a curt note to Churchill criticising him for not having sent a draft to him first: 'Would you think it unreasonable of me to ask that in future if you are going to speak with particular reference to foreign policy, you might let me see in advance what you had in mind to say'.)[8]

At the beginning of the Winter War, Finland appealed to the League of Nations for war material and diplomatic and political support. In response, the League encouraged its members to supply aid to Finland and expelled the Soviet Union.

As a result, Finland received a great deal of support, including aid from the UK and the USA (despite the latter being neutral). However, this assistance was not entirely altruistic as papers from the time show how concerned the British government was about Swedish iron ore falling into German hands. Finland's stoic resistance to the Soviet invasion resulted in a great deal of domestic pressure for the government in Britain to take some tangible action in its defence, and by January 1940 serious consideration was being given to how best to aid the Finns. Options included sanctioning the dispatch of military volunteers 'on the Spanish precedent' (many people had volunteered to fight in the International Brigade during the Spanish Civil War) and the Winter War actually attracted 11,000 volunteers, mostly from Sweden (again officially neutral).

On 22 December, in a note labelled 'Most Secret', Churchill wrote: 'Urge Sweden and Norway to help Finland, and offer then an Anglo-French guarantee that if they are subsequently invaded, either by Russia or Germany, we will come to their aid with adequate forces.'[9] (This was in fact further than the French were prepared to go. Later, on 22 February 1940, Neville Chamberlain informed the Cabinet that the proposal that M. Corbin had transmitted seemed to show that the French government had taken no notice of the suggested timetable for the operations in aid of Finland.)[10]

Later on the same day, his comments were noted in the War Cabinet minutes, which invited the Chiefs of Staff to consider the character and extent of the indirect assistance that could be rendered to Finland, with particular reference to the dispatch of technical missions and the supply of material. What assistance could, in practice, be given to Sweden and Norway against the possible consequences to them of such direct or indirect assistance as they might afford to Finland.[11]

Meanwhile, growing concern over the prospect of a Russo-German exploitation of Swedish iron ore encouraged the development of plans for sending British and French forces to the region:

> A Foreign Office appreciation of the situation in Scandinavia weighing the possibilities of a German intervention in the south if the Russians attack in the north.
>
> Sweden may very likely intervene on the side of Finland, but Norway and Denmark are determined on neutrality. Probably Germany will try to dissuade Russia from seizing Northern Norway and Sweden because in that case the iron ore, upon which Germany so much depends, would fall into Russian hands ...[12]

But preparations for an expeditionary force proceeded slowly, and neither the Norwegians nor the Swedes were ready to agree to give free passage to such a force through their territories. It was stated in the British War Cabinet on 27 December 1939, that '... the First Lord of the Admiralty thought that Finland was still in great danger. He understood that they had only one month's supply of ammunition'.[13] In the War Cabinet minutes, dated 17 January 1940, it was suggested that 'it should be pointed out to the Swedish government that the destruction of Finland, with which the country had a close relationship, was being consummated before their eyes. Finland, however, would not be the last small neutral country to go down before the war was terminated.'[14]

By February 1940, Britain was still considering sending help and Churchill suggested that Brigadier Ling (retired), who was working for the War Office, should
visit Finland and offer assistance to Mannerheim. The War Cabinet also considered that Finland would need between 30,000–40,000 men if they were to repel
the Russian forces. It was felt however that this would be impractical as the only
men of use would be those who could ski, and at the time there were only 360
British soldiers able to work in snow conditions.[15] Nonetheless, Churchill was
determined that some aid should be forthcoming, if only to save the ore fields:
'... Even if the Finns were driven back and our troops with them, there would
be a reasonable chance that, in the course of their retirement, they might all
secure possession of the Galivare ore fields and thus deny them to Germany'.[16]

Despite further discussion in the War Cabinet ab1 out landing forces to
help the Finns, and the French commenting that 'the loss of Finland would be
equivalent to the loss of a great campaign',[17] little actually happened. So, with
Finnish military losses mounting, promises of Allied reinforcements and aid
not forthcoming[18] the government in Helsinki had little choice but to sue for
peace. On 12 March 1940, the Russo-Finnish Treaty was signed in Moscow.

The 105-day Winter War cost Finland a great deal as 20,000 soldiers died,
1,500 disappeared and 45,000 were wounded. In addition, almost 500,000
Karelians had to be repatriated from the area ceded to the USSR, and Finland
lost the cities of Viipuri, Kakisalmi and Sortavala. The Russians also took part
of Kalastajasaarento, an island near Petsamo, to provide them with access to
the Arctic Sea, and they leased Hanko as a military base for fifty years.

Yet, this was an uneasy peace and there was the constant threat of a new
war. Having accepted defeat in the Winter War and now geographically isolated from Britain by Germany's successes in the west, the Finns sought to
counter further Soviet pressure by looking to Berlin for diplomatic and
military support. Germany had become more interested in the strategic
importance of the country and it was said that 'Hitler spread his umbrella
over Finland'. In these circumstances, the British increasingly came to
regard Finland as a pro-Axis power. The Finns, in their turn, responded
to the British effort to blockade their overseas trade by severing diplomatic relations, and it came as no surprise to London when, in June 1941,
German troops were granted access to Finnish soil in advance of Operation
Barbarossa, and Finland became a co-belligerent with the Axis Powers.[19]
Finland was unwilling to be the aggressor and so waited for the Soviets
to declare war, which they did on 25 June 1941.[20] The Finns attacked in
July and attempted to occupy the Ladoga region of Karelia. The old border

was reached in two months. This was then followed by a long period of trench warfare. Hitler proposed that the Finns should help in the attack on Leningrad or take part in the cutting of the Murmansk railway, but both suggestions were rejected by the Finnish authorities. They were fighting their own war as their goal was to regain the Finnish areas lost in 1940.

With Finland a *de facto* ally of Germany, and the British now allied to the Soviet Union, Churchill had no doubts as to where Britain's loyalties should lie. In a letter to Anthony Eden on 5 July 1941 he stated:

> The Finns, having definitely entered the war on Hitler's side, deserve severe treatment. I presume we have taken all their ships found at sea, and that the Finnish Minister (Georges Gripenberg) is deprived of all facilities, cipher and otherwise. There is no need to declare war, but it seems to me they should have much the same treatment as if they were at war.

On 10 July: 'Most Secret. I think you should be pretty stiff with the Finns. They cannot march with the Germans and expect to have any conveniences from the sea or any immunity for their ships'. On 16 July he added: 'In view of the obnoxious and aggressive attitude of Finland, I trust we have already seized all the Finnish ships and subjected the Finns to every inconvenience in our power ... one cannot be on two sides at once.'[21] But, well aware of Finland's dilemma, Churchill was reluctant to see the Finns put 'in the dock with the guilty Axis powers',[22] and hoped that Helsinki could be persuaded to halt its offensive against the USSR. On 10 July 1941, Mannerheim issued a declaration stating that the Finns were determined to cross their 1918 borders and invade eastern Karelia, held at the time by Russia. As a result, Churchill commented that the Finns should be informed that if they went over the borders, Britain would declare war.[23] Yet, on 15 September he told the War Cabinet that, 'As regards Finland ... we should neither threaten nor issue a declaration of war unless strongly pressed by the Soviet Government'.[24]

Despite the misgivings of Anthony Eden his Foreign Secretary, the Prime Minister, in a personal message to Field Marshal Mannerheim, appealed once more to him to halt Finland's offensive:

> 28th November 1941
> Personal, Secret and Private
> I am deeply grieved at what I see coming, namely, that we shall be forced in a few days out of loyalty to our ally Russia to declare war upon Finland. If we do this,

we shall make war also as opportunity serves. Surely your troops have advanced far enough for security during the war, and could now halt and give leave. It is not necessary to make any public declaration, but simply leave off fighting and cease military operations, for which the severe winter affords every reason, and make a de facto exit from the war. I wish I could convince your Excellency that we are going to beat the Nazis. I feel far more confident than in 1917 or 1918. It would be most painful to the many friends of your country in England if Finland found herself in the dock with the guilty and defeated Nazis. My recollections of our pleasant talks and correspondence about the last war leads me to send this purely personal and private message for your consideration before it is too late.[25]

When Mannerheim issued what was, at best, an equivocal reply, London telegraphed Helsinki on 6 December committing Britain to war with Finland from midday on the 7th:

4th December 1941

Personal, Secret and Private

… I thank you for your courtesy in sending me this private message. I am sure you will realise that it is impossible for me to cease my present military operations before my troops have reached positions, which in my opinion would give us the security required. I would regret if these operations, carried out in order to safeguard Finland, would bring my country into a conflict with England and I would be deeply grieved if you consider yourself forced to declare war upon Finland …[26]

After the German defeat at Stalingrad, the Finns held secret talks with the USSR and Paasikivi again travelled to Moscow. (Paasikivi had been the intermediary before the Winter War and led the Finnish-Russian negotiations in Moscow. When ambassador to Moscow 1940–1941 he was, by necessity, isolated from the most secret decision-making initiatives held by the government in Helsinki, and when he found out that they were contemplating entering the conflict on Germany's side, he resigned and retired for a second time.)[27] Having seen that Stalin did not intend to change his policies, he supported compliance with some of the Russian demands. After this unsuccessful diplomatic mission, Paasikivi was cast aside from political activities until September 1944, when the peace treaty was finally negotiated and Mannerheim, now President of Finland, asked him to be Prime Minister.[28] (He later became Finnish President from 1946–56.)

At the talks, Stalin's terms were harsh and he insisted that Finland should break off relations with Germany, return to the 1940 borders and pay reparations of around £450,000. They were all rejected.

In 1944, the Russians started a huge attack on the Karelian Isthmus and succeeded in breaking through the Finnish lines. The Finns were forced to retreat and abandon Viipuri. Although the defence lines remained intact, Mannerheim had to order the evacuation of eastern Karelia.

Germany was concerned that the Finns were negotiating a peace and offered to supply weapons and food in order to keep them in the war. As a result, President Ryti wrote to Hitler promising that they would not accept a separate peace. This was called the 'Ribbentrop Agreement' and the new supplies resulting from it enabled the Finns to reinforce their front line and halt the Soviet advance. Stalin was in a hurry to get to Berlin first, and as further attacks by Russian forces failed in the Karelian Isthmus and eastern Karelia, an Armistice was agreed. President Ryti resigned and Mannerheim was elected President under a special law of 4 August 1944. The Soviet-Finnish Armistice was signed on 4 September 1944 resulting in loss of land and the requirement that Finnish forces should remove the German army from the country.

On 15 September the 'Lapland War' began. The Germans were taken by surprise and sought revenge. They used the tactic of 'scorched earth', burning almost every building within the whole Lapland area, and laid mines in order to slow down the advance of Finnish troops. The area was virtually destroyed. On 23 September 1944, actually during the conflict, the evacuation of the population of northern Finland took place. A total of 127,000 Finns and Laplanders were moved, out of which 56,000 went to northern Sweden with the help of the Swedish army and the Swedish Red Cross. Many of those who were displaced never returned to their homes again, but resettled in Sweden. The 'Lapland War' ended on 25 April 1945, but the last battle between Finnish and German forces did not take place until two days later on the 27th.[29]

Although Finland was never occupied, and was the only country that had achieved independence at the end of the First World War to remain an independent sovereign state in 1945, it lost approximately 96,000 people, around 2.6 per cent of the total population, which at this time was around 3.7 million. Of these, almost 2,000 were civilian deaths caused as a direct result of bombing.

Within all this conflict, the movement of the children to safer areas in Sweden, Denmark and Norway was taking place. As a result of their close links, the Swedes wanted to support the Finns during the Winter War of 1939–40, and although militarily Sweden was not, according to Prime Minister Hansson,[30] a 'War Waging Country',[31] there was no specific declaration of neutrality. However, the humanitarian help offered by Sweden was very much suited to its own policy of Swedish non-intervention, especially in regard to the help offered to the Finnish children.

The initiative for the child-transports, as they were called, came from Sweden and the major driving force behind it was not the government, but Maja Sandler, the wife of the Swedish Minister of Foreign Affairs Richard Sandler, and Hannah Rydh, the head of the Fredrika Bremer Association.[32] They established an organisation called *Centrala Finlandshjälpen* (The Central Help Organization for Finland) and contacted the Finnish authorities on the matter of moving children to Sweden. The Finnish Ministry of the Interior declined the offer stating that it would prefer material help delivered to Finland instead. The *Centrala Finlandshjälpen* organisation was not discouraged and in December 1939 members held a press conference in Finland, outlining their plans and inviting children to Sweden. Three days later, as a result of this appeal, the *Pohjoismaiden Avun Suomen Keskus* (The Finnish Centre of Nordic Help), was set up in Helsinki.[33] Its main task was to take care of the transfer of people from Finland to Sweden, and the Ministry of the Interior gave the organisation full powers to act. The Ministry set the top age at which the children could be transferred at twelve, and mothers could accompany their offspring if the children were no more than three years of age. Pregnant women and elderly people would also be included in the transfers.

The final endorsement of the evacuation of children was given when the Finnish child welfare organisation, *Mannerheimin Lastensuojeluliitto* (The Mannerheim League for Child Welfare) and its founder, Marshal Mannerheim, at the time Commander in Chief of the Finnish Armed Forces, gave its support.

The first official transportation of children from Finland to Sweden left on 15 December 1939.

This initial evacuation was to become the model for future schemes. At this time about 9,000 children, the small ones under three years of age with either their mothers or with a *Lotta* (a member of the Finnish voluntary women's organisation), were evacuated along with 3,000 mothers and some elderly people. Some were also sent to Denmark and Norway, but the majority of these returned when both countries were later occupied by the Germans.

(The re-evacuation from Norway was particularly dangerous as it took place at a time of active fighting between German and Norwegian forces.) Many other families made private arrangements, and although the exact numbers of these are not known, they can be estimated to be at least 3,000. The Winter War ended on 13 March 1940, and all but around 1,000 children (who were to remain in Sweden) returned to Finland. In the early summer of 1941, before the Continuation War began, a visit to Sweden was organised for children. Around 2,000 made the trip, either through the official organisation or privately.

There were political factors involved in the Finnish-Swedish evacuations. The Swedish Prime Minister Hansson, who had a cool relationship with Finland, was criticised for not doing anything to help the Finns, especially as the child-transports had started by private initiative. So, in response to severe personal pressure, Hansson nationalised this private committee, a very unusual event in Sweden, members of the Royal Family were put in control, and the Swedish government paid all the administrative costs. This sort of humanitarian help suited Hansson very well as there was no risk of getting involved in the war, which the government feared.

When the Continuation War began in June 1941, the issue of continuing the transfers of children was raised again. However, the Finnish officials' attitude towards the idea was once more unenthusiastic. As in 1939, they would have much preferred to have received war material instead. Nevertheless, despite this initial response the Swedes made a further offer in September 1941 when they not only asked to take and look after Finnish children but, in addition, promised to pay all the costs of transportation. Amid some controversy in Finland, Karl August Fagerholm, a very pro-Swedish Finnish Minister of Social Affairs,[34] accepted the offer at once and a committee was established called *Lastensiirtokomitea*, 'The Committee for Transporting Finnish children to Sweden'. Its brief was to organise the transportation of children out of the country, and it was to remain in place until 1948. One of the reasons for now permitting the children to go was that some Finnish officials were concerned that had they not allowed the child transfers, Finland might not have received any other war-related help from Sweden.

At first those children who were allowed to go overseas were mostly Karelian and the children of mothers who had gone back to Karelia to start rebuilding the area after the Winter War. Others came from areas where there was a shortage of food, which was a specific concern of large and poor families. Children of war-invalids, children whose homes had been destroyed during the bombing raids and war orphans were also permitted to travel. In 1942 the criteria were further relaxed, and more and more were allowed to go, usually for domestic, social and economic reasons made worse by the war situation.

In December 1941, the Swedish relief organisations wanted to provide help to those Finnish children considered to be in need. Nothin, leader of the organisation and politically a very influential figure in Sweden, made an appeal to the Swedish government asking for help to deliver food and clothes through the International Red Cross, to children in Finland. The government did nothing and there are no notes in the files of the International Red Cross relating to any such activities by the Swedish authorities. The reason for this could have been a fear of the rescinding of the so-called 'Gothenburg Traffic', whereby the Swedish marine fleet was guaranteed safe conduct during the Second World War by both the British and German navies. In addition, they may have been concerned about the possibility of British counter-measures had great amounts of food and other help been delivered to a co-belligerent of Germany. As a result, providing humanitarian aid to Finland challenged the vital commercial and political interests of Sweden. As Sweden got vital supplies via 'Gothenburg Traffic', including all her oil for her air-force and navy, it was vital that she was seen to be an independent non-aligned country. As a result, Hansson was not prepared to take any risks that would contravene the country's neutrality. An attitude supported to some extent by the Swedish Foreign Minister, Gunther, who stated that the country was ready to give Finland all the help possible 'within the limits of their resources and political interests'. Therefore humanitarian aid to Finland from relief organisations did not materialise.[35]

The child transfers during the Continuation War can be divided into two distinct phases. During the first phase, from September 1941 to June 1943, approximately 22,000 children were sent to Sweden. The second occurred in early 1944, when Helsinki was heavily bombed, resulting in the movement of 31,000 children together with an estimated total of 15,000 who were evacuated privately. This gave an all-round figure of approximately 67,000, of whom 5,000 were sick, many suffering from tuberculosis, and the effects of malnourishment. In addition, a total of around 4,000 others went to Denmark; 850 in 1941, 2,606 in 1942 (580 returned during the same year) and 303 in 1943 (when 2,000 returned). During 1945, a further 364 children came home from Denmark. In 1942, the situation on the Finnish front lines had changed and it was now less of a mobile war and more one of entrenchment. As a result, the number of child transfers was decreasing and by 1943 about 9,000 children had already returned to Finland, and although the armistice was concluded in September 1944, the majority of children remained in Sweden.

Throughout both the Winter and Continuation Wars, approximately 80,000 children, representing 2.1 per cent of the Finnish population, left the country. It is worth noting that 8.6 per cent of the total Finnish population comprised of children, and those below fourteen years of age, 928,100, made up 25 per cent of the whole population. Thus any movement of children within this age group was certain to have some sort of effect on Finnish culture and way of life.

During the Winter War of 1939–40, the aim of the transport policy was to take the Finnish children away from the bombings and horrors of war, especially in the large cities such as Helsinki, but during the Continuation War the aims were slightly different. The first wave of evacuees to Sweden was primarily concerned with ensuring both the physical and mental health of the young Finns, and that the future generations returning to Finland would be strong and in good health. The emphasis on the second wave, which took place in 1944, was to remove the children from the threat of a possible Russian occupation and from the heavy bombing of the capital.

However, although the evacuation of the children sounded good in theory, in practice it was not without its problems. They travelled in groups and were not separated until they got to their destinations. Those who arrived in Denmark already had their billets allocated, but as the pressure increased on the Swedish fostering authorities, the hosts went to distribution centres to collect their children, very similar to the situation in Britain. Again, not dissimilar to the UK, their stay in these centres was often traumatic. It was often the case that hosts took the small children and the fair-haired girls first, while the older, dark-haired boys were left until last. The plan had also been that siblings would be billeted together, and where this was physically impossible they would go to foster homes that were close to each other. In reality, this was often not the case and many were separated, not to see each other until after the war, again a situation which not only happened in Finland, but also in all the other countries that had decided to send their children away.

Children went either by train, ship, or in some cases by aeroplane. But, as with the British evacuees going overseas, their safety could not always

1 Children of Woodmansterne Road School, Streatham, arrive for morning school in Caio, Carmarthenshire

2 Children setting off from Myrdle School, Stepney, 1 September 1939

5 Finnamore Wood Camp when being used as a Young Offender's Institute, 1970

Above: 6 Finnamore Wood, 2007

Opposite above: 3 LCC teacher Miss Betty Hall comforts Lennie Bassie, an evacuee from London to Dartington Hall, Devon. She was in charge of forty evacuees from Blackfriars and Gravesend, all under six and some as young as three

Opposite below: 4 Evacuees at Dartington Hall, Devon, looking at the horses on the farm

<u>Circular A.C.5</u>

Children's Overseas Reception Board
Contributions from Parents

There seems, in some quarters, to be a genuine misunderstanding of the terms of the Children's Overseas Reception Board Scheme. The position is as follows.

Parents in this country pay a weekly contribution to the credit of the Children's Overseas Reception Board. These weekly payments go towards the heavy expenses of the evacuation of the children overseas including the cost of transport by rail in the United Kingdom and of the sea voyage, all the Welfare arrangements at the hostels, and the provision of doctors, nurses and escorts for the voyage. They also include provision for illness or other special expenditure that may arise in the Dominion. The Dominion Governments have undertaken the responsibility for the welfare of the children when they arrive, the cost of transport within the Dominion, and the provision of suitable homes and education.

Before accepting any offer of hospitality, the Dominion Authorities have explained to the prospective hosts that they will be responsible for maintaining the children at their own expense, and that they cannot expect to receive any payment, either from the Dominion or the United Kingdom Government. No child is placed with a host who has not satisfied the Dominion Government of his ability to provide proper maintenance.

In the case of children who are sent to friends or relatives nominated by their parents, the position is sometimes a little more difficult. If the friend or relation decides that he is unable to provide adequate maintenance, the Dominion Authorities will place the child in a home, if possible in the same district, where expenses can more easily be met. If, therefore, a host who has been nominated by a parent in this country finds that he cannot meet the expenses of providing hospitality for the child, he should explain the circumstances fully to the representatives of the Dominion Government who are now responsible for the child's welfare. The first obligation of parents, however, is to make the weekly payment due from them to this Board through their Local Authorities or direct to the Board. No host in any Dominion may demand payment from a parent in this country and it must be remembered that attendance at special schools other than those provided for children of the neighbourhood has never been undertaken as part of the Scheme.

In the case of Canada parents should understand that under Treasury regulations no money may be transferred by any individual from the United Kingdom to Canada.

January, 1941.

7 Letter from CORB explaining the misunderstanding about payments, January 1941

Opposite above: 8 Margaret Wood's (*née* Banyard) CORB Identity Disc

Opposite below: 9 Some of the CORB escorts and crew on the *Llanstephan Castle*, September 1940

RAIN DID NOT DAMPEN the spirits of these South African women, bound for England in the Carnarvon Castle to rejoin their husbands. This picture was taken on New Year's Eve. The vessel resumed her voyage this afternoon.

UNION-CASTLE LINE

S.S. "LLANSTEPHAN CASTLE"

Children

TEA

———

Filleted Fitness

Soused Hasty Words with Toasted Tempers

Bright and Breezy Salad

———

Thinkandthank aux Pleeze

Kurtesy Kake

Brisk Buns

———

White and Brown Bread and Butter

English and South African Jams   Marmalade

Tea   Cocoa   Milk

September 3, 1940

Passengers are requested kindly to refrain from
smoking in the Saloon.

Above: 10 CORB evacuees bathing in 'tank' of seawater on board *Llanstephan Castle*, September 1940

Left: 11 Humorous children's tea

DAILY ROUTINE ON BOARD SHIP

We established a strict routine as quickly as possible and the days went something like this:

MORNING   Before breakfast P.T. for those who wished and mass and holy communion.

8.00	Breakfast
9.30	Medical Parade (every child saw the doctor every day.)
10.15	Boat drill (Captain's presence)
10.30-11.00	Religious Instruction (it was considered most important that full use should be made of the opportunity to give the children a complete course.)
11.00 -	Break - escorts drank beef tea.
11.30-12.00	Lecture -

Various subjects were taken - some of the escorts who knew S.A. gave them talks about the country, showed photographs and generally stimulated the children's interest, not a very difficult task. A little elementary Afrikaans was introduced, the children were very keen about it.

There were art lessons for the babies, and Miss Thompson told them about schools of the Empire. The doctor told them about how he was torpedoed at the beginning of the war. It was Friday the 13th and he said they waited up till midnight and then went to bed, at 2.00 am on the Sat 14th it came. However they all knew their jobs, did them and then time spent in the boats seemed almost a pleasant - according to him. A day or two later I found my boys in bed in all their clothes overcoats and life jackets. "It's Friday the 13th" they said.

Right: 12 The CORB evacuees daily routine on the *Llanstephan Castle*

Below: 13 CORB evacuees' first sight of South Africa

As the liner arrives at Table Mountain, these evacuees, many of them children, catch their first glimpse of an historic part of the British Commonwealth. They belong to the first group of over 300 to be sent from Great Britain.

Mr. and Mrs. Banyard have heard of the safe arrival in South Africa of their daughter, Margaret.

CIT LAT (SPOR

Cape Argus

CAPE TOWN, SATURDAY, SEPTEMBER 21, 1940.

[POSTAGE ON TH INLAND, INCLU]

GUEST CHILDREN AT WESTBROOKE: When they left the ship at Table Bay docks yesterday afternoon the guest children from Great Britain were taken to Westbrooke, where they had tea and were registered. All who have come in contact with the children are favourably impressed by their general bearing.

Left: 14 *The Cape Argus* reporting the arrival of CORB evacuees at Westbrooke SA, 21 September 1940

Below: 15 Radio link-up with CORB evacuees in South Africa

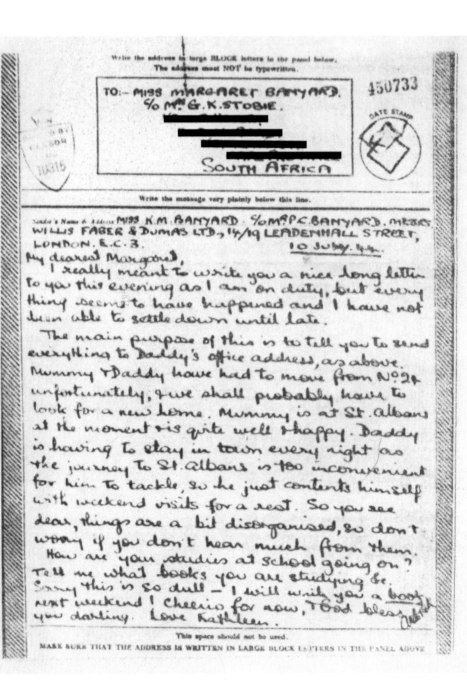

TO:- MISS MARGARET BANYARD.
C/o MRS G.K.STOBIE.
██████████████
██████████████
████████████
SOUTH AFRICA

450733

Sender's Name & Address MISS K.M.BANYARD. C/o MR P.C.BANYARD. MESSRS
WILLIS FABER & DUMAS LTD., 14/19 LEADENHALL STREET,
LONDON. E.C.3.   10 JULY. 44.

My dearest Margaret,

I really meant to write you a nice long letter to you this evening as I am on duty, but everything seems to have happened and I have not been able to settle down until late.

The main purpose of this is to tell you to send everything to Daddy's office address, as above. Mummy & Daddy have had to move from No 24 unfortunately, & we shall probably have to look for a new home. Mummy is at St. Albans at the moment & is quite well & happy. Daddy is having to stay in town every night as the journey to St. Albans is too inconvenient for him to tackle, so he just contents himself with weekend visits for a rest. So you see dear, things are a bit disorganised, so don't worry if you don't hear much from them.

How are your studies at school going on? Tell me what books you are studying &c. Sorry this is so dull — I will write you a book next weekend! Cheerio for now, & God bless you darling. Love Kathleen.

16 Letter sent to Margaret in South Africa

UNION OF SOUTH AFRICA
UNIE VAN SUID-AFRIKA

Oversea Children Reception Administration
Administrasie vir die Ontvangs van Oorseese Kinders

DEPARTMENT OF SOCIAL WELFARE,
DEPARTEMENT VAN VOLKSWELSYN,
PRETORIA.
February 11th, 1946.

TO ALL WHO HAVE ACTED AS PARENT-HOSTS TO THE CHILD-GUESTS FROM THE UNITED KINGDOM, 1940-1946.

With the departure of the "Carnarvon Castle" for England in January, 1946, all but a handful of the children evacuated to South Africa from the United Kingdom in the dark days of 1940 have returned to their own country and to their own homes, and the time has come to bring to an end the organisation which the people and the Government of the Union created to provide for their welfare. The National Advisory Council of the Oversea Children Reception Administration, now in process of winding up its affairs, has asked me to write to you on its behalf and convey its warmest gratitude for the magnificent work you have done as parent-hosts during the last six years.

It is the unanimous opinion of all those, in the United Kingdom and in our own country, who have been concerned in the official evacuation scheme, that it has been an unqualified, indeed an unparalleled success. Our child-guests not only escaped the dangers of death and mutilation, and the privations of their war-locked home country: they also enjoyed advantages and privileges which are almost unique in the history of war's forced migrations and disruptions of family life. They return to their own homes enjoying abundant health, well-nourished, well-educated, unspoiled, and admirably equipped for the life that lies before them. From you they have had affection bestowed on them without stint; they have made friends of their own age; they have the memory of a country beautiful and with spacious ways of living, to inspire them both with a love for it and the desire to make the world as a whole a better place. In character as well as in material well-being, they have gained enormously. When they grow older—and wiser— they will realise even more clearly than they do now how much they owe to the patriotism and beneficence of their temporary parents, and will remember them with gratitude and affection.

The success of this experiment in human rehabilitation is due almost entirely to you and your fellow parent-hosts throughout the country. Your task involved sacrifices, of leisure, energy, money, that grew beyond computation as the war years became increasingly long and arduous. You endured them without limit and without complaint. The many delicate and complex problems of adjustment with which you were confronted were solved to the admiration of us all by your patience and skill, firmness and kindness. Not only the two Governments but also the people of South Africa are deeply in your debt. You have raised the prestige of our country in the eyes of the civilised world, and contributed not a little to that fund of gentleness and selflessness on which the future of civilised ways of living so greatly depends.

On behalf of the National Advisory Council of the Oversea Children Reception Administration, which has represented the people of South Africa in the organisation of the child-guest scheme, I thank you once again.

J. K. Gray

—————————————
Chairman, National Advisory Council.

H.W.V. 82621—2/46.

17 A letter of thanks to the foster parents in South Africa, February 1946

LATE WAR NEWS SPECIAL

Good Whisky —
JOHNNIE WALKER

NO. 13,956 — MONDAY, SEPTEMBER 23, 1940 — ONE PENNY

MERCY LINER TORPEDOED
83 Out of 90 Children are Drowned

BOATS SWAMPED IN HEAVY GALE

By Daily Mail Reporters

EIGHTY-THREE children on their way to Canada under the Government scheme and 211 other people have been lost in a British liner which was torpedoed in the Atlantic by a U-boat. Only seven of the 90 children being officially evacuated were saved.

The ship was battling with a storm more than 600 miles from the British coast when the submarine struck at 10.30 p.m.

Lifeboats and rafts were lowered in the dark, but they stood little chance in the mountainous seas.

Some of the children were trapped in the ship or killed by the explosion.

Others suffered from exposure in lifeboats and on rafts, which were swept by wind, waves, rain, and hail for hours before they could be picked up by a British warship.

Mr. Geoffrey Shakespeare, Under-Secretary for the Dominions and chairman of the Children's Overseas Reception Board, declared in a statement issued yesterday :

"I am full of horror and indignation that any German submarine captain could be found to torpedo a ship over 600 miles from land in a tempestuous sea.

"There was little chance for passengers, whether adults or children, to survive. This deed will shock the world."

A number of grown-up people on the point of giving up the struggle gave their lives to the task of children who kept telling them help would soon arrive.

Of the 406 passengers and crew in the liner only 152 were saved, 294 lost. The saved are 13 children, seven of them evacuees, 18 women, and 82 men, 38 of them Lascar seamen. They have now been landed at a northern port.

"There is no chance," it is officially stated, of there being any further lists of survivors." On the other hand, parents of children being evacuated have no need to worry if they have heard nothing, for the parents of all those lost have already been officially informed.

Only two of the nine grown-up escorts with the children were saved. One of them, Mrs Towns, managed to get all her 13 charges into a boat, then had to watch all but one of them die from exposure one by one.

ALL FOUR

Most of the children were from London, Middlesex, and Liverpool. Eight were travelling independently of the Government scheme with their parents.

The storm added greatly to the tragedy. Two children died after reaching the safety of the rescuing warship.

The liner sank in about ten minutes. The captain stayed on the bridge until the last few seconds, then he dived overboard. He was lost.

His last words were : "Get into the boats and look after yourselves." Then a series of explosions shook the ship and she sank.

One of the happiest survivors was Mrs Barn, of Hyde Park-mansions, London, W. She was travelling to Montreal with her three children, Barbara aged 11, Sonia 11, and Derek, 9. All were saved.

Mrs Barn said to me : "I believe I was one of the last to leave the ship. I got two of my children, Sonia and Derek, on to a raft and Barbara into a lifeboat.

"Then I jumped overboard, and by some miracle landed on the raft which held Sonia and Derek.

"Twice during the many hours we drifted in the terrible sea Sonia was washed off the raft. A man helped me pull her back to safety each time.

"Hour after hour passed. I had almost given up all hope. I slept on to my little girl." 'Daddy, I think we'll take off our umbrella and go to sleep in the water.'

HEELING

" 'But Sonia said, 'Oh, no, mummy, don't do that yet. I'm sure we'll be picked up.'

"A few minutes later a warship came into sight and we were saved.

"I'll never forget those hours on the raft. Waves swept over us. Hailstones and rain bit through our clothes.

"One man saved my three—Mr. Eric Davies, of the B.B.C.

"He was on the raft. We were close to the liner, which was heeling over on top of us.

"He swam with one arm and with the other pushed our raft away from the ship. We got lost

BACK Page, Column ONE

A Child's Faith Saved Mother

THREE of a family—Sonia and Derek Barn and (lower pictured) their mother—lay on a raft. Sonia, she is 11, was washed overboard. Both time Mrs. Barn pulled her back. Then the mother tired. "We'll take off our lifebelts . . . sleep in the water," she said. "Don't do that yet, mother. I'm sure we'll be picked up," urged Sonia. A warship appeared . . .

" I GOT my 13 children mustered "—Daily Mail picture (left) of Mrs. Lilian Towns, one of the two Government escorts saved. Other survivors — pictures, BACK PAGE.

The Seven Saved

Rex Ernest Thorns, aged 13, of 10, Derwent-gardens, Wembley (sister dead).

Jack Sidney Keeley, 8, of 138, Cowley-road, Brixton (sister dead).

John Baker, 7, of 40, Townsend-road, Southall (brother dead).

Linda Bernard Walder, 10, and Beezie Annie Walder, 13 (brother and sister), of 33, Rhyl-street, Kentish Town ;

Eleanor Wright, 13, of 1, Livingstone-road, Sunderland ; and

Elizabeth Mary Cummings, 14, of 55, Kingfield-road, Liverpool.

18 *Daily Mail* report on the sinking of the SS *City of Benares*, 23 September 1940

Left: 19 A young boy scavenging for food in Hamburg, July 1946

Below: 20 One-room accommodation in Hamburg, 1946

21 A new use for an old vehicle. A derelict bus now used as a home in Hamburg, July 1946

22 This cellar in Hamburg housed nine children and four adults

Above: 23 Very basic shelter, Hamburg, 1946

Below: 24 Relief section of the British Red Cross. Members of the Salvation Army dispensing cod liver oil to German children

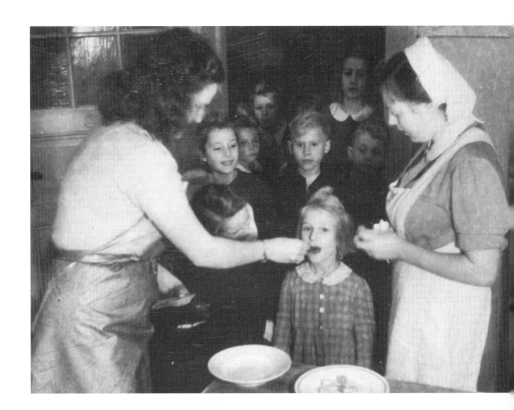

25 Hamburg. A three-power Medical Commission comprising French, American and British doctors inspecting a German war child, 15 August 1946

Above: 26 Poster appealing for contributions to help starving children in Germany, 1947

Right: 27 'Have you forgotten us?' A Finnish poster appealing for Swedish foster parents to take in Finnish children

Below: 28 A child soldier

be guaranteed. In January 1940, one of the ships carrying children was attacked by a Soviet submarine, but fortunately there were no child casualties, although one of the escort ships was destroyed and many sailors died.[36] This was the reason why transfer by ship ended, very soon to be followed by the cessation of air travel and trains as even the remaining rail transportation was not entirely safe. In March 1940, a train travelling north to Haparanda in Sweden collided with another one and as a result fifteen children were killed.[37] The journeys themselves were also traumatic. In some cases it took ten days for the evacuees to get to their destinations as they often only travelled by night due to the possibility of air raids, and once they arrived at the dispersal centres some, especially those who had been allocated to hosts in the countryside, had another long journey within Sweden itself. This also raised health issues as it was very easy for disease to spread among children in confined spaces. According to an alarming report from the Swedish National Board of Health Department in March 1944, some children died of diphtheria and other infectious diseases contracted during the transfer, and about 20 per cent of the children, who at the outset had been perfectly healthy, had to be hospitalised once they reached their destinations.[38] It is interesting to note that the Finnish National Board of Health did not have a regular member on the Committee for Transporting Finnish Children to Sweden, which could be regarded as a crucial absence in the planning of the whole operation.

Over the years, many children forgot their Finnish roots and biological parents, and their relationships with their Swedish foster parents grew stronger. This especially affected those who were separated from their mothers for long periods of time, while those under the age of three, with few or any memories of home, forgot all about their families.

One of the hidden agendas of the evacuation to Sweden was that the arrival of the Finnish children helped fill the population gap that had been created within the country when the birth rate declined in the 1930s. Two Swedish scientists of demography, Alva and Gunnar Myrdal, had written an alarming book in 1935 called *Crisis in the population*, and a committee had been set up by the government to find ways to solve this problem, mainly by giving economic support to families.

As in the UK, for many of the children the parting with caring foster parents and returning to Finland at the end of the war was possibly a more devastating experience than the original departure from their homeland. This is the central theme of a recent, well-acclaimed feature film entitled

Mother of Mine. In some instances, the children returned to a family where new siblings may have been born, and the father may have been killed or wounded. Also, in many cases, they lacked language skills as they had forgotten their Finnish, and while away had learned to speak fluent Swedish. This may also have affected their academic progress as studies have indicated that war children coming back from their evacuation did less well in school than those children who had remained in Finland for the duration of the war. In addition, those children who did not speak Finnish any longer were picked on by their peers and sometimes even by their teachers. Many of the homes in Finland, especially those in the previous conflict zones, were in a serious state of decline after the war and some of the children who had stayed with wealthy foster families in Sweden now returned to a life of poverty and deprivation.

Sirpa Kaukinen returned to Turku and found herself 'missing paradise: her room in Sweden, the spaciousness of it all, the fields, the food ... the certainty of it all'. She remembers the return to Finland as the greatest trauma she suffered, far worse than leaving on the outward journey.[39]

As regards their general wellbeing, it has been found that the health of Finnish war children raised in Sweden was more or less the same as that of their friends who grew up in Finland, but over the years they have suffered from more psychosomatic symptoms. In addition, it is interesting to note that the mortality rate of those who remained in the country was higher than among those who had gone to Sweden.[40] It needs to be remembered that the negative experiences were not shared by all the children who returned from overseas. Some had become homesick in Sweden and desperately wanted to return to their families. In some cases their reintegration into Finnish life was smooth and some were even encouraged by their parents and their schools to keep in touch with their foster families in Sweden. The majority of the war children recall their time in Sweden as a positive experience and, once they became adults and able to make their own choices, many of them returned to the country in the emigration wave of the 1960s. (One Swedish study by Eric de Geer found that one in six of the Finns who had settled in the Gothenburg region in the 1960s was a former war child.[41] So it is possible that the number of Finnish war children now in Sweden is bigger than the number of children who stayed after the war without ever returning home.)

But there were some who had suffered during their evacuation. Marja Bell, sent to Sweden when eight years old, was fostered by a dentist who insisted on showing off her good teeth. The new clothes she had been sent away in had been burned in case they harboured lice and she was forced to wear outfits which were too small for her. Eventually, after many letters home, she returned to Finland.[42] There are other examples. Soila Ilveskola lived in Sweden for two years with an elderly couple. She was abused and forced to weed complete fields of sugar beet. Anita Lof, called 'Finnish Brat' by her hosts, had to sleep in the kitchen and was not allowed to venture anywhere else in the house.[43]

There were long-term implications. In 1942, the reaction of the Finnish parliament to the evacuation schemes was interesting as they thought there would be a great risk of losing children to Sweden. In response, the Conservative parties suggested that Finland should resign from the 1931 Scandinavian Treaty regarding marriage and adoption.[44] They wanted to have an amendment in the Treaty making adoption of a Finnish child always dependent on the permission of the Finnish Minister of Justice. The Swedes would not have understood the significance of this and the whole process alienated both countries. It is thought by modern researchers[45] that this could perhaps be seen as one of the underlying motives to the whole of the parliamentary treatment of child transports to Sweden. The Swedes may have objected to the number of adoptions being closely monitored by the Finnish authorities.

In Finland, the criticism levelled against the child transports was started by a party close to German politics (IKL, The Patriotic Movement of Finnish People). Fagerholm, as a social democrat, openly criticised German policy so he was well known for his anti-German feeling. According to him, child transports 'were a living symbol of the solidarity between Finland and Sweden', and he believed that the hidden agenda behind the IKL's policy was to alienate the two Nordic countries from each other, and by so doing, increase the German influence. The President of Finland, Risto Ryti, and some other political leaders within the country did not accept Fagerholm's interpretation of events. Nonetheless, there was a serious concern that the political relationship between Finland and Sweden, regarded as very valuable by the Finns, should not be jeopardised in any way. So, from February 1942, all negative criticism of the child transports to Sweden was censored and replaced by a policy of positive propaganda in favour of them. In addition, the Finnish Aid Bureau urged parents to write thank-you letters to their child's host in Sweden so that they could be published in Swedish newspapers.

When one evaluates the effectiveness of the measures introduced by the Finnish government in 1942, one can see that they did not introduce, or even consider, any legislation that would have actually prevented the adoption, and thereby permanent residence in Sweden, of Finnish children. In addition, the written agreement signed by parents stating that the child would 'under no circumstances' be left in Sweden permanently, had no authority after the war. Had the country withdrawn from the 1931 Treaty on Adoption, which required that all legal procedures relating to adoption were carried out according to the legislation in the host country, it would have harmed the political relationship between the two countries. In fact it was still legally possible to prevent adoptions of Finnish children by Swedish parents, but under some circumstances such actions would have been harmful to the child who had wanted to stay with their Swedish hosts, and were not considered to be part of the family.

The fears about the delay in the repatriation of some children after the war proved to be well founded. There was a lot of discussion in the Finnish parliament about the problems of the children remaining in Sweden and in some cases it became a very difficult process to get them home. As a result, according to the Suomi-bureau in Stockholm, around 15,000 children remained in Sweden and a further 500 in Denmark. However, the total number of children staying in Sweden was later shown to be false. An Estonian social scientist and demographer, Alur Reinans, together with Pertti Kaven, calculated that the real figure was about 7,000. Their research was based on the Swedish population registers implemented by the Swedish Church. The number of children staying in Denmark is correct because under the German occupation there was a strict registration of anyone entering or leaving the country.

It was obvious that the children were not returning home in the way the authorities had planned and although the 'Committee for transporting Finnish Children to Sweden' wanted to repatriate them all, it needed to ask the basic question as to why they did not want to come home.

At the end of the war an enquiry was set up and 600 families in Helsinki were asked about their children then resident in Sweden. Surprisingly, only 33 per cent wanted them back. The main reasons given were parental willingness to shed their economic and educational responsibilities and an alienation and indifference regarding the future prospects of their offspring. This is one of the saddest, and perhaps unexpected, results of the evacuation. It has also been suggested that the Finnish children themselves did not want to return to an impoverished Finland, which recent research would show to be true. The return back home to Finland was one of the most difficult experiences of the Finnish war children.[46] To a great extent, the Swedish families who had taken them in were relatively better off than their Finnish counterparts so many of the children, some from very poor rural backgrounds, enjoyed a much better standard of living and, as a result, they were not keen either to return to Finland, or if they did so, to stay for any length of time.

The results came as a shock to the Committee and it demanded that the Finnish government should give a binding order that all Finnish children in Sweden must travel home during 1946. This was not accepted, primarily because of pressure exerted by the Swedish authorities.

On 28 March 1946, the Finns compromised and made the decision that certain categories of children could remain in Sweden. This list included:

Orphans.

Those in a situation where there was either sickness in the Finnish Homes or where the domestic situation was not conducive to their return.

Those where the economic circumstances of the Finnish family was poor.

Those where there was no suitable residence for the child to return to.

Those for whom a return would interrupt occupational and vocational training in Sweden.

A private passport was to be arranged for the children meeting these criteria, and the Committee was given the authority to make a foster-child agreement with both the Swedish and Finnish parents to ensure the legal status of the children remaining in Sweden. These decisions contradicted the wishes of Parliament expressed in 1942. The Committee, on which the criticism of the child transports in Parliament in 1942 had made a great impact, wanted tighter regulations. The list of those eligible for residency meant that almost all the children could stay in Sweden. But the Committee was in a difficult position. If they made a formal request that the children should return home, there was a possibility that general Swedish humanitarian aid to post-war Finland would be affected. Throughout the war there always seemed to be some sort of economic concern underlying the war-child situation. The Finnish government's motives cannot always be seen as being entirely philanthropic. One does get the impression that the children became pawns in a bigger political game where the maintenance of good relations with Sweden was a major factor.

In 1949, a new committee was established called *lastenkotiuttamiskomitea*, 'The Committee for the Repatriation of Finnish children'. Its brief was to look at the legal issues surrounding the return of the children remaining overseas. They even sought expert opinion from psychiatrist Professor Martti Kaila about the possible psychological damage that a return to Finland would cause.[47] But this happened too late to have any effect. By this time very little could be done and the requirement of the Committee that Finnish legislation should be used to bring about the return of children had little or no significance.

However, the problem of what to do with those remaining in Sweden did not go away. In 1952, Kaila used his new research to support his original premise that Finnish children returning to Finland had no significant problems of assimilation. He had made a study of seven children who had come home after a very long stay in Sweden (up to seven years), but only by interviewing their parents. Kaila, who was not a child psychologist, found that only one of them showed some minor signs of distress. As a result his testimony was used in some court cases against Swedish hosts who were supporting their claims on their foster children by stating that they would suffer if they ever returned to Finland.[48] Kaila suggested that these problems were exaggerated. One would now question the reliability of this evidence as it only relied on the interviews of a very small number of parents, whose opinion could be seen to be rather biased. They were unlikely to say that their own children would have preferred to have stayed in Sweden. In this respect the later research carried out by Pertti Kaven in 1985 into this original study is very significant. Kaven contacted five of Kaila's sample group and asked how they now felt about Kaila's opinions based on their original interviews with him. Only one agreed with Kaila. The others felt that he had omitted important issues, such as the language problems, and had portrayed their situation as being much easier than it had been in reality. Interestingly, five of the original seven were living in Sweden at the time that Kaven interviewed them.[49]

The argument continued long after the war and heated discussions took place in the Finnish Parliament well into the 1950s. On 15 September 1949, six MPs tabled a motion requesting that the Finnish government should act vigorously not only to get the children home, but also to support the parents who wanted them returned. On 12 May 1950, during a debate in Finnish Parliament, when the representative of the Communist-led SKDL party (The Democratic Union of Finnish People) stated that the government should regard the loss of the children as a loss of the war, even though in some cases the children were leading a better life in Sweden, a member of the Finnish Social Democratic party accused them of wanting to 'pick up an old problem once again'.

The situation was discussed a second time on 23 May when, during a debate, an MP from SKDL made reference to the fact that some MPs regarded the problem as so delicate that it should not be discussed at all. She continued by saying that from a nation's point of view it was not significant to lose 15,000 children. In reply, an MP from the Swedish Minority Party (RKP) argued that if Parliament wanted to say something about the issue it would be simply to thank the Swedish nation for all the care they had given to the Finnish children during a very difficult period. He stated that the matter had been discussed in the Committee of Foreign Affairs and, as it was connected to Finnish Foreign policy, the discussions should go no further. An MP from the Agrarian Party (Maalaisliitto) stated that it was '… unheard of that Sweden did not want to return the remaining Finnish children to their parents.' Another MP from the same party regretted that the discussion had 'become political and children should be kept out of politics'.[50]

A Social Democratic MP suggested that the children should have been repatriated during 1945–46 and that the government was to blame for 'slowing down the return to Finland'. Her idea was that the children had to be repatriated and that the government either had to support the child in their parental home or arrange for a Finnish foster family to take them in. One Conservative MP stated that if a negotiated solution could not be reached then the chances of getting children back were very small, and another agreed that leaving them in Sweden would be a serious mistake.

In the final voting, eighty-six MPs voted for 'No further activities' and eighty-one for 'Vigorous acts'. The total number of MPs in the Finnish Parliament was 200, so thirty-three MPs abstained. The vote was very much on party lines and as such was related to the interest the parties had, or had not, taken in the transportation of the children. All of the forty-six Social Democratic MPs voted for no action, which was obviously a party decision. All twelve MPs from the Swedish Minority Party, which had been very much in favour of the transports and was both socially and politically very much aligned to Sweden, also voted for no action. Three members of the right-wing Progress Party also voted for no action. The Conservative Party, which in 1942 had heavily criticised the transports, were split with fifteen wanting nothing to happen and eleven voting for vigorous acts. The Agrarian

Party was again split with forty-three going for Vigorous Acts and seven who did not agree. On the other side of the Chamber, The People's Democratic Party was also divided when twenty-seven wanted Vigorous Acts and three did not. For them, this was an excellent weapon against the Social Democrats when fighting for the votes of the Finnish working class after the war. In 1948, there was real fear of a takeover by Communists who wanted to loosen the ties with Sweden. Consequently, the children were used by the party as a means of maintaining the possibility of a rift between the two countries.

The result was that nothing was done to get the children back.

However, the problem of repatriation did not go away and was taken up once again in 1952 when ten MPs questioned the Finnish government: 'Is the Government aware of the tragic effects regarding the parents who cannot get their children back home from Sweden despite their requests? What is the Government going to do to ensure that these people get all the interpretation, legal and medical help they need?'

In his answer, the minister in charge said that in 1951 the government had made an allowance in some specific cases to finance the trials regarding the repatriation of Finnish children. He continued by explaining that the amount of these cases was very small compared with the numbers of children transported to Sweden, although these cases got more attention in newspapers. Finally, the minister assured all the participants that the government would give all possible help to the parents and would also take other possible measures to ensure the return of the children. The ten MPs did not refer to the earlier handlings of the problem.

There was little cohesion in these debates. If one looks at the discussions that took place in the Finnish parliament and within government ministries between the years 1942–52, it would seem that each aspect of the war-child situation – transport, return, long-term repatriation etc. – was dealt with as a separate entity without any inter-connection. Although the initial fears of the political 'Right' were fully realised, the matter had simply gone on too long. The individuals who had made the decisions about the transportation of the children had no idea of the emotional and psychological effects on the evacuees, or indeed the risks posed to the long-term development of the country. Little account had been taken of the fact that some of the children were certain to have been influenced by living in a country with a higher standard of living than they had been used to.

What was the final result of this '*Sotalapsi*' operation? The initial aims had been to save the human resources of Finland during a very difficult time and eventually have the children return in a good physical and mental condition so that they could rebuild the country. So was it basically a question of population policy? It is now recognised that the medical treatment and improved nutritional programmes put in place in Sweden at the time saved the lives of around 8,000 war children. These included those suffering from tuberculosis that could not have been treated in Finland. As 7,000 children remained permanently in Sweden, either through continued fostering or adoptions, one could argue that the Swedes also benefited from the scheme at a time when their own population was declining.

However, while acknowledging that the experience for some of the war children has had long-lasting effects, it has to be recognised that the greatest benefit of all was gained by those whose lives were saved … no matter which country they live in today.[51]

10

The Children of Collaborators

As soon as I started coping with my war-related problems, I knew that my feelings of guilt were not well founded, because I was not responsible for my father's guilt. But knowing and feeling are two different phenomena.

Gonda Scheffel-Baars.

One area of study that is often overlooked when dealing with children in conflict is that of the offspring of collaborators, either actual or perceived. Whenever and wherever countries were occupied by an aggressor, some of the local population had been accused of being collaborators by their peers, and in many cases by the relieving powers. To what level this collaboration actually took place was very much up to the specific circumstances and individual involvement and it is too easy to generalise. However, unlike those who 'resisted', collaborators were perhaps more identifiable. They were members of the populace who were deemed to have worked with, slept with, or gained financial, social and political benefit from the occupying forces. In some areas of Europe, including the Netherlands and Norway, the Germans could not have administered the countries effectively without the support of collaborators. After the war, the head of German security in Amsterdam claimed that, 'the main support of the German forces in the police sector and beyond was the Dutch police. Without it, not ten per cent of the German occupation tasks would have been fulfilled'.[1] However, it is a fact that whatever the collaboration was deemed to be, the children of such people were affected, sometimes for the rest of their lives.

One area of occupied Europe that to some extent has now come to terms with its 'collaborative' past, is the Netherlands, largely through the work of the Herkenning ('Recognition') group.[2] What has to be remembered of course is that, like the children in Spain during the civil war, the sins of the fathers were very often passed on to the children who themselves had no political allegiance whatsoever, and in some cases were even too young to understand what was going on. At the end of the war over 200,000 Dutch people were investigated as collaborators, 50 per cent of these were imprisoned, some for as little as being seen to give the Nazi salute. As well as this, 17,500 civil servants lost their jobs and forty people were executed. What this has led to is a generation of Dutch people, many of whom have now retired, who have had to live their lives under the shadow of being a 'child of a collaborator'.

Many of their problems can be traced back directly to their parents either being members of the Dutch National Socialist Party (NSB)[3] or in some other way siding with, or expressing a tolerance or admiration for German National Socialist policies.

As with the Finnish situation, in order to understand the problems facing Dutch children, both at the time and since, it is necessary to look briefly at Dutch history immediately pre-war.

The NSB was established in Utrecht in 1931 at a time when the leaders first favoured the fascist ideology of Mussolini, and then gradually turned towards the ideals of German National Socialism. However, unlike the latter, the party before 1936 was not anti-Semitic and even had Jewish members. Although they may have supported the general Nazi philosophy and ideals most of the founders, including Anton Mussert[4] who became the party's leader and Cornelis van Geelkerken[5] who was in charge of the youth organisations, and many of its members, were first and foremost nationalists and only a minority supported the idea of a Greater German Reich. In the elections of 1935, the party got 8 per cent of the votes, and two seats in the Eerste Kamer.[6] For the first time other political parties became concerned about its apparent success. As in many other European countries, the NSB policies appealed to the large numbers of unemployed people who hoped that the new party would somehow solve the economic problems that the government seemed at a loss to confront. Others considered Dutch democracy as the cause of the country's social and national problems and welcomed a more authoritarian alternative. There was also an historical link as the Dutch tended to identify more with the German nation than with the British, especially after the latter's war against the Boers in South Africa at the turn of the twentieth century.[7] In 1936, under the influence of Meinoud Rost van Tonningen,[8] the party became openly anti-Semitic. Rost van Tonningen began to question Mussert's leadership and with the support of the German NSDAP, created internal divisions within the party. This resulted in decreased support for the party as a whole and led to a strong anti-fascist reaction from other political parties, trade unions and churches.

By 1937, members of the party and their families were becoming more and more isolated within their communities. The majority of the Dutch people disagreed with their National-Socialist convictions and condemned the increasing amount of violence and aggression displayed by the semi-paramilitary organisations marching through the streets. Jews left the party, civil servants were forbidden to join and gradually more and more people disassociated themselves from those in the NSB. Neighbours, friends and relatives reduced their contacts or even broke off relationships. The children in the streets and one-time friends in school bullied and teased the offspring of party members, and even teachers were known to discriminate against them, a situation that was to occur again in the immediate post-war years. Those children who wore the distinctive uniform of the party's youth organisations the Nationale Jeugdstorm were an easy target for personal harassment. Children, who were members because of their parents' political leanings and not through their own choice, were embarrassed to wear the uniform, whereas others were proud of it, feeling that they belonged to an elite group.

So despite its initial success, in 1937 the NSB got only 4 per cent of the votes and four seats in the Tweede Kamer, but expanded its seats in the Eerste Kamer to five. In Parliament, the NSB MPs showed little respect for the parliamentary procedures and many were called to order by the chairman for both physical and verbal assaults. In the provincial elections of 1939 the party again only amassed 4 per cent of the local votes and one could hypothesise that it might have disappeared altogether had the Germans not attacked the Netherlands in May 1940.

After the surrender of the Dutch army in May 1940, a large number of people considered by the staunch pre-war members as simply opportunists, applied for membership of a party that was soon to become the only recognised political party in the country because, as in other areas of the greater Reich, all opposition was suppressed. Even the children of NSB members, who before the war had been isolated and vilified, were now tolerated to some extent because of the fear of reprisals.

The Dutch had not been prepared for war, either physically, materially or psychologically. Economic policies had seen a reduction in the armed forces, both in terms of soldiers and weaponry, and there was a strong pacifist movement. The Dutch had not been involved in a war for almost 100 years since they had fought against Belgium during the wars of independence between 1830 and 1839,[9] and even these were diplomatic rather than militaristic. It had not been since the latter part of the eighteenth and the early part of the nineteenth century, when the French had occupied the area,[10] that they had actually confronted an enemy. Naively perhaps, the Dutch thought that the Germans would honour the Netherlands' neutrality as they had done in 1914, but significantly this was not to be the case in 1940. The Dutch strategy, planned as early as 1935, of opening dykes and flooding fields against an advancing enemy, proved to be a useless defence against German airborne troops dropping from the skies on parachutes. In a very short time these front-line troops had controlled the bridges across the Rhine before they could be blown up by the defenders. So for four years there was a period of mutual, rather than necessarily peaceful, coexistence.

On 4 September 1944, the Allies recaptured Antwerp and there was an expectation that the Netherlands would soon be liberated. During the war the members of the NSB party and their children were seen as intrinsically linked with the policies of National Socialism, so when the war ended, and non-party members needed a focus for their anger, this body of people became the obvious group on which to project all the negative experiences that they had gone through from 1940–45. This is where one sees the beginnings of the collaborators and their children taking on all the post-war ills of the Dutch. Even the treatment of the Jews and other identifiable groups within the Third Reich was laid at the door of the Dutch collaborators.

This is a situation with which many of us today, especially in those countries not occupied by the Axis forces, cannot emphasise.

Gonda Scheffel-Baars, herself the daughter of a collaborator, states that by transferring and projecting guilt onto this group '… (the Dutch) could prevent themselves from seeing their own lack of courage during the war, their accommodation to the occupiers and turning a blind eye to the dramatic decrees that led to the elimination of the Dutch Jews'.[11]

The party leaders feared reprisals from both the Allies and from the Dutch people, and advised the group's members to send their wives and children to Germany. On 5 September, on what was known as *Dolle Dinsdag* (Mad Tuesday), most of the NSB leadership fled to Germany and the party's infrastructure fell apart. They requested special trains for their transportation and about 65,000 people – among them only a handful of men – went to the northern provinces of Germany where they found temporary shelter in provisional refugee camps in the triangle of land between Hamburg, Hannover and Brunswick. Gonda describes the journey:

> My mother, sister and I headed to Luneburg. My mother had never travelled abroad before. I was a child in nappies, my sister was 4. Mamma did not even know where Luneburg was. She knew we had to avoid the big cities like Hamburg and Hannover. We found shelter in a small village of Tangendorff, with 60 other Dutch women and children, and some men who had worked on the NSB radio programmes and propaganda … I spent several days in a hospital in Luneburg and I always thought this was because of the dysentery I suffered and that my mother had no other choice but to abandon me for my own good. However, I recently found out that the people in the camp were fed up with my crying and so I was taken to the hospital … [12]

These 65,000 represented only 25 per cent of the total number of party members. The others stayed in the Netherlands, although most of them moved to places in the northern and eastern provinces. Thus, most of the NSB families left behind their homes and personal belongings. They became uprooted and this affected the children deeply. The latter missed their familiar surroundings, their toys and their school mates and had to build up new relationships in an environment that was often hostile to them.

In January 1945, the evacuated families were ordered to leave the German refugee camps because these were now required for the increasing flood of Germans fleeing the eastern provinces in front of the Russian armies. As a result, the NSB families went to the northern provinces of Netherlands because it was the only area where the railway system was still in use. The party leaders forced people to house the families returning from Germany, who were, of course, not welcome at all. Thus, most of the NSB families again left behind homes and belongings. They became totally uprooted, some for a second time.

One person has described the problems of leaving Germany to return to the Netherlands. Although this was written anonymously, for the purpose of this account and future references we will call him Jan: [13]

> It was an awful trip which took a long time by train and on wagons. We had to leave virtually all our possessions behind including the sewing machine.

When we approached the Dutch frontier the group of returnees became larger. We were hungry and had no opportunity to wash ourselves. At each resting place we had to undergo delousing treatment …

When the allied armies liberated the southern provinces of the Netherlands, many party members and their relatives were arrested and taken to internment camps. The small children were often accompanied by their mothers but many of the older children were left behind. Although some neighbours, friends or relatives took care of these children, many did so reluctantly, not wishing to be associated with them or indeed be stigmatised for providing help. As a result many children found no homes at all and shelter had to be found in temporary children's homes, which were often housed in schools, barracks or vacant houses that had previously been used as German offices. Many of those who were taken in by friends and neighbours were required by circumstance to show that they were extremely grateful which meant that in some cases they were exploited, either domestically, by having to do the housework, or in some cases sexually.

In the beginning there was a noticeable lack of personal and material comforts. There was little food, few clothes and even fewer beds. In addition, it was not easy to find women who were willing to take care of these children within the children's homes in any official capacity. Many of those who agreed to help had few, if any, qualifications and were certainly not equipped to deal with the emotional problems of their charges. They were often unaware of what the children had gone through both physically and psychologically and, as a result, many of the children felt abandoned and alone. There was also a distinct lack of support and tenderness on the part of the majority of the helpers, some of whom took revenge on the children for the years of occupation and for what they had suffered at the hands of the German forces.[14]

In many of these homes, children over the age of ten, i.e. those who may have been tainted by the political allegiance of their parents, were forced to take part in a re-education programme in democracy. However, it was delivered in such an authoritarian way, that it defeated the object.

Jan describes why he eventually ended up in a camp: 'The uncle we were living with got tuberculosis and I was sent to a camp in Breda. We were continually moved around …'

The Bureau Bijzondere Jeugdzorg had the responsibility for looking after the children of NSB families and it supervised many children's homes from its headquarters in Den Bosch. Some of the homes did provide a semblance of support for the children. One in particular 'Huize Lievenshove', a converted large villa, is remembered by one former war child:

> The leaders tried to do something special, even though food was scarce, especially if one of the children had a birthday. There was always a nurse in the room during the night and the Matron tried to maintain a personal relationship with us all. The majority of children and staff were Roman Catholic, but one of the Protestant nurses used to tell stories and sing songs to the Protestant children on Sunday mornings …[15]

During the latter stages of the war, other Dutch provinces were liberated and more members of the NSB were arrested and interned. As in the children's homes, many of the guards in the internment camps were not well qualified for such work and several of them took out their own personal feelings of hatred on the internees. In many camps violence was a way of life, resulting in the deaths of some inmates. The Canadian consul described the way in which internees were treated as 'Nazi methods'. It is estimated that the number of people in the camps totalled around 10,000. Among them were hundreds who had never collaborated at all, but were falsely accused by relatives and neighbours in order to 'settle scores' for perceived wrongdoing, a situation that was replicated in many other areas of previously occupied Europe. Others were interned by association, these were usually women who had no personal allegiance to National Socialism but whose husbands were in the party or those who had married members of the occupying forces. As a result, many children were left behind to fend for themselves. Taking legal action against such a vast number of people took more time than the government in exile in London had envisaged, and as a result many innocent people stayed in the camps for months, in conditions which were far from ideal.

Gonda describes her life in the camps:

> In February 1945 we were summoned back to Holland. We were lodged in one of the northern provinces in the house of a family who were forced to take us in. Despite the circumstances, they were kind and thoughtful. In April, the province was liberated and the wives and children of NSB members were ordered to go to a provisional internment camp in an old factory. The inhabitants of the village stood alongside the road shouting 'traitors' and spitting at

us, venting on us the frustration of five years of German occupation. They did not ask themselves whether the women and children were guilty or not. That is the moment that they threw us out; we were 'expelled' by our own people. Over the years I have overcome my feelings of guilt and shame, but never managed to feel Dutch. I resented them becoming our oppressors … In the internment camp my sister and I became seriously ill and I would have died had not an aunt taken us out. My mother remembered how we walked out of the gate, hand in hand with our aunt, not looking back for one moment, not raising our hands, no single sign of goodbye. The pain of that moment stayed with my mother for years …[16]

Gonda's mother was eventually released after an investigative committee found her not guilty of any links with the NSB. The war haunted Gonda's mother for the rest of her life. However, by the end she had come to terms with the fact that the past could perhaps be put behind her and she could die in peace.

After the German occupying forces signed the surrender on 6 May 1945, the NSB was outlawed and Mussert and other members of the NSB were arrested. Only a few were convicted, including Mussert who was executed on 7 May 1946, and there were no attempts to continue the organisation illegally. Most of those who were eventually convicted were given a three-year or a five-year sentence and all the collaborators lost their Dutch nationality and their right to vote for a period of ten years.

During the war, hundreds of Dutch children had stayed in Germany, Austria and Czechoslovakia, many as part of the *Kinderlandverschikung* scheme and others employed on the land. Some of the unemployed men had even been forced to take jobs in Germany in order to get their ration cards. However, when they tried to return to the Netherlands at the end of the war, often on foot, they were prevented from entering at the borders and were subjected to intense interrogation about their possible Nazi sympathies. When some eventually reached their homes they found them either closed up or other people living in them and it was often very difficult for them to discover the whereabouts of their parents and family. Jan describes the scene when he returned to his village:

We arrived at the town of … in June 1945 and members of the Red Cross took us to the house of our aunt, who was expecting us. However, when we went on to our own house we found another family living there and our shop had been taken over by a company. The family were shocked to see us and we were unable to enter the house because a number of policemen arrived. Some of my siblings stayed with my Uncle and the others with neighbours. We were not allowed to go into the street because of bullying from the other children. Eventually we moved away to live with an Aunt in a village where nobody knew about my father. However, because I had spent so much time in Germany I had to relearn Dutch …[17]

His father was released from internment in 1949, but it took another six months before they could return to their own home. However, Jan has always had a feeling of rejection. Although his father reopened the shop there was still a great deal of anti-NSB feeling to the extent that one villager removed her child from a church group because Jan was leading it.

Gonda's house was not available to her family either. It had been sealed up and confiscated by the government. At first they lived with her paternal grandmother in a very small apartment and then moved to the maternal grandparent's house. However, they were not really welcome, merely tolerated, although Gonda's grandmother risked imprisonment by rescuing some of the family's belongings before the house was finally sealed.

In Dutch society a split became apparent between the 'bad guys' (the 5 per cent of the population who had been collaborators, and seen as 'the embodiment of evil') and the 'good guys' (all the others, although only 5 per cent had been active in the resistance movement). This dichotomy influenced the collaborators' children a great deal. In Holland the 90 per cent 'others', who had just attempted to survive the war, allied themselves with the 5 per cent of the resistance. It is interesting to note that the Dutch label of 'bad' or 'wrong' goes beyond the normal recognised meaning. The 'good' did not consider the 'bad' to have made the wrong *choice* of political allegiance, but they were simply 'wrong'. Even those who had been members of the original NSB and then resigned their membership in protest of the party policies were still labelled as 'wrong'. According to Gonda Scheffel-Baars, if one's membership of the party becomes known, even today, one is labelled with 'wrong' – which amounts to a life sentence. She refers to the opinions of a Dutch journalist, who wrote a book called *When did Harry Mulisch become anti-fascist?* (Mulisch is a famous Dutch author). He accused Mulisch of being 'wrong' because he had been a member of the National Socialist Youth Organisation. Subsequent research has revealed that Mulisch had not been a member. However, what is important about the book is the comment made by the journalist that a collaborator is never able to disassociate himself from his former ideals and past. 'Once a collaborator, once "wrong", always "wrong"'; unfortunately, according to Gonda, the opinion of many Dutch people today.[18]

This attitude not only affected the 'political' collaborator. It was also apparent that *Moffenmeiden*,[19] Dutch women and girls who had had relationships with German soldiers, were stigmatised in the same way. The German authorities were very keen that children of such liaisons should be dealt with fairly, and those born after March 1943 had to be registered with the German Civic registries that had been established in the Netherlands in 1941.[20] According to Monika Diederichs, there are no exact statistics available as to the number of children born in the Netherlands to German fathers. However, on the basis of some figures gathered by the NSV,[21] it has been estimated that there were between 8,000–10,000 illegitimate births in this category. Yet, as these figures only related to those children brought up in children's homes etc., one can assume that the actual figure would have been a lot higher. Also, many women gave birth to their children in homes for unmarried mothers, established by the Dutch Federation of Institutions for Unmarried Mothers (FIOM), or in local hospitals, rather than the childbirth clinics set up by the NSV. The first of these was opened in Amsterdam in February 1942, and others flourished in Rotterdam, The Hague and throughout Friesland. The latter were specifically for those women who had been subjected to allied bombing. These establishments had been authorised by a Fuhrer Decree of July 1942, which had stated that 'for the preservation and promotion of racially valuable Germanic stock in the occupied Norwegian and Dutch territories, the Reichskommissar must take measures to guarantee special care and attention, at the request of the Norwegian and Netherlandish mothers, for their children parented by members of the Wehrmacht'.[22]

Although the children in these homes were brought up in a relatively secure environment and the information about their births was kept confidential, there were very serious problems post-war.

After their eventual release from detention and internment, the problems of the collaborators were far from over. There was a lack of housing, and although this was a concern for many Dutch people, for the collaborators it was made even harder by the unwillingness and intransigence of local government officials who either refused to help or provided sub-standard accommodation. Once a house had been found there was the problem of furnishing it. Even though it was strictly forbidden under the terms of the Dutch constitution, many collaborators had had their personal possessions confiscated, including their children's toys and savings accounts, and although they were later compensated, the sum received was nowhere near the original value of the articles they had lost. Buying replacements was also problematic as there was little or no domestic income. Many employers were not prepared to take on collaborators or even their children, social welfare was not always forthcoming and many were denied access to basic living requirements. As a result many of the children were forced to give up school and find a menial job to provide money for their families. This has always been a source of frustration for many Dutch children who found themselves in this situation, as they were never able to fully develop their potential. Gonda's mother was forced to work as a housemaid in her own parents' home, earning just enough money to survive on, although the question of domestic income and poverty was to be a problem for them for a further twenty years.

Gonda's father was released in 1948 and, like many other former members of the NSB, he had difficulty in finding employment. In 1949, he eventually got a job in a shipyard until his past was 'revealed' by a local pastor as late as the 1960s. Although the local manager wanted to sack him, the company owners had different ideas and he was later sent to Brazil to save a shipyard from bankruptcy. After initial problems with his visa, as he had been denied citizenship for ten years, the family eventually went overseas, where they spent eighteen months away from the NSB discrimination. Many never found any escape from the stigma and even those who moved to townships where their past could be hidden, lived in permanent fear of the inhabitants finding out about their background. For many, the simple solution was to remain silent so as to not give something away inadvertently. Previous 'official' isolation now became self-isolation simply for pragmatic reasons and gradually some of the children became integrated into a community in a physical sense, but rarely emotionally. They simply internalised the rejection of the Dutch people to themselves, or even their parents. They remained outsiders and 'different'.

Although there are no accurate figures, it can be assumed that there were between 200,000–300,000 children of Dutch collaborators, some of whom suffered greatly because of the transgressions of their parents. This was a significant proportion of the next generation of Dutch citizens who were to be socially abused, denigrated, harassed and dehumanised for something that was not their fault or of their own making. They were to suffer in many ways for the rest of their lives and few would remain unscathed.

One other country that felt the full impact of German occupation, and consequently the long-term effects of collaboration, is Norway. According to Professor Baard Borge,[23] there are at least 100,000 people in Norway today who are children of parents who belonged to the Nasjonal Samling (NS)[24] party during the war. This was the collaborationist movement led by Vidkun Quisling, a name now synonymous with 'collaboration' and 'traitor'. It is interesting to note that the history of the NS is very similar to that of the NSB in the Netherlands. Before the war the party failed to gather a great deal of support in local and national elections but nonetheless, despite never winning more that 2.5 per cent of the vote, the party did polarise the right wing of Norwegian politics. All the other established political groups saw it as an offshoot of German National Socialism and refused to have anything to do with it. As in other countries, including England where there was also an interest in the 'right' with Mosley's British Union of Fascists, many of the planned rallies and marches of the NS were either banned or subjected to violent reactions from the opposition. As with the NSB, the NS was also affected by internal divisions. Not all members supported the policies of anti-semitism and anti-free masonry, or the close alliance with the NSDAP in Germany, and although the party had close ties with German National Socialism during the occupation, it was more similar to the Italian Fascist Party in terms of ideology. By the time war broke out, the party was in fact little more than a sect on the fringes of Norwegian politics, but during the German occupation the NS became the official party and formed a puppet government. Party members also dominated the *Reichskommissariat*, the German civilian administration under Reichskommissar Josef Terboven.[25] Terboven[26] shared his authority with the Commander in Chief of the military forces, General von Falkenhorst.[27] In Hitler's decree of 24 April 1940, Terboven was entrusted with the executive power in Norway and was subordinate only to the Fuhrer, but his authority was limited to civilian affairs. In military matters, von Falkenhorst exercised authority over all the other German institutions in Norway. However, Quisling was not given a formal political position until 1 February 1942, when he became Minister President in a NS government.[28]

Many of the children who were brought up in NS households were labelled 'NS-barn' (NS-child) and, as such, experienced problems growing up in post-war Norway because their parents were considered to be

'Quislings' or traitors. Even today, many of the NS-barn choose to keep silent about their past for fear retribution or of being ostracised, even by their close friends. One such child was quoted as saying: 'We still fear being condemned and rejected because of our parents, just like many of us have experienced throughout childhood'.[29] This plight has been recognised by some social scientists within Norway who state that: '… there can be no doubt that the NS-children got an unfair and painful childhood'.[30]

As in the Netherlands, there is a great deal of stigma attached to being on the 'wrong' side during the war, and although a new generation of researchers and scholars have been working on this topic, there are still a number of people in the country who feel that concentrating on the predicament of those children on the 'wrong' side, is disrespectful to those on the 'good' side who fought in the resistance etc. Borge makes a very good point when stating that one of the reasons why research should be done with the NS-children is actually for their own well being. As many of them have remained silent over the years, they have perhaps not realised that there are more of them than they first appreciated. They may have grown up feeling that they were the only ones tainted with the sins of their fathers, whereas, in truth, there are many thousands in the same situation.

Again, similarities in war-child experiences are in evidence. It has long been argued by some historians and psychologists[31] that the children in war zones have been branded as being 'wrong/bad', 'quislings', 'collaborators', and so on, purely on the basis of the politics of their fathers. They were not of an age to have had any influence whatsoever in either the political choice of their parents, or indeed their country. For some who lived through the Second World War, it is easy to forget that at the time these events were happening the people we are now dealing with were children and as such were the 'invisible victims'. Some have become the scapegoats in order to assuage some of the guilt felt by those who perhaps consider that more should have been done. For others, the act of attaching blame has become something of a cathartic response.

As Borge points out, many older Norwegians who lived through the war hold negative feelings, not only towards the Quislings, but also to their children. One correspondent stated that: '… regrettably, my generation, whenever we encounter, or read of, individuals who were on the wrong side, we 'ignite' right instantly. This can also be the case as far as their children are concerned, I am sorry to say.'[32]

This reaction is not only confined to Norway. When I was first invited to attend a conference on German War Children in Frankfurt in 2005, and subsequently to work with the German Kreigskinder, a few members of the Evacuee Reunion Association in the UK threatened to resign their membership. According to them, 'I should not work with the children of the enemy'. Although I respect their views, I pointed out that as children they themselves had had no influence over who should be the wartime Prime Minister or the governing political party in the UK, in the same way that their German counterparts did not elect Hitler.

Like their peers in the Netherlands, many of the NS-children have suffered discrimination in areas such as employment and housing. Why this should be the case, considering that in relative terms the German occupation of Norway was not as extreme as in other parts of the greater Reich and the NS regime was not as repressive as other 'puppet' governments, is something that has occupied historians for many years.[33]

According to new research carried out by Professor Borge, one reason could be that civil resistance against the Nasjonal Samling manifested itself in the form a social boycott by those who were not members of the party. This resulted in NS members known to be in the local communities being ostracised. This not only included the adults, but their children as well, as 'non-party' children were forbidden to play and associate with 'party' children. The final outcome was that at the end of the war it was deemed a criminal offence just to have been a member of the NS, even if the individual's role had been a passive one. This resulted in many thousands of children growing up in post-war Norway with parents who were convicted traitors. One other similarity with the Netherlands, was the need for a post-war social identity, which, by its very nature, meant that those who had sided with the enemy and were therefore 'wrong', were no longer considered part of a country that had stood up to the invader, and therefore they were 'unworthy' of membership. The opposite of 'loyalty' is therefore considered to be 'treason', hence the discrimination.

According to a recent survey,[34] almost 66 per cent of former NS-children stated that their lives had been made more difficult by the fact that their parents had been members of the party. Interestingly, 21 per cent, a significant number, said that it had had no effect at all. A total of 53 per cent had been regularly bullied at school, but again a large number, 38 per cent, had not. But, as with UK, Finnish and Dutch war children, one has to take into account what they would recognise as bullying or harassment. This would very much depend on their individual circumstances and experience, and therefore it is very difficult to generalise. Another factor is quite simply

what criteria are used for such behaviour. What might well be considered
bullying and harassment today, would have been commonplace in the 1930s
and 1940s. The action has to be seen within its historical and sociological
context. When questioned about school experience, the NS-children were
almost equal in those who had had a good time and those who had not,
although many did explain that they had been concerned whenever the
topic of the war, or the NS was raised in class.

One very valid result has come out of this research. It would appear that
the amount of influence the NS had on the life of the child seems to depend
on the year in which the child was born and therefore the amount of time
it experienced the harassment first hand. Only 10 per cent of those children born after 1955 complained that their lives had been seriously affected
because of parental links to the party, against 86 per cent of those born
between 1930 and 1939. However, significantly the figures show that even
up to 1949, 77 per cent of the children had been affected 'absolutely' or
'partially' by the association with the NS.

One of the common traits among such children who did not experience
the war first hand, is the problem inherent in finding out from other people
that their parents had acted in the way they did. One could say that they
have been labelled on the grounds of 'by association, once removed' and
have become drawn back into the NS/NSB/NSDAP debate that had taken
place years before. Paradoxically, those who were aware of their parents'
actions may have been able to cope better with the situation than those
who found out by default and who had not built up the inner resilience
that people, such as Gonda and Jan, had developed during their time as war
children.

Another group to consider are the Norwegian women who had children with German fathers. Like the *Moffenmeiden* in the Netherlands, these
'*Tyskertøser*', or 'German hussies', were also harassed and ostracised. It is estimated that 10,000–12,000 children were born as a result of such liaisons,
although in reality this figure could be higher as some mothers may not have
wanted to admit the name or nationality of the father for fear of recrimination. As in the Netherlands, these children came under the protection of the
same German policy that had been established under the Führer Decree of
1942. In Norway, the responsibility for implementing this came under the
remit of an SS-subsidiary organisation called *Lebensborn*, which established
maternity and children's homes across the country to house both mothers
and children. There is no truth in the post-war media speculation that these

homes were in fact Wehrmacht 'stud farms' set up to create 'blond haired, blue eyed Aryans'.

After the war, there was serious debate as to what should happen to these children. Bearing in mind the post-war Norwegian nationalism and their response to the 'Quisling' children, the authorities were concerned that, should there be another war, these children would already be in the country as potentially a pro-German fifth column. (It is interesting to note that they still considered that Germany may be a future enemy.) There was also serious concern, which was basically anti-war child propaganda, that many of these children would be 'mentally deficient', so something needed to be done to remove them from Norwegian society. A government committee, *Krigsbarnutvalget*, was set up to look into the matter and, after a suggestion by an Australian delegation visiting the country in November 1945 wishing to boost their emigration policy, there was a serious recommendation that all the children, but not the mothers, should be sent to Australia *en bloc*. The scheme failed to materialise because of transport problems. In reality, some of these children, now regularly referred to as *Tyskerunger* or 'German brats', were housed in orphanages and children's homes, in often austere and harsh conditions. Some were sent to Sweden and, for a while, there was a serious proposal to send all the others to Germany, an idea that again amounted to nothing. Within a year the problem of these children was not high on the political agenda and the situation regarding them was allowed to dissipate. Nevertheless, in many instances their individual circumstances remained difficult. As the children of mixed liaisons – and therefore not Norwegian – they had been denied basic human rights. As a result, very few received financial social benefits and, even though they had remained in the country, some lost their citizenship, which they had to reapply for when they were eighteen.[35] In addition it now transpires that a government post-war campaign to make sure that these children did not suffer from bullying or harassment was never instigated, resulting in many of them having to put up with recriminations throughout their lives.

However, in the same way that 'Quisling' children are divided in the effects that such anti-social actions have had on their lives, the same applies to the 'German brats'. Although many have suffered hardship and lack of rights, others have led what they consider to be normal lives, created mainly by individual strength, will power and their desire to survive. Not all fit the downtrodden stereotype described in the press and the media. But, it needs to be recognised that even within this group, some have still had to cope with feelings of shame, guilt and inferiority as a result of their parents actions.

In recent years there has been a willingness in Norwegian political circles to put 'right' a number of historical 'wrongs'. This has included a number of incidents, the treatment of the 'German brats' being just one example.[36] Norway is one of the few countries that address the issue of discrimination against vulnerable minority groups in peacetime as well wartime on ethical and moral grounds. For the past twenty years, media investigations, televised and press interviews and the search by some of the children for their German fathers, have kept the topic in the public domain. However, it was one particular story that stirred up a hornets' nest and ultimately resulted in legislation being passed in the Norwegian parliament. On 15 March 1998, it was reported in many of the national newspapers that in 1956 West Germany had given Norway a reparation payment to the equivalent of £10 million. This money was to be shared among those people who had suffered as a direct result of the war, and was to include the children of German/Norwegian liaisons. However, the latter never received any of this compensation; instead it transpired that it had been confiscated by the government of the time. This story served to draw attention to the predicament of the German-Norwegian children, both at the time and since. In 1998, the administration set up an enquiry and as a result of the initial research work carried out by Kare Olsen, it soon became known that State and local officials had discriminated against war children and their mothers. Another report was commissioned, which led to a larger investigation from 2001–05. Once the ill-conceived Australian emigration scheme of 1945 came to light it was widely agreed that the children and mothers had been harshly dealt with and that the government was to blame for the mishandling of the situation. The 'children', now nearing retirement, were now seen as victims. As a result, seven of them sued the State of Norway for contravening their human rights, and even though the case was thrown out because it was deemed to be 'outdated', the war-child situation was now a serious political issue and one unlikely to go away. In his Millennium address in January 2000, the Lutheran Prime Minister, Kjell Magne Bondevik, made an unreserved apology to the war children on behalf of the State. This was followed up by one from the Parliamentary Justice committee in December 2002 and in April 2005, after a heated debate on *how much* rather than *if* compensation should be paid, a Reparation Law was passed by the Norwegian Parliament – almost sixty years to the day that the Second World War ended.

Another important occupied European country, and of course one-time ally of Britain at the beginning of the war, was France. From previous experience, the government had realised the possible vulnerability of Paris from an air attack in the case of a future war. In consequence, they had organised their civilian evacuation of the city as early as 1931, as a British document dated 17 December 1937 and headed 'ARP Intelligence Branch' indicates. In February 1931, Marshal Petain, as Inspector General of Aerial Defence for France, established a plan for the evacuation of the city which was based on the premise that 1 million citizens would leave voluntarily. The information about evacuation was to be contained in a leaflet of which 1.5 million were to be distributed throughout Paris.

The French Scheme was to take two forms:

LONG RANGE: Those persons who did not have public or private duties to fulfil or whose presence in the city was not essential were to be removed to areas as far away as possible from the vulnerable centre. Their departure was to be implemented at the first threat of war and they were to remain in their reception areas throughout the duration of hostilities. It was estimated that two days' mobilisation would be enough to remove 200,000 citizens from the area. The actual numbers were to be decided by the Mayor of each district.

In the reception areas, approximately 150 kilometres to the south-west of Paris, the billeting arrangements were to be organised by the Prefects of the Departments involved. Each person to be permanently evacuated was to be issued with a card to act as a rail ticket. On it would be marked the name of the billeting area, entraining and detraining stations, the day and time of departure and the number of trains. Arrangements were to be made for coaches to transport the evacuees from the train stations to their billets.

SHORT RANGE: This evacuation was to be either permanent or on a daily basis. However, it was not to be implemented during an air-raid warning. This daily evacuation was primarily concerned with the officials, shopkeepers, tradesmen and other workers, who had to work in a vulnerable area during the day, but who could leave at night to join their families in a safer place outside the city. It was estimated that this would affect 250,000 Parisians.[37]

The population of Paris had been advised to construct their own air-raid shelters in their gardens, unlike residents in the UK who had been given Anderson or Morrison shelters, or indeed close access to street shelters. However, in a similar response to residents of London, the Parisians were advised to take shelter in the Metro, should the need arise.

Again, with striking similarity to London, the French evacuation scheme was tested briefly during the Munich crisis. However, although the British equivalent was never evaluated, the French scheme was thought to be in great need of improvement.

In line with the original plans of earlier years, the idea was to send the non-combatant population of the twenty-five Departments closest to Germany, and those in the cities of Paris, Lyon and Marseilles to those areas that the planners presumed would be well away from any military operations. This movement was to be done entirely by rail, which, as it turned out, was to cause a great deal of congestion.

On 31 August 1939, the same day that 'stand-by' orders for evacuation were issued in London, 16,313 Parisian schoolchildren were evacuated from the city on twenty-seven trains. However, the process was not without its problems. The town of Chartres was told to expect children from two schools, in the event eighteen schools arrived, which caused all sorts of logistical problems for the local authorities. The main evacuation took place on Friday 1 September. Notices and leaflets informed the French population in the designated areas that they could only take 30kg of belongings per person, including bedding, a cooking pot and food for three days. Rather than the paper and cardboard luggage labels draped round the necks of British and Finnish evacuees, French children under seven were to have their labels containing personal information sewn into their clothes.

Although the evacuation was to be by train, many people lived a long way from the designated assembly points. As a result, they were required to travel long distances which meant that roads were full of walkers, some with handcarts, and tractors and trailers. Once they arrived at the stations the sheer vastness of moving so many people meant that there were long waits for overcrowded trains. Behind the exodus remained the detritus of the population movement ... redundant carts and bicycles, excess baggage and the abandoned cats and dogs that were not permitted to travel.

Not all incoming evacuees were welcomed in the reception areas. According to Lynn Nicholas, 250,000 inhabitants of Strasbourg were evacuated to the then primitive region of the Dordogne. Speaking their Alsatian/German language they were referred to by the locals as *boche*.[38] Their designated lodgings lacked the basic services, such as electricity and running water, and amenities like beds and cooking stoves, and they were expected to cook on tripods with stew pots hanging over open fires.[39]

Generally food distribution became a problem in the area, especially butter and milk, and finding a local job was almost impossible. While the threat of invasion existed people were willing to accept the hardships but, as time went on and nothing happened, they became less tolerant and the local inhabitants were especially critical of the incomers spending all their time sitting around in cafes and on benches. This was similar to the response of some inhabitants in British reception areas during the 'Phoney War' period.

The situation in Paris was slightly different, especially for those who had been moved only a short distance away. Rather than put up with the privations in the reception areas it was easier to return home. Even so, 520,000 of those who did leave the city did not return and remained in the country. After a short time, with nothing happening on the war front, the 'collegiate spirit' was declining. There had been a few air-raid warnings, but nothing in the way of actual raids and the Parisians were becoming less inclined to take precautions.

The Paris blackout was not implemented fully and restaurants began to open again, although sometimes just in the basement. Although there was a semblance of rationing, it was rather odd. One Cabinet Minister, on a designated 'meatless day', made do with oysters and grilled sole.[40] It is interesting to note that although it was reported in January 1940 that France was way ahead of Britain in terms of home front organisation, Colonel Baldwin-Webb, the Conservative MP for Wrekin in Shropshire, returned from a fact-finding tour of the country where he found there was virtually no blackout, no evacuation and no rationing. As a result of his trip he questioned whether Britain was justified in applying stringent home-front controls thought necessary for safety.[41] Life in France returned to some normality, some schools were reopened and horse racing and dancing was now permitted, although those events with the potential of attracting large crowds in confined stadia were banned because of the potential loss of life in an air raid. In the mountains ski resorts reopened and hotels on the south coast prepared for an influx of overseas holiday makers.

This was all to come to an abrupt end when the German infantry crossed the Meuse River on 13 May 1940.

There has always been a reluctance in France to address the true extent of collaboration or resistance of the French people. If one believes the speech of de Gaulle made in Paris on 25 August 1944 one would assume that everyone had been working towards liberation: 'Paris! Outraged Paris! Broken Paris! Martyred Paris!, but liberated Paris! Liberated by the people of Paris with the help of the armies of France, with the help and support of the whole of France, of France which is fighting, of the only France, the real France, external France.'

If however, one reads some of the comments made about the resistance groups themselves, one can detect a certain hidden agenda and selfishness regarding French post-war politics.

Disagreement about resistance tactics between the Communists and the groups following de Gaulle reflected basic ideological and political differences, which never ceased to divide the French Resistance. Each group regarded the other with deep suspicion as to its long-range political goals for the country. Both were keenly aware that a new France would be built out of the Resistance; each group's future role in post-war France would depend on its position within the Resistance at the end of the war'.[42]

Whatever stance one takes, the undeniable fact remains that for four years France was occupied by an enemy force comprising (depending on the period of the war) between 400,000 and 1,000,000 of men between the ages of twenty and forty. Although sexual relations between the German soldiers and French women were forbidden because, unlike their peers in Norway and the Netherlands who were deemed Aryan, they were considered to be of 'inferior race', they did of course take place. Although marriages were proscribed, it was possible, mainly for the SS, to obtain a certificate of 'pre-nuptial intent' or permission to marry from the Führer himself.

However, despite some semblance perhaps of a loving relationship, many of the women became pregnant by such liaisons and were left to fend for themselves when their German lovers were often posted elsewhere. In some cases these encounters had taken place while their husbands were being held by the Germans as Prisoners of War. Therefore, they not only had to live with the moral condemnation of having slept with the enemy, they were also labelled as traitors of France. Many sought abortions and others simply 'disappeared' for a while until after the baby was born. In December 1941, Vichy brought in a law that enabled women to have their children anonymously. This meant that it has been difficult to calculate the actual numbers of German-French children, as not only were there serious consequences for anyone violating the confidentiality of the woman, but after the birth the babies were usually put up for adoption. As a result it has been impossible for some of these children to find out who their birth mothers were. Some women kept their babies and in some areas special facilities were established to deal with them. In Cozzèze, in October 1941, the Prefect reported the setting up of 'a secret maternity hospital for pregnant prisoners-of-war wives' and he estimated that there were 300 such pregnant women in his area.[43]

Fabrice Virgili has interviewed a small number of children of German soldiers (*enfants de Boches*) and has estimated that there were 120,000–200,000 German-French children born during the occupation.[44]

These children were of great concern to Vichy, and to some extent the German authorities, who although not interested in all the children, did consider those born to women in the Normandy region, or the northern areas of France, worthy of attention as they were more likely to meet the ideal racial stereotypes of the Nazi party. Yet, despite this initial concern little was done to provide for them.

Although there seems to have been only slight 'official' discrimination of the children, for many of them who knew that they had German fathers, life could nonetheless be hard. This could be apparent even within their own families, where their grandparents, who had lived through the privations of the First World War, now found themselves with a German grandchild, and certainly in their local communities where their background was known. They were often called *boche* or *fritzouille*, and as a result many suffered from serious depression and some attempted suicide.

In *Enfants Maudits*, (Cursed Children), Jean-Paul Picaper retells a number of examples of how so-called *fils de boche* were humiliated by people in their neighbourhood. One interviewee, Daniel Rouxel, who was forced to sleep in a locked chicken coop because his grandmother was so ashamed of his birth, went on to describe a situation where a local official forced him to stand up at Mass and said to him, 'Do you know the difference between the son of a boche and a swallow? I'll tell you: The swallow takes its babies with it when it leaves France. But the boche leaves them behind.'[45]

Some of Virgili's interviewees describe themselves as '… guilty for being born'; another '… the teacher really emphasised the brutality of the Germans, the monstrousness of these barbarians, and she kept reiterating it throughout the entire lesson, so that I felt she was speaking to me, singling me out'.[46]

Some children were even abused by their own parents because they were a living reminder of the mother's guilt.

Although there has been some assimilation, France, unlike Norway and the Netherlands, has yet to really address the problems of its war children. It is as delicate a subject as the collaboration/resistance debate and as such is affected by individual experiences, personal reactions and, in some cases, guilt. According to Picaper, 'the French have a habit of only celebrating the glorious moments of history. Napoleon is portrayed as a benefactor, the revolution only brought human rights, not one drop of blood. Everyone knows there is more to it than just that.'[47]

The post-war politics of de Gaulle were based to some extent on the myth that all the French people had fought in the anti-Nazi resistance and by ignoring the fact that collaborationist Vichy had ever existed. At the Liberation it was relatively easy to purge the memory of the so-called *collaborateurs horizontales* by the ritualistic shaving of the women's heads,[48] but, at the very time that this was happening, the government and French society as a whole were condemning the children of such 'collaboration' to the shadows.

As in other countries within the former Greater Reich, the realisation later in life that one is the product of a German/French liaison is often difficult to comprehend, but few speak out and the silence remains, usually out of respect for the mother and, in some cases, the biological father who may still be alive and with a new family of his own.

It would be very difficult to compare the French situation with those in other countries as the research efforts, similar to those recently carried out in Norway, are not likely to be done until the French really admit that collaboration took place. It is also very unlikely, at least in the foreseeable future, that the compensation arrangements, now in place in Norway, will ever be attainable in France. Fathered by the enemy and ignored by their country, these children, now in their sixties, are still very much 'children of war'.

11

Child Soldiers

No one … not the United Nations, not governments or civil society groups
… has done nearly enough to counter the power, greed and political expedi-
ency with which adults countenance the criminal sacrifice of children in
war.

Graça Machel.[1]

Despite the hope and optimism at the time, the Second World War was
not to be the last major conflict in the world. Today, as you read this, there
are around thirty-one armed conflicts taking place around the world in
Colombia, Sri Lanka, Nicaragua, Iraq, Afghanistan, Tsetshenia, Rwanda,
El Salvador, The Ivory Coast, Sierra Leone, Darfur, Palestine, Lebanon and
Nepal … to name just a few. All these war zones contain children and many
of them are experiencing conflict and its results first hand. One simply has
to look at the television news for the evidence. Look beyond the immediate
images and see the children in the background mimicking their brothers
and fathers. See the photographs in newspapers and magazines of children
in the Middle East inscribing artillery shells with propaganda or inflam-
matory images. The situation really has not changed that much since the
Second World War. It is estimated that over 2 million children have lost their
childhood, innocence and ultimately their lives as a result of being forced to
join government armies or local militias.[2] A further 6 million have received
disabling injuries and, so far, in 2007 an estimated 250,000 continue to be
exploited.[3] Despite evidence that these children in modern-day war zones
are, and will be, affected even into the late twenty-first century, and in spite

of work being carried out by UNICEF, Save the Children and the Human Rights Watch, their plight is still being largely ignored by countries and those with a vested economic interest in such conflicts, in the same way as that of their forebears in the Second World War.

There are also other factors to consider, again some of which were apparent during and immediately after the Second World War. At that time there were around 13 million displaced people wandering around Europe; now there are an estimated 20 million child refugees and asylum seekers still searching for a safe haven, not only in other countries but, in some cases, even within their own. This problem is not only confined to recognised war zones, it is also apparent in so-called social mobility programmes such as that witnessed in Zimbabwe where since 2005 whole communities have been removed from their homelands under the government's urban slum demolition drive. A scheme which, according to UN estimates, has left 700,000 people without jobs or homes.

However, what is new is the modern-day exploitation of children in carrying out actual acts of warfare – a direct violation of Children's Rights. One immediately thinks of the present situation in parts of Africa but according to Ken Caldwell, Director of International Operations at Save the Children: 'The recruitment of vulnerable children by armed groups is not just a West African problem; it is a global one that each year ensnares thousands of children in a web of abuse and hardship'.

What is behind the exploitation? Why has there been a considerable rise in the number of civilians, including children, killed and wounded in war zones where, according to Graça Machel,[4] the total has risen from 5 per cent to 90 per cent over the past few decades?[5] One of the greatest problems at the present time is the globalisation of what in the past may have been viewed as a local conflict. Today these are often fuelled by the more affluent countries which have an economic interest in the local natural resources such as oil, precious stones and minerals, and by drug-related cartels which make vast profits by selling illegal drugs manufactured in third world countries. In order to achieve their aims it is not uncommon for such groups to encourage and manipulate various ethnic, religious and political divisions in order to protect their own interests. Unfortunately, such 'protection' has resulted in very profitable 'spin offs'. Working on the premise that 'he who has the gun has the power', arms dealers make a great deal of money supplying weapons and equipment to insurgent groups. Some of the guns have been developed so that small children can carry them, for example the 'popular' AK-47 rifle is light enough for ten-year-old children to use and costs the equivalent of the price of a goat. In addition they are also able to lob hand-grenades with devastating results, sometimes to themselves, and technological developments have resulted in much lighter child-size body armour. There are also economic factors. As emerging nations find it difficult to cope with struggling debt and rising inflation, they are often required to cut back on social care, basic health provision and public service infrastructures. As a result, many people, including children, are motivated to join rebel factions as a way out of their cycle of poverty. Much of the aid given as emergency relief by Western nations is inadequate and adds further misery to the already existing plight of these children. According to Machel, in 1999, donor countries provided the equivalent of 59 cents per person per day to the 3.5 million people affected by the conflict in Kosovo and south-east Europe, whereas the 12 million in the war zones in Africa received 13 cents per day.[6]

But the main concerns centre on the increasing numbers of child soldiers on 'active service'.

The *Cape Town Principles*, adopted at a symposium on the prevention of recruitment of children into the armed forces, and demobilisation and social reintegration of child soldiers in Africa, organised by UNICEF in 1997, defined a Child Soldier as:

> … any person under 18 years of age who is part of any kind of regular or irreg-ular armed force in any capacity, including but not limited to cooks, porters, messengers and anyone accompanying such groups, other than family mem-bers. This includes girls recruited for sexual purposes and for forced marriages.

It went on to state specific closely defined recommendations, notably that recruitment and use of child soldiers violates children's rights and is a war crime if the children are under fifteen, and that there must be swift disarma-ment, demobilisation, rehabilitation and reintegration of all child soldiers. The latter must include specific arrangements for children ensuring that they have sufficient health care, and are provided with an education and/or skills' train-ing sufficient to make them viable commodities in the job market. Finally, they are to be given help in tracing their families with the long-term aim of reuniting them.

There was also a requirement to respond to the particular needs of girls, many of whom have struggled with the psychological, physical and social consequences of sexual and other forms of abuse, the practice of forced marriage and, in both cases, the possible resultant pregnancy and childbirth. There was also the serious problem of HIV/Aids.

Research carried out by the United Nations suggests that 300,000 child soldiers are exploited in over thirty countries around the world. So why are children still being recruited, despite these guidelines, and what is being done to prevent the practice?

In countries that are already poor, the costs involved in war and conflict, in terms of men and equipment required and then lost, tends to add to the deterioration of the economic and social infrastructure, and often results in soaring inflation thereby forcing families into further financial hardship in order to eke out a basic standard of living. As a result, many children may join armed groups to secure daily food for themselves and their families, thus ensuring their survival, even on a short term basis.

Conflict in all war zones, including those in the Second World War, is also likely to disrupt children's education. Today, in places where schools are permanently closed, children are left with few alternatives other than aimlessly walking around the streets and, as a result, may be more easily persuaded to join up.

When the hostilities are prolonged, armed forces and insurgents are more likely to use children to replenish their ranks. Confusing war and play, many new recruits have little understanding of what combat actually entails and therefore have no idea of the dangers. This perceived lack of fear is often exploited by group commanders who use the children in a variety of roles such as human mine detectors, putting them into the front of the advancing forces and, as witnessed recently in Iraq and Afghanistan, as suicide bombers. Only recently an insurgent leader in Afghanistan explained how he was training children as young as six to take on this role, as they were unlikely to be suspected by enemy forces. In his words '... they go unnoticed'.[7] Few child soldiers reach old age. However, by its very nature, the practice of using children in this way will have long-term effects on the future development of an area or a country as the next generations are being decimated before they reach maturity.[8] As the older ones are killed so the new recruits have to become younger and younger. Not only are these recruits seemingly readily available but also the trend for 'joining up' is facilitated by the child's excitement of handling and using modern small arms and light weapons.

However, not all are attracted by the war lord's propaganda. Other children are 'press-ganged', some are physically threatened and in some cases schools and orphanages are forced to give up any children in their care above the age of fifteen for 'military' purposes. (In Sri Lanka, the 'Tamil Tigers'[9] actively recruit and train schoolchildren and recently had two fully armed units made up of children under the age of ten called the 'Baby Brigade' and the 'Leopard Brigade'.) As a result, all these children are robbed of their childhood and in many cases subjected to extreme brutality by their commanders and their peers for not carrying out their roles efficiently enough. For those who are deemed successful, the rewards are seemingly enticing: promotion, more food, relative material wealth and sexual partners. However, many are drugged or plied with alcohol before being sent out to fight and some are forced to carry out atrocities against their own families and villages in order to destroy family and community ties. In the long term there is a gradual desensitisation that in some ways makes the tasks easier to carry out. The longer such exposure to traumatic situations continues, the more difficult it is for those children who have escaped the clutches of the warring factions or who have been legitimately reintegrated into society, to lead a normal life.

As well as fighting in combat units, children are used for sexual purposes and girls are commonly assigned to a commander and at times gang-raped. As a result, many are infected with HIV/AIDs and tuberculosis which makes their assimilation into a post-war society even more difficult. In addition, such 'killer' diseases again pose a serious threat to the long-term future of the warring nations. In 2000, the UN stated that HIV/AIDs was a significant threat to peace and security and Kofi Annan, Secretary-General, said: '... this cocktail of disasters is a sure recipe for further conflict. And conflict in turn, provides fertile ground for further infections'.[10] Again the spread of disease among an indigenous population is not new. Even as late as 1947 there were approximately 100,000 orphaned and separated children in the British zone in Germany alone, living off the proceeds of petty crime and prostitution. Over 80 per cent of the girls were suffering from venereal disease. However, the main difference is that in the present-day war zones the doctors and health centres, which would have been able to deal to some extent with the HIV problem, have themselves become personal and material targets. As a result, in some areas of Africa, more people are dying from HIV/AIDs than combat, a situation not helped by the fact that as military power is seen as the priority, more money is being spent on arms and ammunition than on tackling these burgeoning serious health issues. Even some of the war-wounded and non-combatant civilians are being treated with blood contaminated with HIV.

A further consideration, often overlooked, is that economically poor countries are unable to afford the high cost of medicines. Although some of the hugely profit-making pharmaceutical companies have been almost 'shamed' into lowering their prices, it does not always bring the palliatives into the hands of those who need them the most. The authorities in some countries, such as Thailand, Brazil and the sub-continent of India, are attempting to overcome this problem by producing their own AIDs drugs, which they hope will be affordable. But, despite these initiatives, in many other countries the whole situation becomes a vicious circle with seemingly little way out.

Unlike the war children of the Second World War, who in the main were very much left to their own devices after 1945, the plight of the present-day child soldiers has resulted in legislation aimed at protecting children. But of course this only works if all countries presently using children for such purposes, will sign up to it.

On 12 February 2002, the Optional Protocol to the Convention on the Rights of the Child came into force. This represented a milestone in the campaign to strengthen the legal protection of children and prevent their use in armed conflicts. Reference was made to the International Conference of the Red Cross and Red Crescent in December 1995, which recommended 'that parties to conflict take every feasible step to ensure that children below the age of 18 years of age do not take part in hostilities'.

The committee specified that for the purposes of the Convention, a child 'means every human being below the age of 18 unless, under law applicable to the child, majority is attained earlier'. Although it did not put a stop to the use of child soldiers, it did lay down strict guidelines relating to their recruitment. For example, it raised the minimum age for direct participation in hostilities from fifteen to eighteen.

It also prohibited the compulsory recruitment by non-government forces of anyone under eighteen, while at the same time allowing nation states to establish a minimum age for recruitment that could be under eighteen. This resulted in a great deal of confusion and created a loophole that has been used by other countries with a recognised standing army, such as the United Kingdom who, although a signatory of the Protocol, stated at the time that recruits under the age of eighteen who were in the armed services would be deployed should the need arise. A statement which has since been rescinded and personnel under age will not now be sent to conflict areas.

The Protocol called on countries to raise the minimum age above fifteen for voluntary recruitment and to implement strict safeguards when voluntary recruitment of children under eighteen was permitted. Four minimum requirements were outlined:

> Article 3. …
> Such recruitment is genuinely voluntary.
> Such recruitment is carried out with the informed consent of the person's parents or legal guardians.
> Such persons are fully informed of the duties involved in such military service.
> Such persons provide reliable proof of age prior to acceptance into national military service …[11]

In the case of non-state armed groups, the treaty prohibits all recruitment, voluntary and compulsory, for anyone under eighteen. The Protocol also made reference to the Rome Statute of the International Criminal Court of June 1998, which came into force on 1 July 2002. This made it a war crime to conscript or enlist children under the age of fifteen and use them in both international and non-international armed conflicts.

In November 1999, the African Charter on the Rights and Welfare of the Child had been the first legislation to establish the minimum age of eighteen as the level of recruitment. However, both the Charter and the Protocol presuppose a number of things. First, that the countries involved have adequate legislation in place for the compulsory registration of births. Some children do not know how old they are and the births of an estimated 40 million children worldwide have gone unregistered. In Afghanistan, where there is no registration, the guideline for the recruitment of boys into the Taliban was whether or not they could grow a beard.[12] (This unreliability of age is not new. Some volunteers wishing to join the British Army in 1914 who gave their age below eighteen, were told to walk around the block and come back when they were the right age. One of the youngest was Valentine Strudwick, who died at the age of fifteen and whose grave in the Essex Farm Cemetery, near Ypres, is visited by many school parties.)

Second, that their parents and/or guardians are *able* to 'give their consent'. Third, do the children themselves realise that the process is voluntary. Fourth, and probably the most significant, bearing in mind the possible confusion between 'reality' and 'play', are they really aware of what military service entails?

The first Peace agreement to recognise the needs of children and plan for their post-war life was made between the government of Sierra Leone and the Revolutionary United Front of Sierra Leone in July 1999. It recognised that the children were entitled to special care and protection of their human rights in accordance with the provision of the International Rights of the Child.

> ARTICLE XXX
> CHILD COMBATANTS
> The Government shall accord particular attention to the issue of child soldiers. It shall, accordingly, mobilize resources, both within the country and from the International Community, and especially through the Office of the UN Special Representative for Children in Armed Conflict, UNICEF and other agencies, to address the special needs of these children in the existing disarmament, demobilization and reintegration processes.

Did it work? On 28 February 2005, there was a violation of a previously agreed cease-fire, which resulted in fighting breaking out in western Ivory Coast. Members of the 'Mouvement de Libération de l'Ouest de la Côte d'Ivoire' (MILOCI), a pro-government militia, launched an attack on the city of Logoualé against a position held by the Forces Nouvelles (former armed opposition group under whose control the northern part of the country had come since the armed insurrection of September 2002). The United Nations Operation in the Ivory Coast (ONUCI) intervened and arrested eighty-seven combatants: all were members of the militia. Two were Liberian children aged ten and eleven who were handed over to UNICEF.

Although thirty-five African states are known to be abiding by the minimum age of eighteen for recruitment of the African Charter on the Rights and Welfare of the Child, there are still an estimated 100,000 children remaining in armed conflicts in Africa. The Liberian government and rebel forces alone recruited c.21,000 children, some as young as six, and even smaller and lighter weapons are being developed to make it easier for children of this age to bear arms.

One must see the problem of the child soldiers in the Ivory Coast in its broader context and realise that it is linked to issues in Liberia that have not been resolved. Notably, it is the result of previous failures to demobilise properly. In July 2004, the charity Save the Children issued an emergency statement about the situation in Liberia, which outlined key issues and measures that they hoped would alleviate the situation of child soldiers in the area. According to the report, by April 2004 the programme of disarmament, demobilisation, rehabilitation and reintegration had resulted in 48,000 being disarmed by the UN mission in the country at the time, but in total only 4,300 child soldiers were demobbed. At the time of the report there were an estimated half a million displaced persons in the country and although 17,000 had been resettled, many still lived in camps with access to only the basic human needs. As a result of fourteen years of war and civil unrest more than 80 per cent of the population were living in a state of poverty. The economy was highly inflated, there was high unemployment, many skilled workers had emigrated and 50 per cent were excluded from their homelands. Consequently, the country became very reliant on outside assistance for basic requirements. There were also serious concerns as non-combatants in Liberia were passing themselves off as former fighters in order to claim the $300 resettlement grant given out on demobilisation. There were also problems regarding the segregation of women and children in the containment camps while waiting for reintegration, and a large number of girls suffered sexual and physical abuse resulting in a high rise in teenage pregnancies and prevalence of HIV/AIDs, all of which was a recipe for further insurrection.

Within the country there was very limited access to safe drinking water, adequate food and proper sanitation. There were no reintegration programmes and little education, which left the child soldiers with few incentives to do anything positive to change their way of life. In order to simply live, many of them became street children and survived by resorting to prostitution, drug dealing and theft. Some formed gangs that the civilian population continued to fear. With few opportunities to improve themselves, for many of them the temptation to go back to military life was always strong. Consequently many child fighters from previous conflicts 're-enlisted' to continue the cycle of war.

The pressure to return to the armed groups and militia were highlighted in a later report. On 11 November 2005, Save the Children published its 'Fighting Back Report'. It was based on interviews with 300 children and 200 parents/carers in Ivory Coast, Sierra Leone and Liberia. The research found that although some joined armed groups against their will, others joined 'voluntarily' for the following reasons: (Although one has to question the term *voluntarily* in this context as some were given up to rebel groups by their parents or, as in the case of areas of the Congo, by their local community as a duty and form of 'community service', it is important that one does not lose sight of the fact that some of these children genuinely chose to join the armed forces and militia in order to improve their way of life.)

First, a general lack of any alternatives. Many cited a lack of access to education and vocational training.

Second, inadequate care. 30 per cent of ex-soldiers said they had been recruited after becoming separated from their parents and carers.

Third, poverty and hunger. Having sufficient food to eat, or being able to provide for parents and siblings, was consistently described as one of the only benefits of joining up. 'Finding food was a problem … so I told my mother that I will go round to see the fighters'. [13]

Fourth, protection. Some joined to safeguard themselves and/or families and their possessions. 'If you had a gun your friend would not come to your house and humiliate and harass your family. You can also defend them.' [14]

Others referred to personal gain and 'power'. Some ex-child soldiers said they joined to gain power and material wealth and be able to do things they would not normally be able to do. Some boys were accused of joining simply to rape girls. Another was revenge both for personal and family reasons. Some joined to avenge abusive or humiliating behaviour, or the death of a family member by another armed group.

Finally, some expressed a simple need for excitement. Some were lured by a desire to have fun and/or adventure, make friends, or find a partner.

The report concluded that attempts to change attitudes to the recruitment of children by armed groups, either to act as soldiers or to carry out supporting roles such as cooking and carrying, must be long term, preferably initiated during times of relative peace and stability. Provision also has to be made to prevent hunger and reduce household poverty. In addition, the dangers of and attitudes towards recruitment should be discussed and the reasons behind the child's desire to join should be addressed. Local groups should develop the methods used by children, parents and communities to avoid recruitment by providing at-risk children with alternative life skills training and good quality education, preferably free, and any such help should be context specific. For example, former voluntary recruits may need more persuasion to forget about the benefits of belonging to an armed group.

As many were recruited after being separated from their families and most of those who did not join took the advice of parents/carers, the report also recommended: That there should be previously agreed safe meeting places in case families get separated. Children should be given the opportunity to attend schools close to their homes. Proper mechanisms should be put in place to care for children whilst their parents are being medically treated. They should develop household or community early warning systems to warn when fighters are near. And children should be reunited with their families as quickly as possible when separation occurs. In April 2007, Kenneth Caldwell commented: 'For every child who joins an armed group, many more do not, and by building on existing community-led initiatives to prevent recruitment, as well as tackling the reasons children join, such as poverty and hunger, we can help eradicate this gross abuse of human rights'.[15]

Despite the legislation and reports, the abuse of children is still taking place. In the Congo there are an estimated 300–500 Congolese Tutsi children, some well below the legal age requirement, currently taking an active role in the conflict between the Mai Mai and the Forces for the Democratic Liberation of Rwanda on one side, and the army of the Rwandan government on the other. According to Human Rights Watch, under an agreement to end the conflict, army commanders were to have identified and handed children over to agencies, which were to be responsible for their rehabilitation. Several refused stating that they needed to maintain sufficient forces to protect the Tutsis living in the area of North Kivu and allow the repatriation of Congolese Tutsis presently housed in refugee camps in Rwanda. These camps are also a source of recruitment with many children being coerced to join the North Kivu brigades. The situation in the country had been considered to be so serious that in September 2006 the UN Security Council called on the government there to take legal action against those commanders accused of war crimes against children. But seemingly this has had little effect. On 11 April 2007, the United Nations Mission in the Congo stated that only thirty-seven of 267 children[16] who had been identified as members of the Kivu forces had actually been demobilised, despite the Congo being a signatory to the Optional Protocol on the Rights of the Child.

In Sri Lanka the situation is little better. It was reported in January 2007[17] that the 'Karuna' group, led by a former commander of the Liberation Tigers of Tamil Eelam (Karuna), which split from the Tamil Tigers in 2004, are forcibly recruiting children in eastern Sri Lanka, with the compliance of the national government. The latter is fully aware of what is going on but sees the LTTE as a useful ally in its fight against the Tamil Tigers, and is therefore prepared to turn a blind eye to what is going on. The Karuna group have been active in abducting many children from their homes, schools and even from the roadside. They generally target poorer families and those who have already had children recruited by the Tigers. Lack of government intervention is highlighted in the movement of these children into the training areas. According to Jo Becker, Child Rights Advocate for the Human Rights Watch, the abducted children are first held in the nearest office of the political wing of the LTTE, usually guarded by Sri Lankan police, and after a few days are transported to one of their training camps. In order to do this the children are taken through a number of police and army checkpoints; a journey that would be totally impossible without the cooperation of the Sri Lankan government. In addition, the Sri Lankan police in the area actively ignore complaints from the parents of the children about their abductions. When asked about the situation Karuna denied the allegations, stating that there were no combatants in his forces below the age of twenty. He even offered the UN access to his camps and to check. However, despite assurances and a willingness to penalise anyone under his command recruiting children, there is no sign that such commitments have been honoured and abductions are still being reported across the region.

One area known for its exploitation of children, but often forgotten, is Burma, where the government is active in forcibly recruiting children into its army. Although it appointed a 'Committee to Prevent the Recruitment of Child Soldiers' in 2003–05 and adopted the resulting action plan, there has been no positive impact on the present situation. Children as young as eleven years of age are abducted from transport centres, schools, roadsides and even market places. Many of them end up fighting against ethnic minority groups where they are forced to carry out human rights abuses. Some of these latter groups also actively recruit children, which mean that in some areas it would be possible to see armed children fighting against armed children.

In Nepal, there are an estimated 3,500–4,500 children fighting in the army of the Communist Party of Nepal (Maoists). As a direct result of this, thousands of others have had to flee their homes in order to escape abduction and forced recruitment. Despite a ceasefire agreement between the Maoists and the Nepalese government, which specifically committed both groups to stop recruiting children under eighteen, the abductions continue and few, if any, of those already in the armed forces have been demobilised. One of the main reasons for this being that the Maoist forces and the Nepali government do not have in place the social service infrastructure necessary to ensure that all of the demobbed children can be effectively assimilated into society. Although none have been actively involved in the fighting since the ceasefire, there is evidence that the Maoists and local militia groups are continuing to train child soldiers. One method used to entice the children to join is a promise that once Maoist forces are integrated into the National Army, they will either get monetary compensation or be given vocational training if they leave. Others are simply kidnapped, often from schools, or indoctrinated by subversive propaganda campaigns that attract them as 'volunteers'. In some areas of the country, the Maoists had a 'one family, one child' policy, which simply meant that each family had to provide a recruit to the army, or face severe sanctions. Once recruited, the child was tied into the army as they believed that any attempt to escape or desert would result in their whole family being punished. The Maoists have always denied that they have actively recruited in this way but since 2002 the group has been cited in three UN reports for violating international standards on the recruitment of children. Although they agreed in August 2006 to allow Child Agencies to gather information about child soldiers and subsequently plan the social reintegration of them into their communities, there has still not been an official order to cease child recruitment. They continue to actively conscript children under the age of fifteen, a practise that will carry on, albeit illegally, until plans are put in place to actively persuade children to leave the insurgent groups. For this to happen, an educational system, both academic and vocational, needs to be initiated in order to ensure that the 'release' of these children into society does not lead to further armed groups of disenchanted youths wandering around the towns and country-side. But, as in other countries where individual economic need is a 'push' factor, the whole state of Nepal is poor and it is very unlikely that, even when educated, these children would be able to find gainful employment.

One area that has had more success than others in releasing children from armed groups is Burundi, but not all have benefited from the process. Since 2004, more than 3,000 children have been demobilised by the Burundian Army and various civilian and militia groups who signed the Arusha Accords in 2000.[18] However, there is one exception. Despite peace talks in Dar es Salem in May 2006, the National Liberation Forces (FNL)[19] persists in using children not only as combat troops but also in support roles. The result is that whereas the signatories to the Accord are allowing their children to leave and pursue 'normal' lives, supported by aid and financial packages, those who fought with the FNL and have been captured or deserted are now in government custody, with few legal rights. They are held at two sites, some are detained in prison and others in an internment camp. Ironically, some children only joined the FNL forces during the time of the peace negotiations, believing that when any ceasefire was announced they would benefit from any aid packages on offer. In reality there was no demobilisation programme and they received neither money nor material help.

Many of the children who had been captured or had deserted were often used by government forces as informers and guides to FNL camps, receiving just food and a little money in return. These children found themselves in a very difficult situation because, as they are in government custody, they were unable to refuse. Those presently interned in the camps have few rights and have little or no access to education or medical services, although they do receive food and are able to exercise freely. In May 2006, the prison in Bujumbura contained thirty-one children in very overcrowded conditions, all charged with being members of an armed force.[20] In contrast to the children in the camps, this group has no access to fresh air and exercise, receives little food and has to sell part of their food ration in order to buy the fuel to cook their own meals. Bearing in mind that many of these gave themselves up to the government forces after having escaped from the FNL their subsequent treatment would seem harsh. However, as with other countries using child soldiers, the influence of personal economic factors are reflected in the children's attitudes to their incarceration. In interviews carried out by the Human Rights Watch, the children stated that they would be prepared to stay in prison longer if it meant that on their release they would gain some financial support. Few wanted to be released if it meant giving up the possibility of a demobilisation package.[21] In order for the situation to be resolved the Burundi government needs to take the initiative and treat all ex-combat children, including those linked with the FNL, in a fair and consistent way. This should not only include economic, medical and educational aid, but assistance in reintegration into their communities. In addition, the government should halt the use of children as informants and guides because the present practise is contravening the Worst Forms of Child Labour Convention No. 182, which Burundi ratified in 2002.

Some countries are now taking seriously the issue of child soldiers and their responsibility towards them. Largely in response to the US State Department's report on Human Rights Practises, published in March 2006, which discussed 'the nature and extent of the compulsory recruitment and conscription of individuals under the age of eighteen by all armed groups in every country, and what steps have been taken by governments of the respective countries to eliminate such practices', the first ever Congressional hearing on 'Casualties of War: Child Soldiers and the Law' took place in the USA in April 2007. Senator Richard Durbin from Illinois recognised that: '... the law provides special protections to children, the most vulnerable members of our society, but during wars, they are often the most exploited'.[22] Senator Tom Coburn from Oklahoma commented that: '... the United States can begin by carefully evaluating the assistance it is providing to countries that use children as soldiers'.[23] He went on to say that the USA had supplied military assistance to fourteen countries where children, under the age of eighteen, had taken a direct part in hostilities or had been forced to support government-backed armed groups or non-state militias. Nine of these countries had recruited children as soldiers within their own forces. As a result of his concern, he was co-sponsoring The Child Soldiers Prevention Act 2007. If this becomes law the United States will determine which countries are exploiting children as child soldiers. Those that are identified as using children in this way within their own government forces will be eligible for US economic aid *only* to end the practise and modify their recruitment procedures accordingly. However, perhaps one loophole in the Act is the statement that: '... the Bill would not automatically cut off aid to countries that are identified by the State Department as using or tolerating child soldiers'. Instead, there would be a two-year transition period before this was implemented.

Some of the countries involved are heavily reliant on fiscal aid from the USA. Over the past eight years vast sums of money have been paid to states abusing Child Rights. For example, according to the 2006 report, the country of Chad, where it had been reported in October 2004 that the government was using child soldiers and pictures of children engaged in military activities were published in the press, received a total of $4.2 million for International Military Education and Training (IMET), $6.8 million for Foreign Military Financing (FMF), and $27.9 million for Foreign Military Sales (FMS). In Colombia, where it was reported that 20 per cent of the Revolutionary Armed Forces of Colombia were minors and that most guerrilla fighters had joined as children, 11,000 in all, the financial aid from the USA is staggering. It received $25.1 million for IMET, $680.2 million for FMF, $630 million for Direct Commercial Sales and $1.7 billion on FMS.[24] It would seem from these figures that this would be an obvious lever with which to bring some of the countries into line. (See Appendix 1.)

In addition, Senator Coburn suggested that the US immigration laws should be amended so that children who had participated in conflicts as child soldiers should not be debarred from entry to the country as refugees on that account alone. However, those who have been involved in the recruitment of child soldiers should not be able to seek refuge with impunity and should be held accountable for their crimes.[25]

Since the 1980s, the use of child soldiers has gone from simply a moral dilemma, which many in the developed world found reprehensible, to being a criminal violation of international law. Those countries that signed and implemented the Optional Protocol to the Convention of the Rights of the Child demonstrated their commitment to outlawing the use of child soldiers and supporting their reintegration into society. The continued use of children in this way has posed a threat to the security and stability of those communities directly involved and those allied to them. However, the situation is now changing. Within all the gloom surrounding child soldiers there is hope. On 20 June 2007, a special court in Sierra Leone, established in 2002 to 'prosecute those who bear the greatest responsibility for war crimes against humanity and other serious violations of international humanitarian law', convicted three members of the Armed Forces Revolutionary Council (AFRC) for crimes against humanity and the recruitment and use of child soldiers. Thousands of children had been used by all combatant groups during the conflict in the country. These included the Revolutionary United Front, the AFRC and the pro-government Civil Defence Forces. (Other prosecutions are in the pipeline including commanders of the Lord's Resistance Army in Uganda and the Democratic Republic of Congo.)[26] This landmark case has been seen by the Human Rights Watch as important in ending impunity for military commanders and personnel who use children in conflict zones across the world.

How is War Depicted in Children's Picture Books, Novels and Textbooks?

It is hard to say just what effect the books we read in childhood have on our later life, but we all know they do have an effect – in images that will not be erased, in people as real as those we know, in conversations heard as echoes.[1]

The global nature of war gains a deeper dimension when young people are able to read not only stories from their own national background, but also those created for children of another country, reflecting that nation's perspective on the conflict.[2]

One of the problems of tackling the topic of 'Children in Conflict' is that over the years children themselves have had little exposure to it, in or out of the classroom. It is not a subject on the school curriculum and at present only one university in Britain teaches it as a self-contained module.[3] There has always been debate about which subjects are appropriate for children's books. For example, in the past, war was not considered a suitable topic in books for the very young and when war was dealt with in literature aimed at older children it was primarily used as an historical topic rather than as one of current concern.

Unless they have been directly caught up in, or had tangential experience of a war zone, they only learn about it from books and other media. Consequently, their exposure very much depends on the accuracy of the historical content in the book(s) and the writer's willingness to explore and depict the true nature of warfare. It is only in very recent times that authors dealing with children's books, in whatever format, pictorial, novel, poetry, non-fiction, have dealt with the reality of war and terrorism with all its attendant emotional and psychological trauma. But there are still areas where the historical knowledge is subsumed within the literature to the point that there is a possibility that it is 'lost' completely. One example is the study of War Poetry, where the notional portrayal of a soldier in the front-line, writing lines of poetry depicting the horror of the situation, is sometimes the only illustration of what life was like in the trenches that some children, studying English and not History, get of the First World War. To some extent, it could be argued that it at least gets the non-history student interested in the topic, but on the other hand, there is a tendency for it to get overplayed. To illustrate the point, there is a famous cartoon where a soldier about to 'go over the top' turns round to his friend and says, 'Do you know I shouldn't really be here because I've not written a poem in my life!' Without the history contextualising the poetry and the poet, the poem is only a work of literature in its own right. It needs to be supported by the history if children are to get some idea of the real conditions.

Books concerned with traumatic and often taboo war experiences such as death, disease and violence, are now more common despite the reservations on the part of some adults who wish to see the 'innocence' of childhood preserved.

During the First World War, children's stories tended to celebrate bravery and patriotism. These were often published in comics such as *The Dreadnought, The Boys'/Girls' Own Paper* or Christmas albums such as *Brave Boys and Girls In Wartime* (1918). The tone was strongly anti-German and often jingoistic.

Between 1939 and 1945, literary heroes in books and in the children's comics of the day were given story lines and characterisations which enabled them to 'do their bit' and defeat either 'the Hun', 'the Nazi' or 'the Jap'. Recent studies have provided a variety of examples in children's literature, including comics and book series, to suggest that during the Second World War, literature for children was primarily used as a form of war-effort propaganda, to stimulate recruitment and convey a nation united in bravery and patriotism in the bleak times of war. Captain W.E. Johns,[4] the author of the already popular 'Biggles'[5] books was even asked by the Air Ministry to create two more characters to promote recruitment, hence the introduction of Captain Lorrington 'Gimlet' King as 'Gimlet King of the Commandos' who appeared in ten books, and Joan 'Worrals' Worralson, who, essentially a female 'Biggles', featured in eleven books in order to aid enrolment into the Women's Auxiliary Air Force.

Between 1945 and 1970, novels concentrated more on looking ahead than behind. Children's literature in the victorious Allied countries was not so much concerned with war or its aftermath but more about escapism, and 'Comics', especially those aimed at the male market, were in abundance. These included the evocatively entitled 'The Victor',[6] which was a story paper in comic book format. Each week the front cover story was related to how a particular individual in the British or Commonwealth forces had won a medal during the First World War and the Second World War, such as Albert Mackenzie VC on the Zeebrugge Raid in 1918 and Merritt VC at Dieppe in 1942. Regular characters included a pilot, 'Braddock VC', and 'Sniper Dennison'. Other stories focused on some characters that were considered cowards until they carried out some heroic deed in the war.

The other famous publication, which is still available, now as *Commando For Action and Adventure*, was *Commando War Stories in Pictures*, simply known as *Commando Comics*. Again, the themes for all the self-contained stories were stereotypical deeds in wartime such as heroism, cowardice, patriotism, dying for one's country, friendship, and enmity etc. With very few exceptions, they were, and remain, somewhat dated; glorifying the wartime actions of allied soldiers while at the same time depicting the enemy as cruel, stupid, barbaric and ignorant. It first came out in July 1961 as a fortnightly publication and surprisingly, despite its black and white cartoon strip format, remained more popular than the weekly comics. As these comics were widely available and were cheap, it could be argued that at the time that they were popular comics had a far wider impact in shaping children's responses to war than recognised quality fiction chosen by parents, librarians or teachers.

Between 1970 and 2000, faced with radical changes in child readership, publishers tended to shift their titles towards the 'realistic' novel. Instead of always portraying the central character as a hero serving in the front line or in a war zone, some novels now depicted conflict in the context of the civilian experience, those not actually fighting in the war, through the interpretation of a 'child' as a central character, many of whom were deprived of parental security in some way. In their treatment of later wars, authors have been more concerned with the suffering of the civilians, both adults and children in war, rather than the combat itself. There has been a greater emphasis on current conflicts, the waste and suffering of war, explicit anti-war and pacifist attitudes and, significantly, more satire against the folly of war. There has been a clear moral certainty and conviction within the texts. At the same time, the comics continue to provide the actual fighting of the war on the battlefields.

Another area that has gained in popularity is the picture book, and not only for younger readers. Toshi Maruki's *Hiroshima No Pika* (1980), depicting the dropping of the first atomic bomb, and Ian McEwan and Roberto Innocenti's *Rose Blanche* (1985), which explores a Gentile girl's experiences of the Holocaust in Germany, deal with subjects that would have been unthinkable only a few years before. Then, the promotion of the suffering of individuals in these publications would have not been considered by those in authority to be in the best interests of the potential readership, and therefore were not thought to be worthy of publication. To some extent this was almost the fate of *Rose Blanche* when, due to its controversial nature, it was deemed inappropriate and banned from publication in some states in the USA simply because it showed the Russian army rather than the American forces liberating the fictional German town. (The same thing happened to *The Silver Sword* (1956) by Ian Serraillier, when the main characters of the book, four refugee children searching for their parents in post-war Europe, were befriended by a Russian soldier.) Visual images are a powerful way of conveying information and in recent years some of the most memorable of them, both static and moving, have been of ordinary children and adults caught up in the terrible crossfire of war. There are numerous examples, from Vietnam, the killing fields of Cambodia, the plight of the starving children in Biafra, to the present conflicts in Palestine and Iraq. In many ways, pictures show things no words can ever convey. In addition, they not only capture our attention, but in many cases demand an emotional response of some kind, be it anger, remorse, sadness or frustration.

Some picture books, such as *The Conquerors* (2004) by David McKee, are allegorical and can be seen on a number of levels. What on the surface looks to be a very simple book on 'conquering and assimilation' of a population because the conquerors have 'the Cannon', is in fact much more than that. Often referred to as the 'Master of the modern fable', David McKee deplores the fact that picture books are automatically labelled as young children's books and he likes to aim his work at adults and children at the same time. In the book his pictures stress the uniformity of the Conquerors in contrast to the individuality of the 'small country' and its rural people. The aggressive reds and blues of the army contrast with the pastel shades of the occupied land. Having overrun the country, the Conquerors 'go native' by joining in with the culture of the 'conquered': even their facial expressions change. The furious General replaces this now ragged army of newly individualised soldiers with a fresh batch of regimented ones. Eventually, even the occupying forces the General leaves behind abandon their uniforms and become literally like the natives. Though the Conquerors celebrate victory, there is an insidious invasion of the culture of the 'conquered' little country. Even the General is affected by it, and sings bedtime songs of the little country to his son. The endpapers suggest peace has broken through like the sun after the smoke of war: furious cross-hatchings are replaced by calm horizontal lines. On first viewing this looks as though it is a book about any war in history for young children, whereas in fact it was published in 2004 as McKee's reaction to the Iraq war and was written for both an adult and child readership. The rights were sold to fifteen countries but rejected by eighteen publishers in the USA.

In some respects, the picture book aimed specifically for children has been well ahead of the 'adult' novel when it comes to looking at very up-to-date acts of terrorism, especially '9/11'. Some authors included the post-9/11 environment and government propaganda in fictional terrorist events and narrative picture books. One good example of the latter is *Lucy and the Liberty Quilt* (2001) by Victoria London, which tells the story of a twelve-year-old girl in New York. It became the first book on the topic of 9/11 to be published as part of American history.[7] Another is *The Day Our World Changed: Children's Art of 9/11*,[8] which incorporates eighty-three paintings, drawings and works of collage in the days and months immediately following the tragedy. It tells the story of 9/11 through the eyes of the actual children affected. However, the drawings do more than document the physical and emotional suffering; they also present images of rebuilding and renewal, enabling the children and adults to move on from such catastrophic events. Art Spiegelman, the Pulitzer Prize-winning graphic artist and author of the famous books *Maus I* and *Maus II* dealing with the Holocaust, wrote the 'comic' book *In the Shadow of No Towers* (2004). It relates to his own experiences and, according to Spiegelman, was written to 'reclaim himself' from the post-traumatic stress disorder he suffered after the attacks.

A recurrent theme in children's 'conflict' literature has been the powerlessness of children in wartime and their seeming inability, initially at least, to influence adult decisions. The image of the evacuee arriving defenceless at a strange place is one that is repeated time and time again in children's fiction, and although this would have been true in the majority of cases, it wasn't the same for all. Probably the best novel dealing with British evacuation is *Goodnight Mister Tom* (1981). Written by Michelle Magorian, it tells the story of William Beech, a very quiet, artistic although illiterate, eight-year-old evacuee from London who is taken in by a recluse called Mr Tom (Oakley). William is a bed-wetter, and gradually the full extent of his problems is revealed. He has scars on his back and he has a constant dread of 'going to hell'. Mr Tom realises that he has come from a very abusive background and after a series of incidents, he is determined to give him a better home. After William's mother commits suicide, Mr Tom adopts him. Michelle Magorian tackled the topic of evacuation again in 1984, in *Back Home* the story of twelve-year-old 'Rusty' (real name Virginia) who, after five years as an evacuee in the USA, returns to England in 1945 and is shocked to find war-damaged cities, rationing, austerity and general drabness. She finds it hard to get on with her mother and is sent off to boarding school, where again she finds it difficult to fit in.

Although *Goodnight Mister Tom* is one of the few evacuee books that delve into the psychological aspect of evacuation, it still falls into the 'trap' of only depicting children who are happy in their billets. Few, if any, deal with the abusive host and the problems inherent in living with perfect strangers, often in an alien environment. By taking this line, it is to some extent perpetuating the stereotypical myth of the 'unhappy' working-class evacuee in a 'happy' billet being looked after by caring hosts ... exactly the message that the propaganda of 1940–44 was promulgating. (Hence there are very few official pictures of children and parents crying or showing any evidence of adverse emotion. Evacuees had to 'enjoy' the experience!)

Only a small proportion of quality prose fiction for children has involved its readers in the combat zones of war. Nonetheless, among them are some excellent examples covering not only wars, but acts of terrorism, religious fundamentalism and civil conflict. *The Machine Gunners* was the first book to establish new standards of realism within children's literature. Written by Robert Westall in 1975, it is the story of Chas McGill who, together with his friend Boddser Brown, is always on the lookout for war 'booty'. When a German bomber crashes nearby, they take its machine gun and store it in their underground 'fortress'. Their plan is to use it to defend their families in case of invasion. Stephanie Tolan's *Flight of the Raven* (2001) delivers a serious message about two young people who come together in the face of terrorist violence in the United States. In addition, the complex psychological thriller *After the First Death*, by Robert Cormier (1979) raises the particularly relevant moral issue of self-sacrifice. The novel tells the story of how a bus carrying young school children is kidnapped by hijackers, and looks at it through the eyes of the terrorists and children involved. In *The Terrorist* (1997), Caroline Cooney tells the story of Laura Williams whose life changes dramatically when Billy, her eleven-year-old brother, is killed by a terrorist package bomb on the London Underground. Notice the similarity to the events in London 2005, eight years after this book was first published. It deals with the issues of multiculturalism, learning to accept and understand cultures other than the readers' own; coping with the death of a loved one as well as the act of terrorism itself.

Others include, *Kiss the Dust* by Elizabeth Laird. Based on the true experiences of many Kurdish refugees who had to face such privations at the time, it is the story of Tara, a twelve-year-old Kurdish girl, who has to flee to Iran because of her father's involvement with the Kurdish resistance movement. They were forced to live in a refugee camp to escape torture. Also by the same author, *A Little Piece of Ground* depicts the fate of twelve-year-old Palestinian boy Karim and his family, living under Israeli military occupation. Other fiction novels depicting relations and conflict in the Middle East include Daniella Carmi's *Samir and Yonatan* (2000), when a young Arab boy from the West Bank becomes friends with a Jewish boy. And, Lynne Reid Banks' *Broken Bridge* (1996), which deals with the complex passions of present-day Israel through the younger generation as they join the struggle against the consequences of decades of war. Beverley Naidoo's *The Other Side of Truth* deals with the consequences of being brought up in a family where the parents are critical of the regime under which the family lives. Sade and Femi, offspring of an outspoken journalist in Lagos, see their mother murdered and have to flee to London.

Terrorism is now widely accepted as a legitimate subject in children's non-fiction books and used prominently in books as academic tools. The text *Political Violence and Terrorism*, edited by Mary Hull, provides a worldwide perspective on the problem of terrorism. Anne Gaines' *Terrorism* (1998) focuses on the Middle East and provides children with some insight into how the United States is affected by its involvement. *Caught in the Crossfire* (1995) by Maria Ousseimi incorporates both text and pictures of children around the world whose lives have been affected by civil war, terrorism and violence. Kathlyn Gay's non-fiction book *Silent Death* (2001), aimed specifically at young adults, provides an in-depth explanation of the ease of manufacture and distribution of lethal chemical and biological weapons and the terrorist organisations that have access to them. Laurel Holliday's non-fiction book *Why Do They Hate Me* (1999) features a collection of true stories in which young people involved in conflicts from the Second World War and the Holocaust to Northern Ireland share their innermost secrets of growing up, in stories that started out as simply as secret journal entries.

Writers of fiction and non-fiction books have seemingly felt the need to set the record straight for younger readers, although this has not been apparent in school textbooks, where many of the topics, including evacuation, have been dealt with on only a double-page spread, most of which is usually taken up by pictures and questions. If one examines the textbooks in many schools, they are full of value-laden misconceptions and inaccuracies. If one looks specifically at the question of war children, the greatest omission is that there is no mention of what is going on in the world today regarding children in present conflict areas, or serving as child soldiers. In British textbooks, the main emphasis is still on the Second World War and civilian evacuation where again, there is no mention of war children in other areas of war-torn Europe. Yet, even here there are serious gaps in both knowledge and understanding. Little or no mention is ever made of children going overseas. There is an assumption that all, or the vast majority, of evacuees came from poor areas and suffered from various physical and social disorders. The social problems inherent in the scheme are always dealt with as black and white with very few 'grey' areas. There is no mention of psychological or social trauma suffered by those who took part which, in some cases, extends to the present day. The information made available is often very heavily influenced by unsubstantiated oral testimonies of people now in their late sixties and early seventies who were as young as five at the time of the experience. With regard to using oral testimony as documentary evidence and questioning their content in specific related tasks, no mention is made in any of the texts about the selectivity of memory. Little credence is given to the notion that the evacuation scheme was less than successful. Nothing is said about the return of the evacuees to their homes at the end of the war, the effects it had on their own and their host families, about the aftermath and what happened to evacuees remaining in the reception areas after the war had ended, or about the positive contribution the evacuation scheme had on post-war child care.

One of the major problems is that many textbooks, even those aimed at examination classes, deal with the topic in just a few lines of text. Therefore it is easy to see how these misconceptions and inaccuracies can be passed on. In some cases they occur simply because of the editorial need to be short and precise, thereby not allowing full development of an argument or analysis of available documentary evidence. Instead, they provide a series of non-substantiated, non-supported statements and/or facts, some of which are totally inaccurate. The following extract is taken from a book used today in some year nine and GCSE History classes:[9]

> In September 1939, children were evacuated (sent away) from cities that were likely to be bombed and went to live with families in the country-side. Although the government planned to move 3.5 million children only 1.5 million left home. Many of the evacuated children came from poor backgrounds. This could be exiting or difficult for both the children and their foster parents.

The whole of the evacuation scheme encapsulated in sixty-two words! One should not criticise the authors because they have been given a brief to work to, but in doing so they have left many questions unanswered and created mis-understanding. By allowing this to happen the text creates a much distorted image of what the scheme meant and the reasons for putting it into opera-tion. For example, it says nothing about the 'cities likely to be bombed'. Where were they? Why were they considered unsafe? Why would they be considered a target? '1.5 million children left home' is almost correct, in fact 1,350,629 were evacuated, but it does not say that 826,959 were unaccompanied and the rest went with their mothers. 'Many evacuees came from poor backgrounds' … what is meant by poor? Are the criteria used for this assumption based on finance, class, life experience or something else? There is no mention of mid-dle- and upper-class children who were moved out of target areas, often as complete schools. Some boarding establishments were 'imposed' on schools of a similar type. In *Children in War* (1989), Ruth Inglis devotes a complete chapter to middle-class evacuation, often to working-class homes, but information on this topic does not appear in the majority of textbooks. Also, what about those children who went overseas, either privately, or under the CORB scheme?

To see what the overall learning experience can be for the pupil, it is worth examining the tasks set for this topic. The questions asked in the task section, relate to three sources:

Source 1. 'Before and During Evacuation' shows two black and white photographs. The first could have been taken anywhere but states, 'Arriving at Gravesend for evacuation. Note the name tags and gas masks in boxes.' The second, with the caption 'Evacuees working on a farm', shows a group of boys digging up potatoes.

Source 2 is an account by a twelve-year-old girl and based on oral testimony:

> It was only 10 miles from Manchester but to us it was the country and a big adventure. Buses took us to the church hall. There we were looked over by village people waiting to pick us out. Along with another girl, I was chosen by an older couple who took us to their home in a car. A car was something only 'well off' people had, so it was very exciting. They lived in a lovely large home with a garden front and back. The maid looked after us. I only remember once eating in the dining room with the family and I was never invited into the lounge. We had to be in early and used to look out at our friends still having fun on the swings. Parents just came up for the day.

Source 3 was written by a thirteen-year-old boy from Stepney:

> Everything was so clean in the room. We were given flannels and toothbrushes. We'd never cleaned our teeth until then. And hot water came from the tap. And there was a lavatory upstairs. And carpets. And something called an eiderdown. This was very odd and rather scary.

The questions related to these sources are simplistic in the extreme and, bearing in mind they are aimed at fourteen- and fifteen-year-old pupils, they do not allow them to either develop their understanding of the topic, or question the authenticity and relevance of the sources themselves.

> Look at Sources 1, 2 and 3.
> What do the pictures in Source 1 tell us about evacuation?
> Suppose you were an evacuee. Write a letter to your parents explaining what happened to you during the 'Phoney War'.
> Design a government poster encouraging parents to evacuate their children.

Frankly, the simple answer to (a) would be *nothing* except that the children wore labels, carried suitcases and gas masks and worked on farms digging potatoes. This question cannot be answered from just these sources. Sources 2 and 3 are not referred to at all, but even if they were they would provide a distorted, one-sided image of evacuation, perpetuating the stereotype that working-class children were taken in by middle- and upper-class hosts. Questions (b) and (c) provide no opportunity for the pupil to discuss any of the inherent social and administrative problems in any detail. One has to ask, have the pupils actually learnt anything about the British evacuation scheme by reading this text and doing the exercise?

There are some books that attempt to put over a balanced view of evacuation and allow the pupils to question the relevance of the sources. Although they still have their own inherent weaknesses, these better examples include *The Home Front* by J.F. Aylett and *The Era of the Second World War* by N. Demarco.

It is interesting to note that the quote in Source 3 is used in more than one book and on at least one television programme. The author's experiences are no different than those of many other evacuees, but his comments have been used because he had written a book on his life as an evacuee. However, it was published in 1963 and a great deal of new material is now available for textbook compilers to use.[10] Although his experience as he saw it has not become outdated, his comments should now be viewed in the same way as any other oral history, not independently, but as another source that requires support and verification before being quoted as a correct version of the events that took place. This should either have been pointed out to the readers, or they should have been given the opportunity in the tasks to question its relevance.

Another important issue is that of interpretation. Some of the staff teaching the topic of evacuation, especially at Key Stage 2 where the topic is on the National Curriculum, are not specialist historians and as such are reliant on the textbooks and some of the novels previously mentioned, to provide the information and the 'empathetic' experience for the children in their classes. Many of these teachers do not have the time to carry out further investigative research, or simply find a counter argument, so what they read and pass on to their pupils could easily be taken as a true representation of the facts. The same also applies to 'labels' and 'explanations' in museums and 'experiences' that have not necessarily been written by historians. In some cases where little background research has been done and the 'experience' has been established as an economic venture, what is often provided is a very basic empathetic exercise in which pupils are invited to see what it would have been like to have sat in an air-raid shelter during a raid, then walk down a bombed street to witness the aftermath. Although as a visual and often 'olfactory' experience, this can create some sort of response from pupils, it falls short of actually providing them with any hint of what actually happened because they cannot physically, or psychologically, sense the fear, trepidation, loneliness, heart-searching, bullying, even the independence, that would have been felt by their contemporaries at the time. This is an important factor that one has to consider when dealing with the question of war children in the classroom where it is felt, quite subjectively and wrongly, that the pupils of the same age today can relate to the children of a similar age who experienced evacuation during wartime. They cannot, simply because pupils in today's classrooms are viewing the events from the standpoint of children in the twenty-first century. In the main, their views and opinions can only be biased and few teachers, especially non-historians, have the skills and the resources to deal with the topic objectively. They often have to rely on unsubstantiated empathy exercises to provide children with an unrelated experience. At best, they are only able to scratch the surface, and where the topic is covered as a 'project' or 'topic' the pupils resort to the same books and information providing them with stereotypical views of the events. In addition, as it is usually dealt with on a national rather than a local level, the pupils are not given access to the material pertaining to those areas that had specific needs, requirements and indeed idiosyncrasies. For example, what about those children who were evacuated to isolated hill farms, or went to Welsh-speaking areas of Wales?

Just as important is the fact that present-day pupils are still not being exposed to the sufferings of other war children either during the Second World War, alongside their evacuation studies, or since. Many children, and indeed adults, are surprised to learn that other countries had evacuation schemes as well, and that the trauma suffered by some British evacuees is apparent in their Finnish and German counterparts.

This experience of misinformation is not limited to Britain. In 1965, Saburo Ienago, a Professor of Education in Japan, sued the Japanese government for censoring history textbooks, including those he had written himself. This was to be a long-drawn out sequence of events. Up until this point he had taught what he had been told to teach i.e. Imperial Myths and Divine Right. From 1945 until the end of the American occupation in 1952, there had been a censorship of memory in Japan, and only two events relating to the Second World War, the dropping of the Atomic Bombs on Hiroshima and Nagasaki had been taught in schools. Nothing was said about the Nanking Massacre, the enslaved 'comfort women' in Korea and the Philippines, or the infamous Unit 731 where Japanese medical experiments had been carried out.[11] In 1982, Ienago managed to force a change in textbook descriptions of the Japanese wartime role in Asia when the words 'military advance' were replaced by the single word 'aggression'. In 1993, a court agreed that the Ministry of Education had acted illegally in 'screening' Ienago's passages on the Nanking massacre, a ruling that allowed the subject to be taught in schools. In addition, in 1997 the Supreme Court judged that the Japanese government had again acted illegally in removing a description of Unit 731 from Ienago's texts. Although this had taken thirty-two years and the Supreme Court had ruled against these particular examples, perversely it still condoned the government's right to continue to censor school history books. According to Professor Fujioka, '… our text books have become a tool of international politics, a card sometimes played in the domestic politics of other countries or for foreign governments to secure money from Japan … In international politics once you apologise it merely confirms in peoples' minds that you indeed are that bad'.[12]

According to Marinak (1993), the best way of delivering history to children is via the novel, not the history text:

> … there is a danger that wars will fade into their designated pages in a history book. Students will memorize the events, not feel the struggle. The only way to combat such potential complacency is to turn students into readers … that means abandoning the history textbooks and embracing the work of children's authors and illustrators.

As an historian I do not necessarily agree with this statement but would suggest that textbooks are brought up to date and made more relevant to the needs of the present-day child. To some extent Marinak is correct in that many of the subjects covered in children's literature do not seem to have permeated to the history textbooks, despite the latter being the source of so-called 'proper' evidence. To a certain degree, this is the result of the 'thirty-year rule', an 'understanding' that prohibits in–depth study of historical topics within the past thirty years. As novels are not restricted by this, authors of children's literature can not only deal with up-to-date issues but they are not usually subject to publishing control. There is a tendency now for such authors to deal with the topic of war, conflict and terrorism in a more direct way. They are no longer hampered by the censorship, propaganda, jingoism and militaristic evangelism of their predecessors.

What has been noticeable over the past few years is a direct convergence of child and adult topics within the literature. Subject matter that was once considered to be unsuitable for the young, such as the Holocaust, vivid descriptions of war zones, death and destruction and so on, have become the norm, not only within the modern novel, but also in films and computer games. Access to the internet enables children to view graphic examples of political violence such as suicide bombing, kidnapping and assassination. Children are subjected to images of war and acts of terrorism on the television news, so they no longer have to rely on their own imagination when reading novels, instead, they can now relate the text to the visual images they have witnessed in their front room.

According to Faye Lawson:

> ... Whether cloaked in subliminal messages in popular narrative or presented in graphic factual description, the issues are there through the various stages of childhood. Recent children's literature is beginning to show that the war child experience is changing on a new level. Boundaries are virtually limitless; the unthinkable has become the norm in how issues are presented to children. Ultimately the differential between the adult and child perception of the war experience has perhaps become inevitably and irretrievably fused. [13]

13

The Long-Term Effects

Ashes and Shifting sands have covered the footprints of war … (However) despite the progress of time, and against a tide of forgetting, childhood war trauma, which had been buried for decades, suddenly surfaced, entering the light of consciousness with an immediacy as if these traumas had occurred only yesterday.[1]

Across Europe, the physical traces of the Second World War have been erased. The bombed buildings have been rebuilt, air-raid shelters have been removed, artefacts only remain as personal belongings, in private collections, museums, 'experiences' and where buildings and institutions, such as Auschwitz/Birkenhau have been left as a reminder of man's inhumanity to man. However, what can never be expunged are the memory and the long-term effects that these experiences have had on the children into adult life. There is a tendency to recall what happened to the child *within* the war, but what one now has to do is observe what happened to the child *after* the conflict was over. Too often a line is drawn underneath the 'end of a war', be it a truce, a peace treaty or just a cessation of hostilities. Unfortunately, the effects of the war can be apparent for months and years afterwards and usually it is the mothers, children and elderly who suffer most. For some, just trying to create a semblance of post-war normality was fraught with trials and tribulations:

We are vegetating in a ghost town, without electricity or gas, without water; we are forced to think personal hygiene as a luxury and our hot meals as abstract concepts. We are living like ghosts in a vast field of ruins, where the few remaining buses and trams cart us circumspectly around the animals for the slaughter, where the schools have no pupils, the shops have no goods, the theatres no actors and the churches no congregations … and where the few hospitals still standing are without water, electricity, medicines and doctors … If we want to fetch water, we have to go to the fountains or pumps, where terrified queues form, presenting far too easy a target for the enemy. Often the queues are mown down by shells or mortar-fire, or by lightning artillery attacks.[2]

Nothing works any more: there are no postmen, no milkmen, not a single doctor to be found, and the emergency services, which had until recently been clearing the streets of corpses, have stopped answering the phone. A city once organised and functioning has abandoned its citizens to their own devices: there are no rights any more, and no duties either.[3]

Having studied the long-term effects of the persecution of Jewish child survivors who had been separated from their parents and spent much of their lives in hiding, the Dutch psychologist Dr Hans Keilson introduced a term called 'sequential traumatisation', whereby in a situation where a child has been subjected to more than one traumatic event, the latter one confirms the former and thereby increases the impact. Where the child received support from parents, siblings and others, the trauma was lessened, but where no such support was available, the later traumatic experiences became more intense. Although this research was based on the Jewish child study, the results can be seen just as strongly within other war child groups, certainly those, like the children of Dutch collaborators, who spent some time in internment camps. Of course, 'hiding' can also be a relative term. It does not have to mean 'physical' seclusion, but also 'hiding' in terms of an emotional response. Many collaborators' children remained 'in hiding' trying to keep their family's past a secret.

The same effect is apparent in Germany where children have not only had to live 'with a past', but in some cases they have had to contend with the 'sins of their fathers'. One son of a leading member of the Nazi party commented in an interview, 'I am something like a connecting link between the guilty and the guiltless, the son of the guilty and the father of the guiltless. I feel obliged to give the guiltless a chance. My generation is the generation of bad conscience.'[4]

In some instances it transcends more than one generation:'… while those who came of age during that time complain that when they were young they were told next to nothing about the Nazi era, today's youth complain that all they hear is that they were, and perhaps still are, a nation of murderers and accomplices'.[5]

Some of the later 'grandchildren' found the realisation of what had gone on in their parents and grandparents generations, difficult to accept:

> … of course I knew that there had been concentration camps and that 6 million Jews had been murdered. We'd been told about it in school. But I also learned about the Crusades and later, when I was older, about the French Revolution. And later still about World War Two and gas chambers. But who, for God's sake, had ever told us that our own parents had been there?[6]

Surprisingly perhaps, the psychological situation for the evacuees within Britain was not much better. When many of the children returned from the reception areas, sometimes after five years away, there was little or no support either for them as individuals, as a national group or for the families, both hosts and parents. As a result many were left to their own devices and had to deal with the situation as best they could. Many found themselves completely isolated within their communities and the family unit. In the situation where not all the siblings had been evacuated, those who had now had no common experience to share, and in some cases were even criticised for having escaped from the bombings. James Roffey recalls that his elder brother, who had not been evacuated, once said to him, '… when you came back from Sussex it was like having a stranger in the house, we didn't speak the same language and had little in common'.[7] For James himself, he felt as if he was an outsider looking on:'… The family seemed to talk about things and people that I knew nothing about and they took little interest when I tried to talk about Sussex'.[8]

There were no language problems as with the returning Finnish evacuees. Although some had gone to Welsh-speaking Wales, they had all had sufficient knowledge and basis of English to revert back to it and the vast majority had not had to deal with the issues of feeling guilty for their fathers like some of their German counterparts, but even so there were psychological and social problems. As these were very much dependent on the experience of the individual children, both in the billets and at home, these problems are unquantifiable. It is only possible to view them in general terms or to investigate vast numbers of specific case studies that, in isolation, would not necessarily have any bearing on the experience of a fellow evacuee. One only has to interview ex-evacuees in order to realise quickly that this is the case, and even those child psychologists researching into the effects of evacuation immediately post-war, disagreed and contradicted each other's findings. How can one equate the experiences of a child who had returned from an excellent billet to a poor home background, with a child who perhaps had been abused or ill treated in the reception area? What happened to those who returned to their parents and found it difficult to come to terms with the loss of their independence, especially those who had been overseas? There was also the problem of adolescent children in need of love and care, who reverted to childish behaviour in order seek attention from their parents and siblings. The experiences are vast and varied.

The fact that, while they had been away, their houses had been destroyed and they now found themselves living in temporary accommodation did not help the domestic situation. For some it was simply a lack of space, as the children had grown up during their time away. This was particularly true of those who had been evacuated overseas and had not seen their parents for six or more years. In addition, as the 'label' of evacuee was removed (officially in March 1946) they just became another 'ordinary' child and treated as such. There was no counselling, no account was taken of their lack of schooling, or possible difficulties within the home behind closed doors. In some cases there were serious problems within families, resulting in some instances in a complete breakdown of the family unit, especially where the children were returning from evacuation and the husband from the forces. The Ministry of Health had advised local authorities in the previously evacuated areas to instigate follow-up visits for the returning evacuees to ensure that any problems relating to the re-familiarisation with the family or neighbourhood could be overcome swiftly, although research would suggest that few evacuees knew that this was taking place. In my own extensive research with evacuees, involving many interviews, the general consensus was that little was done to ensure that their return home was dealt with smoothly. The majority were left to get on with their lives. Such was the pressure on some, that those who were near to leaving school took the opportunity to leave home and return to get jobs where they had previously lived as evacuees, in a few examples even living with their previous hosts – now as paying guests.

Some of those coming back from the USA and the Empire countries also found the return difficult to cope with. Again, little was done to help them.

Yet these children were often affected more in sociological and psychological terms than their peers who had been evacuated within the UK. One of
the reasons being that they had left the country for an unknown period of
time, to live in a culture that to some extent must have seemed alien to them,
and were returning to war-affected areas that now were equally as unfamil-
iar. Also, having been sent out of the country for their formative years, they
returned, some not until 1947, to find themselves having to renew relationships with parents and siblings they no longer knew. Barbara Shawcroft
found contact with her family so difficult, and life in 'austerity drab' Britain
so depressing, that within weeks of her repatriation from New England, she
decided to return to the USA and become an American citizen.[9]

Quotes from evacuees returning from Australia indicate the same emotional stress felt by Barbara, which in the following example was brought
about by non-recognition. Barbara Helical recalled how she stood on Leeds
station: 'There was a heavy mist swirling and everyone had gone. I'd passed
this couple three times. They didn't know it was their daughter, and I didn't
know it was my parents. I felt so lonely, as if I was the only person left in the
world ...'[10]

Two sisters, who had been forced to return to the UK against their will
by the courts, found family life in London very difficult. 'We resented having to come back to England and didn't like our parents, especially our
mother'.[11] They were forbidden to receive or send any communications
to their former hosts and were not allowed to have anything to do with
Canada. Totally disenchanted with being at home, they decided to return
to Canada as soon as they were old enough to do so, and when they were
older considered the years in between as a painful stage in their lives. One
sister commented: 'The evacuation scheme separated us from my mother
for the rest of her life. We could not discuss the subject with her. I believe
it was her greatest sorrow that she did separate from us for this long period
of time.'[12]

On the other hand there were children who wished to return from overseas, but were prevented from doing so because of family circumstances.
Michael Fethney recalls one poignant example where four sisters stayed in
Canada and although they enjoyed their lives there, one in particular still
finds the original experience difficult to cope with:

The experience led to the total fracture of our family. I have three sisters
whom I do not know. My father died alone in England without ever seeing

his four daughters evacuated to Canada. And I have never returned to the city of my birth. But some day I will! You ask how long was I homesick? The answer is: I still am![13]

However, it would be wrong to dwell entirely on negativity. To see the positive side of the British overseas evacuee plans, it is worth quoting a statement made by Michael Henderson in a recent journal article:

> ... There may be social scientists who regard the whole overseas evacuation as a big mistake. Many accounts tend to dwell on the trauma of separation and cite examples where it didn't work out well. All I can add, as would many others with whom I have been in touch, we would not have missed the experience for anything. It has enriched our lives and the links with the United States and Canada it opened up to us are a blessing. The final sentence of the report of the US Committee for the Care of European Children reads, 'In the long run, the 861 British children in the Committee's program turned into nearly that many emissaries of good will, who through the personal feelings they developed and provoked added solid substance to the friendliness of British-American relations.' The report described the evacuation as 'an applied lesson in international understanding.[14]

In Finland the situation was perhaps worse because 15,000 never returned to the country after the war was over and it was not until the mid-1950s that legal proceedings to get some of the remaining children home from Sweden were stopped. As in Britain, coming home for some of the children was problematic and they returned to families and siblings they did not know and speaking a language many of them no longer understood. As a result, unless the parents could speak Swedish, or in some cases Danish, basic communication within the family broke down. In addition, they were often bullied and ostracised in schools, in some cases even by the teachers.

Such has been the response to the long-term effects of this separation that in modern-day Finland the media has attempted to demonstrate the difficulties that their grandparents might have faced by showing dramatic reconstructions of the events on Finnish children's television. In addition there was also an award-winning feature film called *Mother of Mine*, which dealt with the problems of not only the evacuation, but also the effect it had on the mothers, particularly in this case the foster mother. Research by Pertti Kaven and others show that guilt was a common factor among the families, particularly the mothers who had sent their children away. They also felt jealous of the fact that in some instances the children were better looked after and enjoyed a higher standard of living than that in Finland. In addition, we have also noted that there were serious problems with some parents simply not wishing to have their children back for domestic reasons or because they were not wanted any more. A situation that must have been very hard and traumatic for those children involved. The sense of rejection was something they never forgot.

It is worth remembering however that the experience for some of the children was not an entirely negative one. Not only were they protected from the ravages of the Winter War and then the Continuation War, but on their return many of their parents allowed them to keep in touch with their foster families. Finland had lost a significant percentage of its young people, and thereby its next generation and as such the return of the children became a political 'hot potato' for the next decade with some political parties demanding immediate repatriation and others exercising caution.

For German children the end of the Second World War did not represent salvation or even liberation, for many it was seen as a catastrophe. They had been led to believe in a Thousand-Year Reich and they had grown up knowing of no other government than the controlling influence of the totalitarian Nazi state. In May 1945, this was in ruins and, for many, the hitherto consistent part of their life … the ideals of National Socialism were gone. Their world had collapsed around them, both physically and figuratively. They now found themselves in a country devastated by war and controlled by foreign powers. There were severe housing shortages and basic accommodation was lacking in many of the cities. Immediately after the war there were few vital services, the black market was rife and the economy was in ruins. Lack of essential foods and amenities meant that some were not equipped to survive the extreme winters of 1945/6 and 1946/7, and many died as a result.

Some authors, such as James Bacque, have attempted to show that the fate of the post-war Germans was not helped by allied intransigence and neglect. He quotes more than 1 million being starved and abandoned, statements which have been refuted by John S. Conway, of the University of British Columbia, who claims that Bacque's figures are based on records of perhaps questionable authenticity, mainly from the KGB archive in Moscow. In *Crimes and Mercies; The fate of German civilians under Allied Occupation 1944–1950,*[15] Bacque declares that 9.3 million German civilians died needlessly and asserts that the silence about their fate amounts to a vast international falsification maintained for fifty years. 'Sometimes the Allies have lied in co-operation with the Soviets, sometimes they have lied to foment hatred against them, sometimes they have lied to cover up their own crimes. They are still at it'.[16]

He claims that the suffering resulted from the allies somewhat vindictive policy of dismantling the industrial infrastructure, which he says was a conspiracy on the part of those people who instigated the policy of unconditional surrender. He states that although only 30 per cent of industrial plant in the Ruhr was destroyed, the post-war production was kept to only 25–30 per cent of pre-war levels. However, along with everything else going on in post-war Europe, one has to place Bacque's comments against the complex nature of the political agenda of the time. It is known that some of the policies implemented within the occupied zones were draconian and inhumane, but this was at a time when few Germans were demonstrating any remorse for the Nazi policies. Although this may not be seen today as an excuse for the allied reaction, such a response does need to be seen within the historical context.

Whether one agrees with Bacque, or indeed Conway, it is true that German children were starving. Immediately after the war finished, the allies had either confiscated, or had refused permission to unload, numerous consignments of food sent by pacifist religious organisations. This was eased in January 1946, when the ban on private help was less rigidly enforced and the Allies set up 'CARE' (Cooperative for American Remittances to Europe), which covered twenty-two American charities supplying aid, to be followed in February by CRALOG (Council of Relief Agencies Licensed for Operation in Germany), which supervised a further sixteen. According to Bacque it was the likes of Herbert Hoover and Victor Gollancz who pressurised the governments to relax the ban on private aid to the German population, thus easing the plight of the civilians. Yet, despite these initiatives, no aid was sent by these organisations until October 1946. In 1945–46, in the British and American zones of occupation, the number of calories per adult, per day was 900 and in 1947 the situation was still so serious that appeals were published in Canadian newspapers on behalf of the Canadian Lutheran World Relief, entitled 'At Christmas remember the starving children in the British Zone of Germany'.[17]

For the children who had been members of the Hitler Youth, life was even harder. They found it difficult to get jobs and few managed to obtain gainful employment. As it had been virtually compulsory to be members of the organisation, this situation affected more than 90 per cent of the juvenile population. Most of the young people claimed to be victims of the system, they had known nothing else. The comradeship that was very much part of the Hitler Youth ideal was, by its very nature, dehumanising. It destroyed the need to be an individual. Within the organisation, from waking to sleeping, food, shelter and clothes were provided, routines were enforced and dictated by the State, while at the same time the daily rigours of existence and personal worries were removed. As a result, the camaraderie within the Hitler Youth was a source of 'decivilisation' which, for some, made it all the more difficult to cope with life 'outside'.

However, after a while, re-socialisation was gradually introduced, first of all in the Allied internment camps and then outside, where youth clubs and social clubs were initiated not only for leisure activities but also for democratisation purposes. This was not accepted by everybody as some of the young people had been totally immersed in National Socialism and therefore found it difficult to accept any other doctrine. Also, some of the teaching and instructional methods on the part of the occupying forces were less than subtle, resulting in abject rejection by many. However, there were some classes such as farming, horticulture, commerce and trades aimed specifically at getting people back into worthwhile pursuits. In August 1946, there was a political amnesty in the American and British sectors, but again this was not accepted fully by the die-hard members of the Hitler Youth. Having grown up in a one-party system they had to be taught the merits of multi-party politics. At the Nuremburg Trial in 1946, Baldur von Shirach stressed:

> It is my fault to have educated the youth in the service of a man who was a murderer of millions. I believed in this man. This is all I can say in my defence, or to explain my actions. I bore the responsibility for youth. I held it in my charge, and hence I alone bear the guilt for these juveniles. The young generation is guiltless.[18]

Yet, despite von Shirach's plea, according to Kater, the Hitler Youth had to be answerable on its own behalf. In only being marginally complicit in what happened in the broader spectrum of war, they nonetheless had become part of the system and as such helped guarantee its functionality.[19] The question of moral guilt is much more difficult to define and depended very much on the position within the organisation and their related functions.

Ulla Roberts, herself a German refugee expelled from Czechoslovakia in June 1945, has been researching the effects of war and memory. She agrees that the suffering of the children must be seen within the context of the pain caused by the Nazi regime in occupied Europe.[20]

Unlike the German children, the British and the Finns were not caught up in the maelstrom of humanity wandering around Europe at the end of the war, desperately trying to find a refuge or a semblance of a home. The figures fluctuate between 12 and 13 million, of whom only 9 million survived. One can only imagine what it must have been like for the hundreds of thousands of children caught up in this exodus and what effect these memories had on their later lives. It is difficult to empathise with those children, including Gonda, who at the end of their journey found themselves in internment camps where there was little in the way of comfort and where the overriding concern was daily survival. Peter Heinl makes a very poignant comment when recalling a child's experience in a Danish camp: '… she and her family were forced to spend several years in the camp where there was neither warmth nor lightheartedness. Even a teddy bear,[21] which might have given her some comfort and company, was unobtainable behind the fence …'[22] (This was almost seventy years ago but the description could equally apply to similar scenes being replicated in the world today.)

It is easy to forget that as well as the Hitler Youth who had been sent to 'colonise' eastern areas, there were thousands of children living within the Greater Reich with their parents, who in 1945 were expelled and forced to return to Germany, some in cattle trucks, some forced to walk, and some in front of the advancing Russians. One of Ulla Roberts' interviewees remembers at the age of four crossing the river Weichsel in Poland:

> The panic stricken face of my mother as we fled across the frozen river. Would the ice hold us? The expression in her eyes warned me 'be quiet, don't speak'. I was struck dumb with fear. I felt completely helpless and unprotected. When I look back I can relate the expression of fear on my mother's face with my own problem of looking somebody in the eyes when I talk to them today.[23]

One woman recalled fleeing from East Prussia at the age of five. By this time she had already been raped, seen her grandfather shot and in the chaotic scenes of escaping she and her younger brother had been separated from their sister. They were now on their own. She relates that:

… during a train journey her brother died in the icy cold. His stiff frozen corpse was thrown out of the train window as they crossed a bridge over a river. There was no grave, no prayer, and no memory as to where this happened'. But the memory of what happened lived with her for the rest of her life.[24]

Although there may be a temptation to think that almost seventy years should have provided a sufficient time to mourn such loss, evidence would suggest that in some cases the mourning has not yet even started.[25]

Many children in such circumstances, and not only in Germany, were conditioned to repress their fears in order to cope with everyday living. In so doing, some entered adolescence and adulthood believing that there was neither a place to call home, nor a relationship they could consider secure:

> I don't have a sense of belonging to a place, a town or a region. I lost my home and became a refugee, a fate shared by millions of other children. I have always grasped at the sense of collective identity, the sense of community, in painful experiences and in the sense of consolation. I believe this was important to me as a child.[26]

Such concerns have led to low self-esteem and lack of identity on the part of the war child; traits that are very apparent in collaborators' children who continue to question who they really are, will they make the same mistakes as their parents, will they ever become a 'person' in their own right?

Even in the UK, where some still assume that the children did not suffer any psychological problems, there is evidence to suggest that a few ex-evacuees still have no sense of belonging:

> All the time I was evacuated I used to tell myself that one day the war would be over and I could go back home. After the war we were living in a different part of London and I made my way back to where I used to live. The whole area had been completely obliterated during the first few days of the Blitz and I was quite unable to find the spot where my house once stood. This happened more than 50 years ago. I have lived in many other places. I now have a grown-up family of my own and I am a grandfather. I now have a lovely house, but somehow I'm still waiting to go home![27]

Some children were not even given the chance to escape and were again interned within their adopted countries, very much a feature of post-war

Czechoslovakia, where German-Czech families found themselves subjected to arrest and imprisonment.

In some cases, parental fears overrode the desire to gain safety. Peter Heinl recalls an example where a woman, living on her own and fearing the advance of the Red Army, instructed her eldest son to shoot her first, then his younger brother, and then himself. He obeyed and a whole family was wiped out, consigned to the pages of history as a simple statistic.

As well as the effects of the 'concrete' aspects of war such as air-raids, death and devastation, one must remember that many of these war-children across post-war Europe (and indeed in parts of the world today), concerned primarily with survival, have memories of environmental and personal experiences that now provide psychological triggers in later life. Their need for food, warmth, and a sense of belonging occur many times within their stories:

> Whenever I recall the time when we fled, I always experience a cold sensa-
> tion. I always feel cold. My feet turn as cold as ice. Nothing helps me to keep
> warm. My nice woollen socks make no difference to this feeling I get. When
> I look outside, the summer landscape which is filled with illuminating green
> trees and vibrant flowers ... suddenly turns white.[28]

This woman had left Danzig and remembers the snow on the road leading to the railway station. One woman, now suffering from depression, had been taken into a children's home and recalled how cold it was in the winter of 1944/5. This 'coldness' and memory of 'cold' has affected her since and her illness was not only more intense during winter months, but she was almost in a suicidal state if the heating in her house failed.[29]

It is easy to forget now they are adults, that at the time many of them were very young children. Depending on their circumstances, some of them were forced to take on roles well above their age and some have never really experienced a childhood. There is a little-known fact that in some instances in the UK evacuation, children just over the age of five were given respon-sibility for siblings under the age of five. Although this was not common, it occurred more frequently than one might imagine and for some of the children involved has had an effect on all the parties ever since. In a recent research project I was carrying out, where the interviews were being filmed rather than just recorded on sound tape, two sisters who had been seven and four at the time of their evacuation were sitting side by side in the studio.

As the older one (A) was recalling her experiences as an evacuee, the younger of the two (B) started to swivel round and ended up with her back to her sister. When questioned about this after the session, B denied that she had done it and was therefore very surprised to see her response when the tape was replayed. Further questioning revealed that all her life B had considered her sister to have been an 'interfering busybody', questioning her fashion sense, her choice of boyfriends etc., so much so that B had refused to allow her own children to stay with her. However, during the filming she had realised that for five years of her life, her older sister had in fact been her mother, a role which she had found hard to give up on their return home, and as a result B felt guilty about her present relationship with her.[30]

There are other examples. Many children grew up during the war and afterwards without a male role model. Not only did this create problems for some children in relating to male figures but in a situation where the mother was left on her own and took on the role of both father and mother, there was often a breakdown in the traditional mother-child relationship. In some cases, as in the example above, children were forced into taking on the adult roles themselves and not only had to look after their siblings, but in some cases their parents. Some of this pressure was actually placed on them by the fathers themselves and comments like 'You are the man of the house now' or 'Make sure you look after your mother and sisters' only added to the burden. (This is a theme in the early part of the Finnish film *Mother of Mine* and it is one of the reasons why Eero, the seven-year-old main character, does not want to go to Sweden as he feels he is betraying his father's trust.)

For some war children this need for a father figure can become very debilitating and has affected the upbringing of their own children. It has also meant that having to take on the parental roles so early in life these children have been denied a childhood and all its inherent features such as play, socialisation and an education.

For others, whose parents were active in the war as collaborators or members of a totalitarian elite, there is always the question of loyalty. On the one hand the fathers and sometimes the mothers are vilified by the State, individuals and history in general; on the other, to the children they remain parents. Even if they were unable to provide the physical and moral support, how can the children address such divergent emotion? Some work through it, others never do.

What became of the orphans? Not only those who were physically deprived of their parents, but those whose parents were so emotionally scarred by their own experiences that they were unable to raise their children in a loving, caring family unit. In my own interviews, many evacuees refer to the difficulties in establishing and maintaining a relationship with their fathers who had returned from the war. In some cases the mothers also found such relations difficult as for the previous five years they had had the responsibility of having to run both a home and maintain a job themselves and now pushed their family responsibilities onto men who were perhaps unable to cope because of their own war experiences. Under such circumstances, the children were the least of their concerns.

For all war children there is an element of distrust. As children they had no say in what was going on at the time, nor indeed their future. As such they were reliant on adults to make decisions for them, some of which turned out to be detrimental to their well being. They became aware that relations, friends, schoolteachers and adults in general could not necessarily be trusted and also that life could be unpredictable. As a result, today some find it difficult to enter into any sort of relationship and where they have there is often a willingness to end it 'before it happens to them'; they can have a fear of rejection and can find it difficult to express their emotions and anger. Barbara Shawcroft has been married and divorced a few times and blames her inability to forge long-lasting relationships on her evacuee experience. In a way the need for a relationship is offset by her uncertainty that it is genuine and there is an ever-present underlying fear that it will be snatched away from her.[31] Some suffer from psychosomatic disorders, and at a simple level, are incapable of saying goodbye to friends and relations.

What present-day research shows is that trans-generational transmission of war trauma does not fit in neatly with historical dates, periods or eras. It does not cease when wars or conflicts end, so it is important that such data is considered by those dealing with children in present-day war zones. The examples mentioned above are not confined to children of the Second World War and the post-war years of the late 1940s and early '50s. The same issues are being witnessed today. It should be the responsibility of governments and child-welfare organisations to make sure that the cycle of trauma is broken at some point.

Some countries have recognised the need to do this and are now dealing with the problems that ex-war children have within their own countries. For the past twenty years there has been a significant change in the way in which the German people have been addressing the question of the Nazi era. Rather than 'burying' it, teachers and psychologists recognise that there is an obligation to keep alive the memories of all of those who took part, both victims and perpetrators, in order to inform future generations. In the Netherlands, largely as a result of the Herkenning group, there is a greater awareness of the discrimination aimed at the children of collaborators. They were not the guilty ones, although, as the title of a recent autobiography *Not Guilty. All the same punished* would indicate the scars still run deep. In Norway, such awareness has led to financial compensation. Surprisingly, the country that has yet to confront the long-term effects of war-child separation is Britain. As has been illustrated, children returned from the reception areas and were left to get on with their lives. Even today, little attention is paid to Operation Pied Piper, which was a massive undertaking, and it is one of the few aspects of the war that not only goes unrecognised but which does not have its own tangible memorial. Many people were involved and all have been affected in one way or another, either as evacuees, hosts, children in the reception areas, or mothers sending them away. Add to the list those who were involved in the administration and transportation, the teachers, the billeting officers, the escorts etc., and one begins to see how extensive and all-encompassing the scheme was. It just cannot be ignored and swept away. It will be remembered and its effects will still be apparent long after the 'evacuee generation' has gone.

One area of war-child study that is often forgotten relates to those children who, for whatever reason, were, and continue to be, caught up in war on their own home front. A great deal of research has been done on the Jewish children in the ghettoes, but little is known of the Russian children who were involved in the siege of Leningrad. An event now consigned to the pages of history, at the time it not only encapsulated all the horrors of war and humankind's inhumanity but was also a demonstration of stoic resistance. Much of the previous work on this area, usually conducted by journalists and social workers, did not draw any distinction between the experience of children and that of adults. But significantly, recent research carried out by Professor Marina Gulina is the first in which the blockade is seen exclusively through the eyes of children and adolescents.

To put it into context, just two months after the beginning of Operation Barbarossa, Germany's invasion of the Soviet Union[32] on 22 June 1941, advancing German troops encircled the city of Leningrad and laid siege to it. According to official figures 2.8 million people stayed in the city during this period, including 400,000 children. The siege was to last for 900 days, from 8 September 1941 until 27 January 1944 during which time an estimated 641,000 people died. (Later estimates put this figure nearer to 800,000.) At the time there was only enough fuel and food for two months and during the ensuing winter there was no heating, no water supply, virtually no power and very little food. Between January and February 1942, a particularly cold winter where temperatures reached minus 40°C, around 200,000 people died of cold and hunger. Water was only available from holes cut into the ice of the river Neva and the canals. Yet, despite all the problems, the industries in the city continued to function, students continued with their studies and life, as far as possible, carried on. Although a few hundred thousand people were able to leave the city via the now famous 'Road of Life' by lorry across the frozen Lake Lagoda in winter and by boat after the thaw, many remained. Even though there were a few plane 'drops' this road was also used as the main route to ferry limited supplies into the city, a dangerous action as it continually came under enemy fire. When it became necessary to initiate rationing on 20 November 1941 the daily allocation consisted of 250g of bread for essential workers and 125g for non-essential workers and for dependents, including children – just about a slice. In January 1942 the rations available to all the inhabitants amounted to 125g of bread per day.

> One day we couldn't get bread in the store in our building and had to go to the Street of the Commune for it. Because of the difficulty of the journey, mamma and I went together. It was getting dark. We walked slowly, saying nothing and supporting each other, carefully planting our feet in the steps left by the slowly winding procession of wrapped shadows heading for the store. One's breath froze. The way seemed endless. Suddenly, a man somewhere in front of us stumbled, took a few uncertain steps … and slowly fell. I often see, exactly as if it were happening again, his tall, emaciated figure in a black overcoat with a black fur sheepskin collar and a black fur sheepskin hat. I see him falling. The dead do stay with us. My heart felt as if it was being squeezed, and my soul was filled with pity. But there was no way to help. We staggered on. Then another person fell, and another, very near us, then another and another, and we all plodded along, barely raising our feet as we stepped over the bodies of the fallen. One step, another step – then a rest. Snow was falling, a white winding-cloth covering the horrors created by the rational minds of the 'supermen.' I don't remember how we got back. Obviously, the last reserves of the human psyche were exhausted. We didn't get any bread. The city's water-supply system had burst.[33]

By the time the siege was lifted on 27 January 1944, only 560,000 inhabitants had survived and remained in the city.[34] All of those involved were affected in some way by what they had witnessed and what they had endured. As many of them were children, the trauma they experienced at the time has remained with them throughout their lives and some are only now beginning to come to terms with it. According to Marina Gulina the children experienced at least two traumas of such severity that few children of a similar age in different circumstances would be able to cope with them. First, they included those relating specifically to the individual themselves such as pain, hunger, cold, loneliness, dependence, isolation and danger from other adults. Second, a fear that the mother or any other person responsible for the child's welfare might not return. According to the present research 'fear for the other' takes precedence over 'fear for one's self'.[35]

Those children left on their own with no support were particularly vulnerable. In her memoirs, teacher L. Raskin described a scene she came across:

> The emaciated children lay in bed with wide-open eyes. They barely moved. The horror they had experienced was frozen in their eyes. The skin of their faces, arms and bodies was coated with impenetrable muck. Fleas crawled over their shrunken frames. Many of these children hadn't seen hot food, even some boiled water, for 15–20 days.[36]

It is impossible for the vast majority of people today to empathise with the emotional problems that these children and their mothers went through at the time. But within the whole area of war-child research one does see commonalities of response. As in other war zones where women were left to fend for themselves and take total responsibility for their children, the need to take specific decisions relating to their safety weighed heavily, especially when the wrong decision could mean certain death. Added to which the general lack of nutrition would have affected their wellbeing. Tiredness, general lethargy and exhaustion would have made simple acts difficult to carry out and any weakness could lead to death. One child survivor of the siege recalls a walk to her mother's factory to collect wood:

> Apart and feeling nothing, I trudge on, hardly able to move my legs, toward the factory, pulling a homemade little sled behind me. If only I can make it. … There is no desperation, no fear, no pain – only weakness. My face is

chilled, becoming hard, the unbearable brightness blinds my eyes, my hands are getting stiff, breathing is difficult; it is too cold. At 30 degrees below zero, air actually thickens … I realise that I can't stand any longer, that I have to go home. If I fall, I won't get up. No one gets up if he falls … I find myself stopping and slowly, slowly, against my will, I go down, my knees bending by themselves, as if someone behind me was carefully pushing me down into the snow. The terrible weakness weighs me down, weighs me down, bending me to the ground, my knees lowering to the snow. I know that I am never, never to do this. I am leaning on my hands in the snow. The cold is attacking from all sides. Cold is spreading over me, over my whole body, from my knees pressing into the snow (my felt overshoes don't cover them). My elbows are in the snow. I am beginning to lean to the left. I clearly understand that this is the end – that I am dying. One more second and I will fall, will fall forever and will lie with them. I try to stand up, but I can't, I can't even lift my hands, if only to free them from the snow. The thought flashed on me: mamma will see me when she leaves work, for I probably won't be covered by snow by then. At this last second, I suddenly saw two familiar figures in front of me. They were walking, holding each other tightly by the hand. The memory of their backs in their quilted jackets is etched in my memory forever! I cried out: 'Roxana!' My voice was so weak apparently that they didn't hear me. I tried to shout again and again … The backs moved off. The end! I can already feel the cold in my left elbow. Pulling together the last bits of strength remaining to me, I shouted one last time. They heard me. They pulled me up. Memory has kept every detail of this moment, every tiny detail that wouldn't even have been noticed normally. This SOS, as it were, left its mark on my consciousness forever.[37]

There was also the question of guilt. In Finland and Germany this was apparent with the mothers who sent their children away, in Leningrad depersonalisation of the mothers and the children was demonstrated by panic and again a sense of guilt that in some examples led to serious cases of self-hate. Since the war many of the 'siege children', like their contemporaries in other war zones, have been affected by severe depression, lack of self-worth and loss of personal development. According to Marina Gulina, some survivors are only able to cope with the effects, and certainly the acute depression, by reverting to various forms of aggression.

In contrast, in terms of personal values, Gulina has found that siege survivors demonstrate a sense of responsibility as a quality that they value in themselves and as a quality that they value in others; similarly, they see self-reliance as an important factor in their survival. For them, such a reaction as taking offence easily has been banished. Characteristically they are more strongly drawn into and interested in contemporary social life and events, and they show an ability to adapt to the changing conditions in the society around them.

When asked how they survived some explained how they had grown seeds, boiled water and 'ate a dog'. In emotional terms they rated family solidarity very highly. As a result there was a collective response to survival. Some told of their faith and spiritual strength and others in the collective spirit of the people. Others indicated that 'sleep' had saved them and many that they simply 'took each day as it came'. One interviewee recalls:

> We lay and were silent for whole days, unresponsive to bombings or shelling, indifferent to everything. We slept 20 hours a day. This wasn't sleep, but it wasn't being awake either but rather a kind of half-lethargic condition of forgetting from which time was absent and not felt. There was no pain, no suffering, no thoughts of any kind – simply the continued existence of living matter and nothing else … The bread rations became larger, but still the death toll from starvation was very high. My mother and some of her workmates were sent to clear Porokhovy Railway Station of bodies and filth. She returned home, said nothing, and almost without taking off any clothes lay down on the bed. She answered no questions. In the morning, she went to work without a word. By this time, her face had an indifferently bitter expression. Her cheeks were sunken. The black circles under her eyes cruelly spoke of the end. Second-stage dystrophy had become final-stage. She began to get a tablespoon of seal oil a day, and I got the same of fish oil. I began giving her my portion. And to this day, I believe that fish oil is the elixir of life: people who reach the stage of emaciation that my mother had don't recover. But she survived. Death backed away.[38]

For some adults who have lived through various conflicts as children, the long-term effects are very similar in nature. The work that Dr Helga Spranger and Dr Peter Heinl have been doing in Germany, the late Prof. Sandelin Benko's research into the Finnish/Swedish scheme, Prof. Marina Gulina in St Petersburg, and my own investigation into evacuees in Britain, have exposed the similarities in the symptoms of war-child separation. One positive result from the Leningrad research is that deprivation of even the most basic necessities, even in very early childhood and for a very long time, does not stop the child's personal development if there is psychological support within the family. In addition, the child in such circumstances can often transform traumatic experience into something positive and creative. The important thing is that some of the children mentioned in this book did not have, and still do not have, the security of a family structure. Many have had to cope on their own with little support from familial and external sources.

Almost seventy years on, those of us working in the field of war children and children in conflict now have a responsibility to study these long-term effects so that present and future governments can be informed and advised on how to provide support, both short and long term, to children in war zones. If this happens, there might be some hope that the mistakes of the past will not be repeated in the future.

Graça Machel is correct when she states that:

> ... the International Community must address the plight of war-affected children and women, with new urgency. Their protection is not a matter of negotiation. Those who wage war, legitimise and support wars must be condemned and held to account as surely the children must be cherished and protected. Children cannot afford to wait.

In conclusion, this is why our research is important. With the exception of the gun-carrying children, the problems being experienced by children in present-day war zones are almost exactly the same as those in the Second World War. Many are robbed of a childhood, miss out on their education, suffer from the lack of family relationships, feel guilty, lack security and have an indeterminate future.

A former child migrant received the following advice from her employer:

> You are the hardest working, most reliable, punctual girl I have ever had the pleasure to employ, but your insecurity stands in the way of promotion with this company. If you want my advice, girl, go out there and find out who you are and come back and see me when you find yourself.[39]

There is also the present problem of the use of children in worldwide propaganda. Not a new phenomenon, as the film *Hearts and Minds* made in

1974 was, according to the National Review, a '… rather blatant piece of propaganda'. This Oscar-winning docu-film was credited with 'humanising' the Vietnamese for the American public. And although not specifically about children during the conflict, it does not avoid the fact that innocent children were killed. Few cannot have seen the famous photograph of a naked Kim Phuc Phan Thi running down the road in a bombing raid, an image used on such a massive scale that Kim had to change her identity; or the images of Gerald Ford bringing babies down from the aircraft during the Pan Am airlift from Vietnam.

Today children are often shown in the newspapers and in news bulletins and the images are used to grasp our attention and attack our emotions. Seeing a figure of a vulnerable child makes us want to help. However, I would suggest that by using children in this way, the media is forcing us to pay attention to the situation as a whole, rather than the plight of the individual child. A photographic-media experiment I do with my university students would suggest the children are still invisible.[40]

This aside, although there seems to be an increasing concern within society for the welfare of children in war-torn areas, the long-term effects are still largely ignored. Those of us working with war children have to make the results of our research known in order to stop the present cycle of war-child abuse continuing. This will be a difficult task, but one which, with dedication, will hopefully have a positive effect on future generations of children.

To quote William of Orange: 'There is no need to hope, just start; there is no need to be successful, just persevere.'[41]

The final comment should be left to Peter Heinl who in a few simple words encapsulates the reason why we continue to research and work with war children:

> … sadly, there is no end in sight for wars on this planet. The childhood sufferers of today will be the suffering adults of tomorrow. Peace stands by helplessly. There is one conclusion, which can be drawn firmly with respect to children in war time, be it victory or defeat: children tend to be the great losers overlooked by history.[42]

Postscript

It is only in recent years that academics have begun to study the long-term and psychological effects that years of separation, or active participation in conflict, have had on war children. Although there have been significant studies of the effects on civilians and the Home Front, the children have often been forgotten. It is also important to remember that they all came from a generation and a time when one just didn't talk about one's own fears, concerns and trauma and just got on with life.

Now things are beginning to change, many of the children caught up in the Second World War especially, have had to raise awareness themselves and as a result have established their own organisations to address the problems, provide counselling, or simply let it be known that the individuals concerned are not alone.

If you have read this book and are an ex-war child yourself, or know of someone who perhaps needs help and support, the following organisations will be able to provide information about their events and membership.

Please don't feel that you have to confront the past on your own.

The Evacuees Reunion Association. era@evacueesreunion.co.uk
The Finnish War Child Association. www.sotalapset.fi
The Swedish War Child Association. www.krigsbarn.se
The Herkenning (Children of Dutch Collaborators). www.werkgroepherkenning.nl
German War Children. www.kriegskinder.de
Norway. www.nkbf.no

Notes

INTRODUCTION

1 A Nicaraguan Child.
2 Margaret Humphreys, Director of the Child Migrants' Trust.
3 Eva Simonsen, 'Children in Danger'. Kjersti Ericsson and Eva Simonsen (eds),
   Children of World War II. (Berg, 2005) p.269.
4 Derechos Human Rights Chile.
5 Erna Paris, *Long Shadows. Truth, Lies and History*. (Bloomsbury, 2000) p.431.
6 Boro Pandurevic. Cited by Paris op.cit. p.385.
7 *Ibid*.
8 Work carried out by Professor Singa Sandelin Benko and Dr Martin Parsons,
   'Child in the Eye of the Storm' project. Universities of Helsinki and Reading.
9 Michael Richards, 'War Children in Franco's Spain', in *Children of World War
   II*. op.cit. p.118.
10 *Divagaciones intrascendentes*. (Valladolid, 1938) p.105 cited in 'War Children in
   Franco's Spain' op.cit.
11 Tony Judt, *Postwar. A history of Europe since 1945*. (Pimlico, 2007) p.21.
12 United Nations Educational, Scientific and Cultural Organisation.
13 Report on the European Situation: War Handicapped Children. UNESCO
   1950.
14 Alan Gill, *Orphans of the Empire*. (Vintage, 1998) p.15.
15 *Ibid*. p.27.
16 *Ibid*. p.14.
17 Anderson Committee Report, 1938.
18 This problem has been dealt with in Finland with the release of a very
   powerful and emotional feature film called (in translation) *Mother of Mine*. It
   looks in detail at the effect the removal of a Finnish child has on the Swedish
   foster family.

19 An estimated 20 million people in Germany had been made homeless, half a million of these in Hamburg. 25 million in the USSR. Judt, op.cit. p.17.

CHAPTER 1: MYTH MAKING

1 Confessions. St Augustine cited in Raphael Samuel, *Theatres of Memory*. (Verso, 1994) p.vii.
2 Luisa Passerini, 'Mythbiography in Oral History' cited in *The myths we live by*. Raphael Samuel and Paul Thompson (eds) (Routledge, 1993) p.49.
3 *Ibid*. Samuel and Thompson, p.2.
4 The last seventy years simply because so many ways to store and retrieve oral testimonies have been developed.
5 Samuel, *Theatres of Memory*. op.cit. p.ix.
6 Jacques Le Goff, *History and Memory*. p.129 cited in *Theatres of Memory*. op.cit.
7 Samuel, op.cit. p.x.
8 Jean Peneff, 'Myths in Life Stories' in *Myths we live by*. op.cit. p.36.
9 A.J. Cummings, 'Propaganda', an article in the *News Chronicle*, 9 February 1937.

CHAPTER 2: BRITISH EVACUATION: THE REALITY

1 Richard Titmuss, *Problems of Social Policy*. (HMSO, 1950)
2 These arrangements were not restricted to the South Coast. At the same time people in North Shields were issued with Evacuation permits and instructions: 'As soon therefore as the alarm is given pack up your blankets, and a change of cloathes (sic) for yourself and children in the coverlid of your bed. Carry also what meal and meat and potatoes, not exceeding one Peck, you may have in the house at the time; but on no account will any article of Furniture, or heavy baggage, be allowed to be put into the carts. One hour only will be allowed for preparation and then set out.' *Dorset Daily Echo*, 2 May 1940.
3 C.F. Carr. Talk to Bournemouth Rotary Club, 17 October 1939.
4 Titmuss, op.cit. p.23.
5 House of Commons Debates, 10 Nov. 1932. Vol. 270 col. 633, cited Titmuss, op.cit. p.23.
6 M. Gilbert, *Winston S. Churchill Vol. V 1922-39*. (Heinemann, 1976) p.573.
7 Sir John Anderson, 1st Viscount Waverley, GCB, OM, GCSI, GCIE, PC (8 July 1882–4 January 1958).
8 House of Commons Debates, 25 November 1937. Vol. 329, col. 1447, cited Titmuss, op.cit. p.26.
9 Exeter Blitz. Box 5. Devon Record Office. Exeter.
10 *Ibid*.
11 PRO HO45/17636.

12 Titmuss, op. cit. p.32.

13 *Ibid.* p.33.

14 In July 1934 Stanley Baldwin had informed the House of Commons that '... so far as I know every country in Europe has carried its work a great deal further than we have carried ours'. House of Commons Debates. 30 July 1934. vol. 1,292 cols 2,335–6, cited Titmuss, p.33.

15 *Ibid.* p.33.

CHAPTER 3: THE ANDERSON COMMITTEE DISCUSSIONS

1 Comment made to James Roffey by a ten-year-old pupil in a London school in September 1996.

2 It is important to remember that some government departments were also moved out of London.

3 In reality the total number of evacuees was nowhere near as high as those predicted at this stage. However, these were the figures that were used during the planning stages.

4 PRO HO45/17636.

5 For example, the Silver Jubilee celebrations in 1935 and the Coronation of George VI in 1937.

6 It is interesting to note that this phrase occurs in many government and official statements of the time. There was a concern that information available to the general public should contain a note of optimism. This continued up to 31 August 1939.

7 During the evacuation some teachers were 'forgotten about' when it came to billeting. In Shaftesbury in Dorset the Town Crier went around the town, with bell, asking people to take in three teachers who had spent the day making sure that their children were suitably housed. Nobody volunteered and consequently they spent the first three nights sleeping in a barn.

8 What is not often reported is that women teachers, who had been required to leave the profession on marriage, were now recalled. Many now had their own families and in some cases their children were not evacuated with them, but with their own schools. As wartime school holidays were more fluid, a few did not see their own children until the end of the war.

9 There were in fact Camp Schools dispersed around the countryside but they were not seriously considered until 1940. Research would suggest that although the children had to contend with two distinct emotional experiences – evacuation and living in a boarding-school situation – the education they received was thought to be better than their counterparts who in many cases shared educational establishments. In Camp Schools teachers were on duty 24/7.

10 Ministry of Health. Government Evacuation Scheme. Memo Ev. 4.Clause 72. 1939.

11 One teacher, whose London school was too big to be attached to the school in the village where they had been evacuated to in Wales, was told that they

would be dispersed to other schools in an area covering 400 square miles of mid-Wales. She was given a bicycle to make her visits!

12 Official Circular. May 1941. p.137 col. 2.

13 W. de M. Egerton. Chief Billeting Officer. Dorset County Council. Correspondence File.

14 R. Titmuss, *Problems of Social Policy*. (HMSO, 1951) p.103.

15 *Ibid*. p.391.

16 He had previously pointed out that all the motor coaches in the area had already been earmarked for ambulance work and therefore would not be available for evacuation. However, although 50 per cent of the city's 6,000 buses had been assigned to carry on the normal service in the area, 250 had been assigned to work with the police, which meant that the remaining 2,750 buses could be used to move a limited amount of the population.

17 PRO HO45/17636.

18 *Ibid*.

19 R. Calder, *Carry on London*. (Cape) p.91.

20 Angus Calder, *The Myth of the Blitz*. (Cape, 1991) p.47.

21 PRO HO45/17636.

22 Sir Ralph Wedgewood, Chief General-Manager of the LNER, Mr G.S. Szlumper, General-Manager of Southern Rail and Mr V.M. Barrington-Ward, Chairman of the Railway Companies Technical ARP Committee.

23 PRO HO45/17636.

24 Tim Bryan, *Great Western Railway at War*. (Patrick Stephens Ltd, 1995) p.13.

25 *Ibid*. p.16.

26 *Ibid*. p.13.

27 Great Western Railway. Circular. London Evacuation Scheme No. 2. Also altered working of through passenger trains. August 1939. Cited GWR. op.cit. p.11.

28 *Ibid*. p.16.

29 James Roffey. Letter to Author. June 1998.

30 J. Rawlins. Private papers.

31 *The Evacuee*. Journal of the Evacuee Reunion Association. June 1996.

32 The *Medway Queen* still exists, although in a poor state, and an appeal has been launched to save her. She has had quite a history. Having evacuated children from Dagenham on 1 September 1939 she took children from Gravesend on 3 September and was then taken to Deptford to be fitted out as a mine-sweeper and became part of the Royal Navy. In 1940 she earned the title 'Heroine of Dunkirk' having made seven journeys across the Channel to Dunkirk and brought back an estimated 7,000 soldiers. *Ibid*. January 1997.

33 *Ibid*. December 1996

34 The *Royal Daffodil* brought 1,600 Frenchmen from Dunkirk but was put out of action when a bomb went through three of her decks. The *Queen of the Channel* brought 600 from the beaches but was hit the following day by a bomb, which broke her back. The *Royal Sovereign* collected 6,856 men over

a period of a few days. The *Crested Eagle* was hit by a bomb at the Dunkirk mole while tranferring 700 men from the *Fenella*, which had also just been hit. The *Crested Eagle* caught fire and was abandoned on the beach. *Ibid.* February 1997.

35 Devon Record Office. Evacuation File. No Date.

36 Titmuss. op.cit. p.394.

37 *North Wales Chronicle*, p.13, cited in Gillian Wallis, *North Wales. A Case Study of a Reception Area under the Government Evacuation Scheme. 1939-45.* unpublished thesis, p.63. Flintshire Record Office. This viewpoint was held by the Welsh National Party throughout the war but was a minority one as the total membership could be numbered in hundreds. They issued a Memorandum in February 1939 expressing further concerns.

38 These volunteers, called 'Visitors', while not being allowed to enter houses for the purpose of obtaining information would have to satisfy themselves that the home was suitable for children and that their presence would be willingly acceptable. It was suggested that the work of the volunteers would be made easier if the Local Authorities were to send a printed letter signed by the Chairman of the Council or the Mayor to all householders appealing for their co-operation with the collection of the data. The content of such a letter was to be left to the discretion of the Council.

39 Visitors were given some interesting instructions on how to deal with farms in rural areas. In wartime the Government planned to increase home production. Therefore, under the Evacuation Scheme it wanted to ensure that there was enough flexibility to allow for the housing of additional labour on the farms but not to the extent that this impeded the farmer's normal activities. They were also to consider the degree of isolation especially where a farm, or other dwelling, was a distance of more than 2 miles away from a suitable school. Memo. Ev. 2 Paragraph 11d. January 1939.

40 PRO HO45/17636.

41 The problem of who was entitled to accommodation was not one that went away easily. Even after the Evacuation scheme had been fully implemented some reception areas that were deemed to be in the front line of evacuee billeting were still having to compete with other agencies for billeting places. On 5 November 1940, the Dorchester Rural District Council discussed this question of billeting at some length. It had been intimated by the Ministry of Health that all suitable empty properties in their area could be requisitioned and now empty, furnished houses could also be used for evacuees. The Chief Billeting Officer, Admiral Egerton, informed the Council that a Co-ordinating Officer was to be appointed to liaise between all parties competing for the same accommodation and maintain an overview of the situation. However, it was thought that although this would be useful for the Ministry, it would not help the Billeting Officer in the villages. *Dorset County Chronicle and Swanage Times*, 7 November 1940.

42 Titmuss, op.cit. p.37.

43 House of Commons Debate, 28 July 1938. Vol. 338, col. 3283. Cited Titmuss, op.cit.p.28.

44 *Ibid.* p.30.

45 Baroness Barbara Castle, who knew him, confirmed that Sir John Anderson was simply a bureaucrat and stated that 'I have more humanity in the top joint of my little finger than he had in his whole body'. Personal conversation July 2003.

46 Jessie Stewart, 'Recuerdos' in *Cambridge Daily News*, p.23. The original intention had been to repatriate the Basque children when the situation in Spain improved. However, the alternative was adoption in English homes and this was the course the Committee took because of lack of food and employment in Spain at this time made it a better option. Therefore the twenty-nine children in the Cambridge area left the hostel and stayed with foster parents in various parts of the country.

CHAPTER 4: THE BRITISH EVACUATION

1 Dorothy Lofts cited in Edward Stokes, *Innocents Abroad*. (Allen and Unwin, 1994) p.4.

2 Dorchester Rural District Council Minutes, 31 May 1939.

3 25 August 1939.

4 *Dorset County Chronicle and Swanage Times*, 31 August 1939.

5 *Dorset County Chronicle and Swanage Times*, 21 September 1939.

6 T.L. Crosby, *Impact of Civilian Evacuation in the Second World War*. (Croom Helm, 1986) p.28.

7 *Ibid.* p.97.

8 *Dorset Daily Echo*, 1 September 1939

9 The evacuation plans did not apply to the cities of Bristol, Nottingham, South Wales or Plymouth. These were designated by the Government as 'Neutral Evacuation Areas' and it was difficult to get children out of these areas unless the parents had the money to do so. Plymouth's designation was changed and fortunately it became an evacuated area. Angus Calder, *The People's War*. (Panther, 1971) p.42.

10 *Dorset Daily Echo*, 25 August 1939.

11 *Dorset Daily Echo*, 9 September 1939.

12 Bradfield C. of E. Primary School. Log Book. Berkshire Record Office. D/P/22/28/3

13 It needs to be remembered that few people had travelled any distances in the 1930s so bureaucrats responsible for allocating evacuees to the reception areas often had no idea of the location they were sending them to. They relied heavily on local billeting officers sorting the problems out at ground level.

14 James Roffey. op. cit. Personal Archive.

15 E.O. Humphreys. Education Officer. Anglesey. Report 'The Education of Evacuated Children.' University College of North Wales Archives. V. 4594.

16 Wallis, op.cit. p.17.

17 *Dorset County Chronicle and Swanage Times*, 29 June 1944.

18 J.Roffey. Letter to the author. 9 June 1998.

19 Sylvia Rose. Letter to the author. 29 January 1998.

20 Didcot Parish Council minutes. September/October 1939

21 E/LB11/5 Flintshire Record Office. Hawarden.

22 Anonymous Account.

23 WRO/F2/850/1-12

24 Written communication with author, 1998.

25 Berkshire County Council Minutes. May 1940.

26 M. Parsons, *Manchester Evacuation. The Exception to the Rule.* (DSM, 2001) p.21.

27 *Dorset County Chronicle and Swanage Times*, 15 February 1940.

28 St Matthews Infants School. Log Book. Hawarden R.O E/LB/11/5.

29 H.C. Dent, *Education in Transition.* (London, 1944) cited P.H.J.H. Godsen,
   Education in the Second World War. (1976)

30 PRO.ED 136/205.

31 E.O. Humphreys. Education Officer Anglesey. Report. 'The Education of
   Evacuated Children'. 27 November 1939. University College North Wales.
   Archives V4594.

32 W. Elliott and Sylvia Lewis. Letter to the author. June 1998.

33 Evacuation Group. Prince Rupert School. Liverpool 1941. Log Book
   Caernarfon Record Office.

34 Bucks. Record Office. E/LB/8/1 19 and 20 June 1940.

35 *Ibid.* 6 June 1940.

36 Bucks. Record Office. E/LB/6/3 30 September 1941.

37 *Ibid.* 18 June 1942.

38 PRO.ED.138/34.

39 Bucks. Record Office. E/LB/8/1. October 1939.

40 Idbury and Fifield C. of E. Primary School. Log Book. Oxford Record Office.

41 *North Wales Chronicle*, 12 May 1939.

42 Clerk of Nant Conway RDC to C.F. Mott. Evacuation File. 23 April 1940.
   Caernarvon Record Office.

43 Miriam Ward, *Evacuation. A Reception Area in Berkshire.* unpublished account.
   Undated.

44 The Boys Evacuated School. Aston Clinton. Bucks. School Diary. Bucks.
   Record Office E/LB/8/1 op.cit.

45 Quoted in the *Dorset County Chronicle and Swanage Times*, 2 January 1941.

46 Berkshire County Council. C/CL/C1/1/42.

47 1941 LCC Evacuee Party 941. Aston Clinton Girls School. Log Book. Bucks.
   Record Office. E/LB/8/1. 28 November 1939.

48 Dorset County Council Minutes. 29 January 1942.

49 T.L. Crosby, op.cit. p.93.

50 Titmuss, op.cit. p.58.

51 *Ibid.* p.409.

52 *Dorset Daily Echo*, 22 December 1939.
53 Tom Hickman, *What did you do in the war Auntie?* (BC, 1995) p.79.
54 Samways, *We think you ought to go.* (GLRO, 1995) p.39.
55 *Dorset County Chronicle and Swanage Times*, 20 November 1941.
56 *The Evacuee*, October 1997. p.6.
57 *Ibid.* 27 January 1944.
58 Titmuss, op.cit. p.544.
59 PRO.HO/45 17635.
60 Mass Observation. Topic Collection 5. Evacuation Folder 2/A. 20 February
   1940. Cited Crosby, op.cit. p.66.
61 *Dorset County Chronicle and Swanage Times*, 5 February 1942.
62 Norman Longmate, *Air Raid.* (Hutchinson, 1976) p.20.
63 Titmuss, op.cit. p.372 et al.
64 Crosby, op.cit. p.50.
65 James Roffey, 'Is he being a good boy?' *The Evacuee*, August 1996.
66 *Yesterday's Children.* Compiled by Lillian Evans.
67 Doc. 10 Chipping Norton Borough Council papers. Town Clerks Office.
   There are no reference numbers except the number of the document.
68 Crosby, op.cit. p.53.
69 Titmuss, op.cit. p.433.

CHAPTER 5: BRITISH CAMP SCHOOLS

1   Beal School for Boys. School Log Book entry. 17 February 1940.
2   Brian Winch. Taped interview.
3   Jim Bartley. Former evacuee. Taped Interview. November 1996.
4   I am indebted to John Bell, a former pupil at Wrens Warren, for allowing me
    access to his personal files.
5   Despite their reassurances there was a serious incident at the camp in the
    summer of 1941 when some evacuees came across an anti-tank mine left after
    a Canadian forces military exercise. It was thrown into a stream and retrieved
    a few days later by another boy who examined the device with a penknife.
    The fuse exploded. One boy died in hospital of stomach wounds, one lost
    a number of fingers and the third remained in hospital for nine months
    suffering from stomach and hand wounds.
6   City of Rochester Education Committee. Letter to parents from Edward
    H. Webb Education Secretary. 1940.
7   Education Journal Vol. LXXIV NO 1911. 25 August 1939. p.176.
8   Education Journal Vol. LXXV No1934. 2 February 1940. p.88.
9   Education Journal Vol. LXXV No 1947. 3 May 1940. p.377.
10 Kennylands School Log Book. 26 February 1940.
11 From an interview with John Gould.
12 B. Winch. Taped interview.
13 *Dorset Daily Echo*, 19 February 1940.

14 Education Journal. Vol. LXXVII No. 2008. Friday, 4 July 1941.
15 From a report by R.L. Arkell, *Home and Country*, September 1942, p.138. cited in *London Children in Wartime Oxford*. op.cit. p.50.
16 Beal School for Boys Log Book entry. 30 September 1940.
17 *Ibid.* 13 May 1941.
18 *Ibid.* 9 March 1945.
19 Interview with Doug Dielhenn.
20 Tony Towner, *An Evacuees War*. Deposit in the Evacuee Archive. University of Reading.
21 One can see why many of the pupils from camp schools found the transition to the services, either during the war or as part of national service, easy. The same 'boxing of beds' and inspection routines would have been very familiar to new recruits.
22 Tony Towner, op.cit.
23 *Ibid.*
24 From M. Parsons, *Manchester the Exception to the Rule*. (DSM, 2003)
25 Ministry of Information 1941. It deals with the ploughing up of non-productive land and how some local farmers and officials were given powers to confiscate land not being used effectively.
26 *Farmers Weekly*, 2 February 1940. p.47.
27 Beal School for Boys Log Book. 31 October 1941. p.189.
28 Mrs Frank Carling in *Farmers Weekly*, 13 September 1940. p.45.
29 *Farmers Weekly*, 2 February 1940. p.25.
30 *Farmers Weekly*, 23 February 1940. p.26.
31 Personal interviews. This usually happened when the host children were not interested in farming and the concern was passed on to the evacuee (now a paid farm-worker) instead.
32 Letter to the author from Joyce Goddard who taught at Kennylands until 1950.

CHAPTER 6: OVERSEAS EVACUATION

1 *Vera Brittain's Diary. 1939-45.* 25 June 1940. (Thorpe, 1993) p.167.
2 PRO.DO131/29.
3 PRO.DO 35/259/B277/4: PRO.DO 35/529/B305/8: PRO.DO 35/529/B305/4.
4 Elspeth Joscelin Huxley (née Grant) 1907–97 was a writer, journalist, broadcaster, colonial officer, environmentalist and government advisor. She married Gervas Huxley, grandson of Thomas Huxley and cousin of Aldous Huxley.
5 As well as Geoffrey Shakespeare, the other members of the Committee were Miss Florence Horsbrugh (Ministry of Health) and Mr J. Chuter Ede (Board of Education). There were also a number of Civil Servants representing all the interested Government departments. A further sixteen members.

6 Report on Inter-Departmental Committee on the reception of children overseas. Cmd.6213: CAB.67/7/172. Minutes 15 June 1940: Official CORB History. PRO.DO 131/43.

7 PRO.CAB.65/7/170. 17 June 1940.

8 Ralph Barker, *Children of the Benares. A War Crime and its Victims*. (Methuen, 1987) p.28.

9 PRO.CA. 65/7/174. 21 June 1940. Sir Martin Gilbert, *Churchill War Papers*. (Heinemann) p.391.

10 Parliamentary Debates. Commons 5th Series. Vol.363.1939-40 col. 358. 17 June 1940: PRO.CAB. 65/7/170 17 June 1940: PRO.CAB. 65/8/179 1 July 1940.

11 Parliamentary Debates Commons 5th Series vol. 362. 1939-40 cols 5-6. 18 June 1940; and *Westward Ho!* Ministry of Information Film soundtrack, 1940.

12 Michael Henderson, *See you after the duration*. (Britannica, 2004) p.28.

13 *Ibid.* p.34.

14 Reuters. 1 July 1940.

15 Reuters. 10 July 1940.

16 Reported in the *Dorset Daily Echo*, 3 July 1940.

17 Martin Gilbert, *Churchill War Papers*. Vol. 2. op.cit. p.543.

18 Sir Geoffrey Shakespeare, *Let Candles be Brought In*. (MacDonald, 1949) p.249.

19 Michael Henderson, op.cit. p.20.

20 *Dorset County Chronicle and Swanage Times*, 27 June 1940.

21 Gilbert, *Churchill War Papers*. Vol. 2. op.cit. p.451.

22 PRO.CAB. 65/7/174. Minutes. 21 June 1940. M. Gilbert, *The Churchill War Papers*. Vol. 2, May 1940–December 1940. (Heinemann, 1994) p.391.

23 E. Stokes, *Innocents Abroad*. (Allen and Unwin, 1994) p.35.

24 *Ibid.* p.36.

25 PRO.DO.131/39.

26 PRO.CAB.65/8/179 Minutes. 1 July 1940.

27 *Dorset Daily Echo*, 6 July 1940.

28 Official communications sent to the parents of Patricia Johnston then living in Liverpool. Patricia went to Australia on the 6 August 1940 on the M.S. *Batory*. The ship was also transporting 1,000 troops. I am indebted to the family for allowing me to use this now rare correspondence.

29 Parliamentary Debates. Commons 5th Series. Vol. 363. 1939-40 col. 21–23, 355–62

30 Martin Gilbert, *Churchill War Papers*. Vol. 2, op.cit. p.542.

31 *Ibid.*

32 *Ibid.*

33 Shakespeare, op.cit. p.256.

34 Letter to the author and personal papers.

35 Shakespeare, op.cit. p.259.

36 *International War Cry*. 6 June 1940. (Salvation Army Publications.)

37 Stokes, *Innocents Abroad*. op.cit. p.49.

38 *Ibid.* p.49.

39 R. Barker, op.cit. p.1.

40 Shakespeare, op.cit. p.271.

41 Fetheney, op.cit. p.132.

42 *The Times*, 2 September 1940.

43 Barker, op.cit. p.43.

44 Heinrich Bleichrodt. Korvettenkapitan was born October 1909 and was Captain of two U-boats – U-48 and U-10. On his first venture at sea, Heinrich sank eight ships which included the 11,081 ton *City of Benares*.

45 DO131/20 (CORB Files).

46 Fetheney, op.cit. p.134.

47 Miss Day. Escort on the *Benares. Ibid.* p.138.

48 Mrs Towns. Escort on the *Benares. Ibid.*

49 There is a memorial to him in the Church of St Jude-on-the-Hill, Hampstead.

50 Fetheney, op.cit. p.149.

51 *Ibid.* p.146.

52 Barker, op.cit. p.153.

53 *Ibid.* p.143.

54 PRO.CAB 79/6 folio 323. Gilbert, *Churchill War Papers.* Vol. 2, op.cit. 23 September 1940. p.862.

55 CAB67/8. Letter to Home Secretary from G. Shakespeare. 25 September 1940.

56 Martin Parsons, *Waiting to Go Home.* (DSM, 1999) p.156.

57 *Ibid.* p.157.

58 Martin Parsons, op.cit. p.160.

59 *Ibid.* p.163. Letter signed by Peter Emrys Evans.

60 Extract from letter from CORB to parents of evacuees in Australia and New Zealand. 20 June 1945.

61 Fetheney, op.cit. p.230.

62 *Ibid.* p.233.

63 *Ibid.* p.239.

CHAPTER 7: HITLER YOUTH

1 Michael H. Kater, *Hitler Youth.* (Harvard University Press, 2006) p.4.

2 Guido Knopp, *Hitler's Children.* (Sutton, 2000) p.176.

3 Kater, op.cit. p.37.

4 Baldur von Schirach 1907–74. In 1931 promoted to the post of Reich Youth Leader. In 1933 he took over the leadership of the Hitler Youth. In 1940 he was appointed Gauleiter of Vienna. At Nuremberg he was found guilty of war crimes and sentenced to twenty years in prison.

5 Artur Axmann 1913–1996.

6 Kater, op.cit. p.22.

7 *Ibid.* p.25.

8 Introduced on 24 November 1942 by Himmler, as Chief of the SS and State Police.

9 H. Boberach (ed.), *Richterbriefe. Dokumente zur Beeinflussing der deutschen Rechtsprechung 1942-44*. Cited in *Nazism. 1919-1945 Volume 4* Jeremy Noakes (ed.) (University of Exeter Press) p.150.

10 Sophia Magdalena Scholl (1921–43). A member of the White Rose non-violent resistance movement. She was convicted of treason and guillotined in 1943.

11 For examples of the broadsheets issued by the White Rose see Noakes, op.cit. pp.457–459.

12 The other core members of the White Rose group were: Hans Scholl, Christopher Probst, Willi Graf, Alexander Schmorell and Jurgen Wittenstein.

13 NSV. National Socialist Youth Welfare

14 Knopp, op.cit. p.196.

15 Noakes, op.cit. p.400.

16 Kater, op.cit. p.177.

17 Noakes, op.cit. p.400.

18 *Schulungsdienst der Hitler Jugend 4*. (1942) p.2 and 22–23.

19 Reichsleiter Alfred Rosenberg (1893-1946). Among other posts he was representative for the comprehensive and intellectual and ideological indoctrination of the NSDAP. Found Guilty at the Nuremberg trial and hanged on 16 October 1946.

20 Head Teacher of St Mary's State Sec. School for Boys. Oldenberg. To the Oldenberg State Ministry of Churches and schools. 30 September 1940. Noakes, op.cit. p.442.

21 Sebastian Haffner, *Defying Hitler*. (Phoenix, 2003) p.231.

22 *Ibid*.

23 Noakes, op.cit. p.407.

24 K-H Jahnke and M. Buddrus, *Deutsche Jugend 1933-45*. (Hamburg, 1989) p.318.

25 Recruitment advertising for the SS Panzer Division. Hitlerjugend. 1944.

26 Knopp, op.cit. p.177.

27 Artur Axmann, 1945. Cited in Knopp, op.cit. p.231.

28 Noakes, op.cit. p.644.

29 Knopp, op.cit. p.237.

30 Constantin Film. Produced by Bernd Eichinger. 2004.

31 Dieter Hildebrandt. Cited in *Hitler's Children*. op.cit. p.173.

32 Willi Rabe. Wehmarcht Officer 1945 (aged twenty). *ibid*. p.256.

33 Gerd Hafner. Cited in Knopp, op.cit. p.240.

34 *Ibid*. p.241.

35 *Ibid*. p.255.

36 Artur Axmann, September 1944.

37 Knopp, op.cit. p.233.

38 Mikhail Pozelsky, *ibid*. p.271.

39 Lothar Loewe and Hans Jurgen Habenicht, *ibid*. p.277.

CHAPTER 8: KINDERLANDVERSCHICKUNG

1 Jeremy Noakes (ed.), *Nazism*. Vol 4. (Exeter University Press, 1998) p.429.
2 PRO HO45/17636.
3 Noakes, op.cit. p.60.
4 'Sending children to the countryside'.
5 Neither was it in the UK. At the time of the threat of possible invasion by Napoleon many people on the south coast were moved inland.
6 Gerhard Debit Brock, 'KLV Essay.' *Children in War*, Journal No. 3. (2005)
7 Baldur von Schirach was the former Reich Youth Leader. In June 1940 he was appointed Gauleiter of Vienna while retaining the title of 'Delegate for the Inspection of the Whole of the Hitler Youth'.
8 National Socialist Teachers League.
9 Notes from a meeting held between Shirach and Hitler, 27 September 1940.
10 National Socialist Welfare Organisation.
11 G. Dabel, *KLV. Die erweiterte Kinder-Land-Verschickung. KLV Lager 1940-45.* (Freiburg, 1981) p.32. cited in Noakes, op.cit. p.428.
12 The management structure in the KLV camps consisted of the following: Camp Head, Camp Team Leader, Deputy Camp Head, Camp teacher, Camp boys/girls section leader, Camp boys/girls group leader, Camp Matron, Personnel for maternal care, Bursar. Noakes, op.cit. p.433.
13 League of German Girls (Maidens).
14 Noakes, op.cit. p.434–5.
15 Later, other areas such as Dusseldorf, Koln and Hanover were involved in the scheme.
16 G. Hock 'Der Fuhrer sorgt fur unsere Kinder …', *Die Kinderlandesverschickung im Zweiten Weltkrieg*. (Paderborn, 1996) p.136.
17 Gerhard Brock. Essay Notes.
18 Earl R. Beck. *Under the Bombs. The German Home Front. 1942-45.* (University Press of Kentucky) p.24.
19 *Ibid*. p.25.
20 Ministry of Health Circular. GES 13. 25 August 1939. Cited Titmuss, op.cit. p.92.
21 'Reichsleistungsgesetz'.
22 Hauptstaatsarchiv Stuttgart E151 cII Bu 748. Cited Noakes, op.cit. p.425.
23 *Ibid*. p.426.
24 From July 1943–October 1944 the child population in West Berlin was reduced by 66.9 per cent compared to only 40.4 per cent in North Berlin. Kurt Pritzkoleit, *Berlin*. (Dusseldorf, 1962) p.55.
25 Richard Grunberger, *A Social History of the Third Reich*. (Pelican, 1971) p.56.
26 National Socialist German Worker's Party.
27 Claus Larass, *Der Zug der Kinder. KLV-Die Evakuierung 5 Millionen deutscher Kinder im 2 Weltkrieg*. (Munich, 1983) p.102. Cited *Nazism*. Noakes, op.cit. p.430.

28 *Ibid.* p.431.

29 Anon. diary account cited in Noakes, op.cit. p.410.

30 'I swear that I will serve the Fuhrer Adolf Hitler faithfully and selflessly in the Hitler Youth. I swear that I will always strive for the unity and comradeship of German Youth. I swear obedience to the Reich Youth Leader and to all leaders of the HJ. I swear on our holy flag that I will always be worthy of it. So help me God.'

31 As an example. The annual school intake in Dresden in 1940 was around 5,500, in 1943 it fluctuated between 8,500 and 9,000. (ref. Frederick Taylor, *Dresden*, Bloomsbury. p.139.)

32 Noakes, op.cit. p.359.

33 During 1943 the number of air-raid alerts had totalled fifty-two, by 1944 this had increased to 151. Taylor. op.cit. p.143.

34 Very similar to concern that the working classes would panic in the UK if they thought there was a war coming. An issue that necessitated the Anderson Committee decisions being kept out of the public domain for as long as possible.

35 Matthias Neutzner (ed.), *Martha Heinrich Acht: Dresden 1944/45.* (Dresden, 2000) p.23.

36 *Sicherheitdienst.*

37 *Ibid.*

38 Hoch, op.cit. p.308.

39 Lynn H. Nicholas, *Cruel World. The Children of Europe in the Nazi Web.* (Vintage: New York, 2005) p.60.

40 Gerhard Brock. KLV Essay, 2005.

41 *Ibid.*

42 A. Hitler, *Mein Kampf.*

43 Peter Sichrovsky, *Born Guilty.* (Basic Books: New York, 1988) p.169.

44 Jost Hermand, *A Hitler Youth in Poland – Erwiterte KLV 1940-45.*

45 *Ibid.* p.49.

46 *Ibid.*

47 Stargardt, *Witnesses of War.* p.381.

CHAPTER 9: THE FINNISH WAR CHILDREN: 'THE SOTALAPSI'

1 Dr Martin Parsons. In conversation with Pertti Kaven. University of Helsinki and ex-war child.

2 In 1906, because of the Russo-Japanese war which Russia lost, there was an attempt to improve Russo-Finnish relations.

3 uho Kusti Paasikivi (27 November 1870–14 December 1956) was Prime Minister of Finland (1918 and 1944–1946). He was President of Finland from 1946 to 1956. He was an influential figure in Finnish economics and politics for over fifty years, and the architect of Finland's post-war foreign policy. He was born as Johan Gustaf Hellsten in 1870 at Koski in Häme Province,

Finland, the son of August Hellsten, a merchant, and Karolina Wilhelmina Selin. He Finnicised his name to Juho Kusti Paasikivi in 1885.

4 'At the Admiralty'Vol. 1. September 1939–May 1940. Martin Gilbert, *Churchill War Papers.* (Heinemann, 1993) Footnote p.445.

5 Baron Carl Gustaf Emil Mannerheim (4 June 1867–28 January 1951) was the Commander-in-Chief of Finland's Defence Forces, Marshal of Finland, an astute politician and a successful military commander. He was the sixth President of Finland (1944–1946). Mannerheim was born in the Grand Duchy of Finland to a notable Finnish noble family that had migrated during the sevententh century to Sweden/Finland from the Netherlands. He started his military career in the Imperial Russian army, becoming the leader of Finnish government forces in the civil war of 1918 and during the Second World War.

6 Historical Papers. Occasional Papers. Documents on relations between Britain and Finland: 1939–1956. Documents relating to British policy during the 'Winter War', 1939–1940. Foreign and Commonwealth Office.

7 Winston S. Churchill. Broadcast, 20 January 1940.

8 Lord Halifax to Churchill. Churchill Papers 23/3. 26 January 1940.

9 Winston S. Churchill. Note. Admiralty Papers. 22 December 1939.

10 War Cabinet. Confidential Annex. Cabinet Papers 65/11. 22 February 1940.

11 War Cabinet. Confidential Annex. 65/4. 22 December 1939. WSC War Papers. op.cit. p.556.

12 16 December 1939. John Colville Diary. Colville Papers.

13 War Cabinet. Confidential Annex. Cabinet Papers 65/4. 27 December 1939.

14 War Cabinet. Confidential Annex. Cabinet Papers 65/11. 17 January 1940.

15 War Cabinet. Confidential Annex. Cabinet Papers 65/11. 12 February 1940.

16 *Ibid.* 18 February 1940.

17 War Cabinet. Confidential Annex. Cabinet Papers 65/12. 12 March 1940.

18 Neville Chamberlain had proposed sending three armed divisions (15,000 men) to Scandinavia to help the Finns, landing at Narvik (Operation Avonmouth) and at Trondheim, Stavanger and Bergen (Operation Stratford), proceeding overland through Norway and Sweden to Finland, occupying the Gallivare Iron-Ore mines on the way. He informed the war cabinet that the expedition should take place by 20 March 1940 'if we are to be sure of forestalling the Germans'.

19 The Winter War caused Hitler to begin to attack Norway and Denmark earlier than he had planned. In addition, the performance of Russian forces during the winter war made Hitler critically underestimate their capabilities. A mistake that was to result in the heavy defeat during the invasion of Russia.

20 General Mannerheim called upon the people of Finland to take part in a 'Holy War against communism'.

21 Winston Churchill to Anthony Eden. Churchill Papers 20/36. 5 July 1941 and 10 July 1941.

22 Winston Churchill to Joseph Stalin. Churchill Papers 20/45. 21 November 1941.

23 Anthony Eden to Sir Stafford Cripps. Foreign Office Papers. 954/24. 4 September 1941.

24 War Cabinet Minutes. Cabinet Papers 65/19. 15 September 1941.

25 Winston Churchill to Field Marshal Mannerheim. Churchill Papers 20/45.

26 Field Marshal Mannerheim to Winston Churchill. Churchill Papers 20/46. 4 December 1941.

27 Paasikivi, *Toimintani Moskovassa ja Suomessa 1939-1941*. (1986). Paasikivi, *My activity in Moscow and Finland 1939-1941*. (1986)

28 *J.K. Paasikiven päiväkirjat 1944-1956. Ensimmäinen osa*. (1985). *The diaries of J.K. Paasikivi from 1944-56. Part one*. (1985)

29 The USSR no longer demanded absolute surrender of the Finnish forces and an Armistice was agreed under the 1947 Treaty of Paris:
   * Defined the 1940 Finnish Border.
   * Reparations of £200,000 to be paid by 1952. (They were paid in full.)
   * The Porkkala Peninsular was to be leased to the USSR as a military base.
   * The Finnish authorities were to punish war criminals and to suppress Anti-Soviet organisations. (Ryti was sentenced to ten years in prison ... although he was released very soon because of ill health.)

30 Per Albin Hansson (28 October 1885–6 October 1946), leader of the Swedish Social Democrats, was Prime Minister four times between 1932 and 1946, including the coalition government which was formed during the Second World War, and included all major parties except the Communists. Fearing a German invasion, Per Albin gave in to Hitler's demands and allowed German troop transports onto Swedish railways to Norway, which had already been invaded and occupied by the Nazis.

31 13 December 1939.

32 Since 1884, the Fredrika-Bremer-Association (FBF) has led the debate on equality between men and women in Sweden.

33 Pertti Kaven, *70,000 Precious Commodities*. (Keuruu: Otava, 1985) p.41–45

34 Karl-August Fagerholm (31 December 1901–22 May 1984) was Speaker of Parliament and three times Prime Minister of Finland (1948–50, 1956–57 and 1958–58). Fagerholm became chairman of the Social Democrats after the armistice in the Continuation War. As a Scandinavia-oriented Swedish-speaking Finn, he was believed to be more in favour of the Soviet Union's leadership than his predecessor Väinö Tanner. However, during Fagerholm's post-war career he was opposed by both the Kremlin and domestic communists.

35 The Swedish National Archive. The Committee to help Finnish children. The letter of Nothin. Signug B:1. Rockberger, Nicolaus, *Göteborgs trafiken*. (1973). Rockberger, Nicolaus, *The Gothenburg Traffic*. (1973) pp.286-291.

36 Kaven, op.cit. p.22.

37 *Ibid*. p.22.

38 *Ibid*. p.24.

39 Sue Saffle, 'Children War and the rhetoric of remembrance. The Stories of Finland's war children.' *Children in War*, Journal. (DSM, Dec. 2006) p.101.

40 Kaven, op.cit. p.101.

41 Eric De Geer, 'The Finnish war-children in Sweden 1941.' Special edition of the book *The Finnish language in Sweden nr 39*. (Stockholm, 1986)

42 Saffle, op.cit. p.101.

43 *Ibid.* p.101.

44 Finland ratified the Hague Convention on the Civil Aspects of International Child Abduction in 1994. The most important features of these national arrangements are the following:

- The Hague Convention rules on the return of an abducted child have been made retroactive.
- Only one court, the Court of Appeal of Helsinki, is competent to receive applications and make orders for the return of children. Besides, an order for the return is always immediately enforceable, unless the Supreme Court, upon appeal, orders the stay of enforcement.
- The 'fundamental principles' exception in Article 20 of the Convention cannot be invoked against the application in Finnish return proceedings. According to Article 20 the return of the child can be refused where the return would not be permitted by the fundamental principles relating to the protection of human rights and fundamental freedoms of the requested State. The first cases indicate that the retroactive application of the Convention provided by the Finnish Act has been less successful. The courts have shown obvious reluctance towards the ordering of the return in these cases whereas in the 'new' cases the Court of Appeal as well as the Supreme Court have generally followed the spirit of the Convention in a loyal manner. 'The Hague Convention on Child Abduction of 1980 and its implementation in Finland.' *Nordic Journal of International Law. Vol. 66 No. 1.* (January 1997.) Abstract.

45 Professor Kaila stated that returning the child to his/her biological family would only cause trauma in exceptional cases.

46 Kaven, op.cit. pp.123–4.

47 Pertti Kaven, the late Prof. Benko.

48 Eila Räsänen, *The effect of the Separation Experiences during Childhood on the Mental and Physical Health and social Well-being in Adulthood. A psychosocial study of the later effects of war-child separation experiences.* (University of Kuopio, 1988) pp.121–123.

49 Kaven, op.cit.

50 *Ibid.* p.124–30.

51 *Ibid.*

52 Dr Olle Elgenmark, 'The treatment of sick Finnish children in Sweden'. *Finnish Journal.* (Huoltaja,1943) pp.439–444 and Dr Bertil Sourander, 'Experiences of the evacuation of Finnish children to Sweden 1941-42'. *Finnish Medical Journal.* (Duodecim, 1942) pp.269–273.

CHAPTER 10: THE CHILDREN OF COLLABORATORS

1 Tony Judt, *Postwar. A History of Europe since 1945*. (Pimlico, 2007) p.39.
2 Herkenning was founded in 1981 by a journalist, a member of the clergy working on radio, a psychologist and a psychiatrist.
3 Nationaal Socialistische Beweging.
4 Anton Adriaan Mussert (11 May 1894–7 May 1946) was one of the founders of the National Socialist Movement of the Netherlands and its *de jure* leader. During the Second World War he was able to keep this position, due to the support he received from the Germans. After the war he was convicted and executed for high treason on 7 May 1946 in the Hague (on the Waalsdorpervlakte).
5 Cornelis van Geelkerken (19 March 1901–29 March 1979) was co-founder of the Dutch Nationaal-Socialistische Beweging. He became director of their youth corps, the Nationale Jeugdstorm. After the German invasion Geelkerken was appointed Inspector-General of the Nederlandsche Landwacht (home guard set up to combat the Resistance). After the war he was sentenced to life imprisonment but released in 1959.
6 The Eerste Kamer (literally 'First Chamber' in Dutch) is the Upper House, or Senate of the Netherlands parliament, the States-General. (The Netherlands calls its Upper House the 'First Chamber' and it's Lower House the 'Second Chamber'.)
7 The Boers in South Africa were descendants of Dutch settlers who had colonised the area in the seventeenth and eighteenth centuries.
8 Meinoud Marinus Rost van Tonningen (19 February 1894–6 June 1945) was a Dutch politician of the National Socialist, NSB Party. During the Second World War, and the German occupation of the Netherlands, he collaborated extensively with the German occupation forces. He is thought to have committed suicide.
9 The conflict began with an insurrection against Dutch forces in Brussels (25 August 1830); Belgium then declared its independence (4 October). Dutch forces attacked Brussels, taking its citadel (27 October), but they could not take the city. Belgian independence was declared by the London Conference (December), which dissolved the Kingdom of the Netherlands. Holland formally recognised Belgian independence 19 April 1836.
10 French occupation (1795–1813). Holland was called the Batavian Republic.
11 Gonda Scheffel-Baars. 'The Role of Dutch Society in the victimisation of collaborators children.' *Children in War*, Journal. Vol. 1 No. 4 (DSM, December 2006) p.106.
12 Gonda Scheffel-Baar, 'Becoming oneself beyond fear and shame'. Personal account.
13 This is from an anonymous account entitled 'We Never Spoke About the War'. I am indebted to Gonda Scheffel-Baars for allowing me access to these private papers.

14 Paul Mantel and Gonda Scheffel-Baars, N.S.B.-*kinderen in tehuizen*, (Collaborators' Children in Children's Homes), MA dissertation.

15 Anonymous personal account.

16 Gonda Scheffel-Baars. Personal Account.

17 Anonymous personal account.

18 Gonda Scheffel-Baars. 'The Role of Dutch Soc.' op.cit.

19 Interesting that according to Monika Diederichs this label was only applied to women who were considered to come from a low socio-economic class. Kjersti Ericsson and Eva Simonsen (eds), 'Dutch Women, German Soldiers, their children' in *Children of World War II*. (Berg) p.161.

20 *Ibid.* p.155.

21 NSV. Nationalsozialistishce Volkswohlfahrt was the German organisation in the Netherlands with responsibility for caring for German/Dutch children.

22 Cited in Diederichs, op.cit. p.154.

23 Prof. Baard Borge, Harstad University, Norway.

24 Norwegian for 'National Gathering' or 'National Unity' the NS was a fascist party in Norway, between 1933–45. It was founded by former Defence Minister Vidkun Quisling and a group of sympathisers such as Johan Bernhard Hjort, who was to lead the party's paramilitary wing, the Hird, for a short time before leaving the party in 1937.

25 It is worth pointing out that there were two strands of administration in wartime Norway, one German and one Norwegian (NS).

26 Josef Terboven (1898–1945). Born in Essen, Terboven was basically dictator of Norway during the war years. Although he had no authority over the occupying forces, he did have control over 6000 'militia', which included 800 members of the secret police. He committed suicide by blowing himself up on 8 May 1945.

27 Von Falkenhorst (1885–1968) was dismissed from his command in Norway on 18 December 1944 for opposing the policies of Josef Terboven. After the war he was tried by a joint British-Norwegian military tribunal for violating the rules of war. He had passed on the Führerbefehl known as the Commando Order, which required captured saboteurs to be shot (several were, including many on the 'Heavy Water Raid' immortalised in the film *Heroes of Telemark*). He was convicted and sentenced to death in 1946. The sentence was later commuted to twenty years' imprisonment. Von Falkenhorst was released on July 23, 1953 due to bad health and died in 1968.

28 Other important ministers were Jonas Lie, who as Minister of Police was head of the Norwegian wing of the SS from 1941, Dr Gulbrand Lunde Minister of 'popular enlightenment and propaganda' and Albert Viljam Hagelin Minister Domestic Affairs.

29 NS Child. Kari Berle. Dagbladet 3. June 1996. Cited in Baard Borge, *The Norwegian NS-Children*.

30 Jarl Eik and Stein U. Larsen (eds), *The Aftermath of War*. (Oslo, 1999) p.259.

31 Dr Martin Parsons (UK), Prof. Baard Borge (Norway), late Prof. Singa Sandelin-Benko (Finland), Dr Peter Heinl (Germany) … to name but a few.

32 Terje Herrem, 9 April 2001. Cited Borge, op.cit.

33 To a degree, the German leniency may have resulted from the Norwegians' high standing within the racial hierarchy of National Socialism. In a written instruction carried by Wehrmacht soldiers during the 1940 campaign in Norway, residents were to be seen on a par with the farmers of Friesland (Friessen) in Germany. Like elsewhere in occupied Europe, food was sometimes scarce and frequently of lesser quality than in normal times. But, unlike the situation in many other occupied areas, civilians never starved, even though the country was dependent on import of food and other vital commodities from Germany and occupied Denmark.

34 The following figures are taken from a recent pilot study carried out in Norway by Baard Borge. I am indebted to him for allowing me access to this material.

35 In August 1945, all Norwegian women who had married a German soldier were deprived of their citizenship, even if they had remained in the country. At the same time, their children also lost their residency. These women regained their passports in December 1950, but their children, technically 'stateless persons', could only become Norwegian nationals by a special government provision or when they reached the age of eighteen.

36 The others involved were the Saami, the Norwegian 'gypsies' (Rom) and ex-pupils of special schools who have been granted special rights to State compensation.

37 Exeter Blitz. Box 16 Group O 188. Devon Record Office.

38 This was a term of abuse that had originated in the First World War, and was aimed collectively at German soldiers.

39 Lynn Nicholas, *Cruel World. The Children of the Europe in the Nazi Web.* (Vintage, 2005) p.174.

40 *Ibid.* p.175.

41 Reported in *Dorset Daily Echo.* 12 January 1940.

42 Sarah Farmer, 'The Communist Resistance in the Haute-Vienne', *French Historical Studies.* Vol. 14 (1985) p.105.

43 Fabrice Virgili, '*Enfants de Boches*: The war children of France' (2005) in Kjersti Ericsson and Eva Simonsen (eds.), *Children of World War II. The Hidden Enemy Legacy.* (Berg: Oxford and New York) p.142.

44 *Ibid.* p.144.

45 Reuters, 1 June 2004.

46 *Ibid.* p.147.

47 Reuters, op.cit.

48 Although in some places it went beyond that. Some were tortured, one woman was kicked to death in Paris and others were stripped, tarred and forced to walk through the streets.

CHAPTER 11: CHILD SOLDIERS

1 Graça Machel, the former Education Minister in Mozambique.
2 Report of the Special Representative of the UN Secretary-General for Children and Armed Conflict, 17 August 2006.
3 *Ibid.*
4 In 1994, the UN Secretary-General asked Graça Machel to carry out research into the global human rights of children in war zones and involved in armed conflict.
5 Graça Machel, *The Impact of War on Children.* (London, 2001) p.1.
6 *Ibid.* p.3.
7 BBC News, 29 July 2007.
8 It is worth remembering that in some African countries more than 50 per cent of the population is under the age of eighteen.
9 Liberation of Tamil Tiger Eelam. This group have been fighting for some years against the Sri Lankan government.
10 UN Press release. 6 January 2000. Cited in Machel, op.cit. p.41.
11 UN Assembly resolution A/RES/54/263. 25 May 2000 came into force 12 February 2002.
12 UNICEF. The Progress of Nations 2000. (New York, 2000) Cited in Machel, op.cit. p.9.
13 Seventeen-year-old girl volunteer quoted in the report.
14 Sixteen-year-old boy from Sierra Leone.
15 Kenneth Caldwell, Director of International Operations at Save the Children.
16 Human Rights Watch, 19.April 2007
17 *Ibid.* 24 January 2007.
18 'A Long Way Home.' Human Rights Watch Report, June 2006.
19 The pertinent definition is: Article 3a. All forms of slavery or practices similar to slavery, such as sale and trafficking of children, debt bondage and serfdom and forced or compulsory labour, including forced or compulsory recruitment of children for use in armed conflict.
20 Senator Richard J. Durbin to third Hearing of the Subcommittee on Human Rights and the Law, 24 April 2007.
21 Human Rights Watch, 2007.
22 Senator Richard J. Durbin to third Hearing of the Sub-Committee on Human Rights and the Law, 24 April 2007.
23 Senator Tom Coburn to third Hearing of the Sub-Committee on Human Rights and the Law, 24 April 2007.
24 Report: 'US Military Assistance to countries using child soldiers. 1990–2007.' (Centre for Defense (sic) Information.) Compiled by Rhea Myerscough.
25 *Ibid.*
26 Daniel Howden and Steve Bloomfield, 'Historic Trial puts Warlord in Dock over Child Soldiers.' *The Independent* (USA), 30 January 2007.

CHAPTER 12: HOW IS WAR DEPICTED IN CHILDREN'S PICTURE BOOKS,
NOVELS AND TEXTBOOKS?

1 Marcia Brown, 1978.
2 Nist, 1981.
3 The University of Reading offers War Child Studies as a module in both the
   Modern History BA and MA courses. It is also the 'home' of the Research
   Centre for Evacuee and War Child Studies.
4 William Earl Johns (1893–1968). The Captain was a made up rank. He had in
   fact been a Flying Officer which equated with the rank of Lieutenant.
5 'Biggles' first appeared in 1932 in the book *The Camels are Coming* published
   by John Hamilton, and made his last appearance in *Biggles Sees too Much*
   published by Brockhampton Press in 1970.
6 *The Victor* was a British comic published weekly by D.C. Thomson & Co. Ltd.
   It ran for 1,657 issues from 25 January 1961 until 21 November 1992.
7 N. Tucker Chill http://www.sparklesoup.com/gpage.html.
8 New York Museum press preview of *The Day Our World Changed: Childen's
   Art of 9/11*: http://www.aboutourkids.org/news/assets/releases/2002/dowcmc-
   nyseptember02.pdf. Children's Literature the next twenty years: www.
   bookstrusted.co.uk/articles/tucker.pdf.p4.
9 Tony and Steve Lancaster, *The Era of the Second World War.* (Causeway, 1993)
10 Bernard Kops, *The World is a Wedding.* (1963)
11 Erna Paris, *Long Shadows. Truth, Lies and History.* (Bloomsbury, 2000) p.152.
12 *Ibid.* Professor Fujioka, University of Tokyo.
13 Faye Lawson, 'How has children's war literature changed from World War II
   and developed into the present day? To what extent has this shaped our views
   on the war child experience?' *Children in War*, Journal, December 2006.

CHAPTER 13: THE LONG-TERM EFFECTS

1 Peter Heinl, *Splintered Innocence.* (Brunner Routledge, 2001) pp.ix, x.
2 Helga Schneider, *The Bonfire of Berlin.* (Vintage, 2006) p.5.
3 *Ibid.* p.91.
4 'Werner' in Peter Sichrovsky, *Born Guilty.* (New York, 1988) p.147.
5 *Ibid.* p.165.
6 'Anna', *ibid.* p.165.
7 Interview with author. James Roffey is founder and Chief Executive of the
   Evacuees Reunion Association in the UK.
8 James Roffey, *Big Boys Don't Cry.* unpub manuscript. p.164.
9 Interview with Barbara Shawcroft. California, 1992.
10 E. Stokes, *Innocents Abroad.* op.cit. p.197.
11 Michael Fethney, *Absurd and the Brave.* op.cit. p.247.
12 *Ibid.*
13 *Ibid.* p.249.

14 Michael Henderson, 'The evacuation of British children to North America in World War II.' *Children in War.* Vol. 1 No. 3. (2005)

15 James Bacque, *Crimes and Mercies. The fate of German civilians under Allied Occupation 1944-1950.* (Toronto: Little, Brown and Co., 1997) p.288.

16 *Ibid.* p.88.

17 In July 1946, around 400 German children were sent to Ireland for three years to get over the rigours of war, and these were followed by a further 100 in 1948. *Ibid.* p.165.

18 Michael Kater, *Hitler Youth.* (Harvard, 2004) p.261.

19 *Ibid.*

20 Ulla Roberts, 'War and Memory: the long shadows of childhood in Nazi Germany'. Conference Paper, Frankfurt, April 2005.

21 Interesting to note that some UK evacuees had their dolls and teddy bears confiscated because they took up too much room in their luggage.

22 Peter Heinl, op.cit. p.71.

23 Roberts, op.cit.

24 Heinl, op.cit. p.5.

25 *Ibid.* p.85.

26 Roberts, op.cit.

27 Jim Bartley and Martin Parsons, *I'll Take That One.* (Becket Karlson, 1998)

28 Heinl, op.cit. p.53.

29 *Ibid.* p.15.

30 Parsons and Sandelin-Benko. Joint (pilot) research project into the long-term effects of war-child separation. Universities of Reading and Helsinki, 2004.

31 Interview with author. California, 1992.

32 The aims of Operation Barbarossa was the rapid conquest of the European part of the Soviet Union, west of a line connecting the cities of Archangel and Astrakhan. The eventual failure of the Operation Barbarossa was a turning point in the fortunes of the Third Reich.

33 Nina Konovalova. From an Interview by Marina Gulina.

34 Most of those who died were buried in mass graves in different cemeteries, with the majority in the Piskariovskoye Memorial Cemetery.

35 Work presently being carried out by Prof. Marina Gulina.

36 Marina Gulina and Julia Borossa. 'Child Survivors of the Siege of Leningrad: Notes from a study on war trauma and its long term effects on individuals.' *Children in War*, Journal, Dec. 2006. University of Reading.

37 Nina Konovalova. From an Interview by Marina Gulina.

38 *Ibid.*

39 Alan Gill, op.cit. p.29.

40 I show them images of war zones that contain children and ask them for the common factor. This year only four out of eighteen said children.

41 William of Orange who led the Dutch revolt against the Spanish in the sixteenth century.

42 Heinl, op.cit. p.x.

Bibliography

I have divided the bibliography into specific sections for ease of identification. I have also included relevant texts for books relating to children in the Holocaust and a section for those readers who wish to follow up some of the other 'novels' and 'children's' books relating to the topic.

BOOKS

Bacque, James, *Crimes and Mercie*. (Times Warner Paperbacks, 1998)
Beardmore, George, *Civilians at War. Journals. 1938-46*. (OUP)
Beevor, Antony, *Berlin*. (2003)
Calder, Angus, *The Myth of the Blitz*. (Jonathan Cape, 1991)
Cull, Nicholas, *Selling War*. (Oxford, 1995)
Gardiner, Juliet, *Britain at War*. (2004)
Gregory, Adrian, *Silence of Memory. Armistice 1919-1946*.
Haffner, Sebastian, *Defying Hitler. A Memoir*. (Phoenix, 2003)
Harrisson, Tom, *Living Through the Blitz*. (Penguin, 1978)
Hickman, Tom, *What did you do in the war Auntie? The BBC at War*. (BBC, 1995)
Holliday, Laurel, *Children's Wartime Diaries*. (Piatkus, 1995)
Johnson, Derek E., *East Anglia at War. 1939-45*. (Jarrold, 1994)
Kater, Michael H., *Hitler Youth*. (Harvard, 2006)
Knopf, Guido, *Hitler's Children*. (Sutton, 2002)
Lowe, Roy, ed., *Education and the Second World War. Studies on schooling and social change*. (Falmer Press, 1992)
Machel, Graça, *The Impact of War on Children*. (Hurst, 2001)
Marwick, Arthur, *The Home Front*. (Thames and Hudson, 1976)
Marwick, Arthur, *Total War and Social Change*. (Macmillan, 1988)

McKibbin, Ross, *The Ideologies of Class. Social Relations in Britain 1880-1950*. (OUP, 1991)

Morgan, David and Evans, Mary, *The Battle for Britain. Citizenship and Ideology in the Second World War.* (Routledge, 1993)

Mosely, Leonard, *Backs to the Wall*. (Weidenfeld and Nicolson, 1971)

Nicholas, Lynn H., *Cruel World. The Children in the Nazi Web*. (Vintage, 2006)

Nicholas, Sian, *The Echo of War. Home Front Propaganda and the Wartime BBC 1939-45*. (Manchester University Press)

Noakes (ed.), *The German Home Front in World War Two. Vol. 4*. (Exeter University Press, 1998)

Paris, Erna, *Long Shadows. Truth, Lies and History*. (Bloomsbury, 2000)

Pelling, H., *Britain and the Second World War*. (Collins, 1970)

Ponting, Clive, *1940. Myth or Reality*. (Hamish Hamilton, 1990)

Radebold, H., Heuft, G. and Fooken, I., *Kindheiten in Zweiten Weltkreig*. (Juventa, 2006)

Ramsey (ed.), *The Blitz. Then and Now. Vols 1-3*. After the Battle. (1992)

Samuel, Raphael and Thompson, Paul, *The Myths We Live By*. (Routledge, 1993)

Samuel, Raphael, *Theatres of Memory*. (Verso, 1994)

Sichrovsky, Peter, *Born Guilty. Children of Nazi Families*. (Basic, 1988)

Screen, J.E.O., *Mannerheim. The Finnish Years*. (Hurst, 2000)

Smith, Harold L. (ed.), *War and Social Change. British Society in the Second World War*. (Manchester University Press, 1986)

Spranger, Helga, *Der Kreig nach dem Kreig*. (Herstellung und Verlag, 2006)

Stargardt, Nicholas, *Witnesses of War*. (Jonathan Cape, 2005)

Strachey, St. Loe, *Borrowed Children*. (John Murray, 1940)

Titmuss, Richard, *Problems of Social Policy*. (HMSO, 1950)

Stevenson, J., *British Society 1914-45*. (Penguin, 1990)

Waller and Vaughan-Rees *Blitz. The Civilian War. 1940-45*. (Optima, 1990)

Ziegler, Philip, *London at War*. (Sinclair-Stevenson, 1995)

British Evacuation

Crosby, Travis L., *The Impact of Civilian Evacuation in the Second World War*. (Croom Helm, 1986)

Holman, Bob, *Evacuation. A very British Revolution*. (Lion, 1995)

Inglis, Ruth, *The Children's War*. (Fontana, 1986)

Parsons, Martin and Starns, Penny, *Evacuation. The True Story*. (DSM, 1999)

Parsons, Martin L., *I'll Take That One. Dispelling the Myths of Civilian Evacuation 1939-45*. (Beckett and Karlson, 1998)

Parsons, Martin L., *Manchester Evacuation. The Exception to the Rule*. (DSM, 2004)

Parsons, Martin L., *Waiting to go home*. (DSM, 1999)

Wallis, Gillian, *A Welcome in the Hillsides? The Merseyside and North Wales Experience of Evacuation 1939-45*. (Avid Publications, 2000)

Wicks, Ben, *No Time to Wave Goodbye*. (Bloomsbury, 1990)

Overseas Evacuation

Barker, Ralph, *Children of the Benares. A War Crime and its victims.* (Methuen, 1987)
Bilson, Geoffrey, *The Guest Children.* (Fifth House, 1988)
Cave, Patricia, *War Guest. Recollections of being evacuated to Canada in 1940.* (Adept Services Publishing, 1995)
Fethney, Michael, *Absurd and the Brave.* (Book Guild Sussex. Republished, 2003)
Gill, Alan, *Likely Lads and Lasses.* (BBM, 2005)
Gill, Alan, *Orphans of the Empire.* (Vintage, 1998)
Henderson, Michael, *See You After the Duration. The Story of British Evacuees to North America in World War II.* (Britannica, 2004)
Horne, Alistair, *Bundles from Britain.* (Macmillan, 1993)
Humphreys, Margaret, *Empty Cradles.* (Doubleday, 1994)
Schweitzer, Pam (ed.), *Goodnight Children Everywhere.* (Exchange Theatre Trust, 1990)
Spokes Symonds, Ann (ed.), *Havens Across the Sea.* (Mulberry Books, 1990)
Stokes, Edward, *Innocents Abroad. The Story of Child Evacuees in Australia 1940-45.* (Unwin, 1994)
Shakespeare, Sir Geoffrey, *Let Candles Be Brought In.* (MacDonald and Co., 1949)

Others

Heinl, Peter, *Splintered Innocence.* (Brunner Routledge, 2001)
Freud, Anna and Burlingham, Dorothy T., *War and Children.* (Medical War Books, 1942)

The Aftermath

Anonymous, *A Woman in Berlin.* (Virago, 2004)
Bader Whiteman, D., *The Uprooted: A Hitler Legacy* (Insight Books: New York, 1993)
Bar-On, D., *Fear and Hope: Three Generations of the Holocaust.* (Harvard University Press: London, 1995)
Bar-On, D., *The Indescribable and the Undiscussable: Reconstructing the Human Discourse after Trauma.* (Central University Press: Budapest, 1999)
Bar-On, D. (ed.), *Bridging the Gap: Storytelling as a way to work through Political and Collective Hostilities* (Köber Stiftung: Hamburg, 2000)
Beaglehole, A., *Facing the Past: Looking Back at Refugee Childhood in New Zealand.* (Allen and Unwin: Wellington, NZ, 1990)
Beaglehole, A. with Levin, H., *Far from the Promised Land: Being Jewish in NZ.* (Pacific Press: Wellington, NZ, 1995)
Beaglehole, A., *Replacement Girl.* (Tandem Press: Auckland, NZ, 2002)
Beevor, Antony and Cooper, Artemis, *Paris. After the Liberation: 1944–1949.* (Penguin, 1994)
Beller, S., *Vienna and the Jews: A Cultural History 1867–1938.* (Cambridge University Press: Cambridge, 1989)

Beradt, C., *The Third Reich of Dreams: The Nightmares of a Nation: 1933–1939.* (The Aquarian Press, 1985)

Bohm-Duchen, M. (ed.), *After Auschwitz: Responses to the Holocaust in Contemporary Art.* (London: Lund Humphries Publishers Ltd, 1995. in association with Northern Centre for Contemporary Art, Sunderland)

Brett, L., *Too Many Men.* (2002)

Dalal, F., *Taking the Group Seriously.* (Jessica Kingsley: London, 1998)

Epstein, H., *Children of the Holocaust: Conversations with the Sons and Daughters of Survivors.* (Penguin: New York, 1979)

Epstein, H., *Where She Came From: A Daughter's Search for her Mother's History.* (Plume Book by Penguin: New York, 1998)

Ericsson, K., and Simonsen, E., *Children of World War II. The hidden enemy legacy.* (2005)

Etherington, K., *Trauma, The Body and Transformation: A Narrative Inquiry.* (Jessica Kingsley: London, 2003)

Grinblat, K. (ed.), *Children of the Shadows: Voices of the Second Generation.* (University of Western Australia Press: Montrose, 2002)

Haffner, S., *Defying Hitler.* (Phoenix: London, 2003)

Translated from the German, *Geschichte eines Deutschen* or 'History of a German'.

Hirsch, R., *Last Dance at the Kempinski: Creating a Life in the Shadow of History.* (University Press of New England: Hanover NH, USA, 1995)

Judt, Tony, *Postwar. A history of Europe since 1945.* (Pimlico, 2007)

REPRESENTATION OF WAR IN CHILDREN'S LITERATURE, MEDIA AND DRAMA

Indicative Reading:

Picture Books

Foreman, Michael and Borden, Louise, *The Little Ships.* [Dunkirk]
Foreman, Michael. *After the War was Over.* [Second World War]
Foreman, Michael, *War and Peas.* [War in general]
Foreman, Michael, *War Boy.* [Second World War]
Foreman, Michael, *War Game.* [First World War]
Hughes, Shirley, *The Lion and the Unicorn.* [Evacuation]
McKee, David, *The Conquerors.* [War in general]
Morimoto, Junko, *My Hiroshima.* [Second World War, Hiroshima]

Novels

Ashley, Bernard, *Little Soldier.* [Child soldiers in Africa]
Bawden, Nina, *Carrie's War.* [Evacuation]

Bawden, Nina, *Keeping Henry.* [Evacuation]
Crompton, Richmal, *William and the Evacuees.* [Evacuation]
Davies, Andrew, *Conrad's War.* [Second World War]
Holm, Anne, *I Am David.* [Holocaust]
Kerr, Judith, *When Hitler Stole Pink Rabbit.* [Second World War]
Laird, Elizabeth, *A Little Piece of Ground.* [Palestine]
Laird, Elizabeth, *Kiss the Dust.* [Kurdistan/Iraq]
Magorian, Michelle, *Back Home.* [Return from Evacuation Overseas]
Magorian, Michelle, *Goodnight Mr Tom.* [Evacuation]
Morpurgo, Michael, *Friend or Foe.* [Evacuation]
Morpurgo, Michael, *Private Peaceful.* [First World War]
Morpurgo, Michael, *Waiting for Anya.* [Second World War, France]
Morpurgo, Michael, *War Horse.* [First World War]
Naidoo, Beverley, *The Other Side of Truth.* [Nigeria]
O'Brien, Robert, *Z for Zachariah.* [Nuclear war]
Serraillier, Ian, *The Silver Sword.* [Refugees in Second World War]
Streatfeild, Noel, *When the Siren Wailed.* [Evacuation]
Swindells, Robert, *Brother in the Land.* [Nuclear war]
Westall, Robert, *Blitzcat.* [Second World War]
Westall, Robert, *Fathom Five.* [Second World War]
Westall, Robert, *Gulf.* [Gulf War]
Westall, Robert, *The Kingdom by the Sea.* [Second World War]
Westall, Robert, *The Machine Gunners.* [Second World War]

Poetry

Grant, Reg (ed.), *History through Poetry: World War Two.*
Harrison, Michael and Stuart-Clark, Christopher (eds), *Peace and War.* [War in general]
Harvey, Anne (ed.), *In Time of War.* [First and Second World War]
Hudson, Edward (ed.), *Poetry of the Second World War.*

Anthologies

Fox, Carol et al (eds), *In Times of War: An Anthology of War and Peace in Children's Literature.* [International perspectives on First and Second World War and more recent conflicts]
Hoffman, Mary and Lassiter, Rhiannon (eds), *Lines in the Sand: New Writing on War and Peace.* [Iraq]

Criticism

Agnew, Kate and Fox, Geoff, *Children at War: from the First World War to the Gulf.* (London: Continuum, 2001)

Fox, Carol et al, *War and Peace in Children's Books*. (Brighton: University of Brighton, 2000)

The Media

Batho, R. et.al, (n.d.) *War and Peace in Children's Books*.
Brians, Paul, *Nuclear Holocausts: Atomic War in Fiction 1895-1984*. (1987)
Chapman, James, *The British at War. Cinema, State & Propaganda, 1939-1945*. (I.B. Taurus, 2000)
Ellis, John, *Visible Fictions*. (1988)
Evans, Alun, *Brassey's Guide to War Films*. (2000)
Flynn, Simon R.D., 'Those Billets: constructions of evacuation and evacuees in the BBC radio programme. Children's Hour.' (*Children in War*, Journal, 2004)
Fox, Carol et al, *War and Peace in Children's Books*. (2000)
Grevatt, Wallace, *Children's Hour. A Celebration of Those Magical Years*. (BBC, 1988)
Hartley, Ian, *Goodnight Children … Everywhere*. (1983)
James, A., Jenks, C. and Prout, Alan, *Theorizing Childhood*. (1998)
Jenks, Chris, *Childhood*. (1996)
Lipschutz, Ronnie D., *Cold War Fantasies*. (2001)
Marten, James Alan (ed.), *Children and War*. (New York University, 2002)
Messenger Davies, Maire, *Do mention the war: Children and media coverage of traumatic events*. (Media War)
Murphy, *Realism and Tinsel. Cinema and Society in Britain 1939-46*. (Robert, 1992)
Nicholas, Sian, *The Echo of War. Home Front Propaganda and the Wartime BBC 1939-45*. (1996)
Rattigan, Neil, *This is England. British Film and the People's War 1939-45*.
Rook, Robert E., *Dr Spock Meets Dr Strangelove: Children During the Cold War*. (*Children in War*, Journal, 2004)
Short, K.R.M. (ed.), *Film and Radio Propaganda in World War II*. (1983)
Stewart, Ian (ed.), *War, Culture and the Media: Representations of the Military in 20th Century Britain*. (1996)
Staples, Terry, *All Pals Together. The Story of Children's Cinema*. (1997)
Trout, Steven, *The Jungle Seem[ed] for a Moment like the Home Countie*. (2004)
Trout, Steven, *Revisiting William Golding's Lord of the Flies*. (*Children in War*, Journal)
Virilio, Paul, *War and Cinema. The Logistics of Perception*. (1989)

Films

Archive/Propaganda
Westward Ho! (Ministry of Information, 1940)★
Living with Strangers. (Ministry of Information, 1941)★
The Village School. (Ministry of Information, 1941)★
★All on a DVD entitled *Keep the Wheels Turning*. Imperial War Museum.
Spring Offensive (1942)

Feature

Empire of the Sun. (Steven Spielberg, USA, 1987)
Grave of Fireflies. (Isao Takahata, Japan, 1987)
Hope and Glory. (John Boorman, GB, 1987)
Äideistä Paryain (*Mother of Mine*) (Klaus Haron Elokvva, Finland, 2005)

Television

Carrie's War. (BBC)
Constructions of the Child in News & Drama.
Goodnight Mister Tom. (BBC)
Into the Arms of Strangers. (BBC)
The Lost Decade. (BBC)

Appendix 1

Total US Financial Aid to countries using child soldiers. 1990–2007. In US Dollars.

COUNTRY	IMET	FMF	DCS	FMS	EDA
BURMA	0	0	0	0	0
BURUNDI	1,442,000	315,000	397,000	65,000	0
CHAD	4,272,000	6,851,000	342,000	27,901,000	0
COLOMBIA	25,134,000	680,284,000	630,004,000	1,781,019,000	57,216,264
CÔTE D'IVOIRE	1,833,000	4,517,000	570,000	2,040,000	0
CONGO	1,995,000	3,736,000	44,000	12,702,000	0
NEPAL	6,298,000	25,322,000	2,073,000	20,116,000	962,648
PHILIPPINES	37,492,000	572,627,000	90,219,000	1,194,571,000	77,778,447
RWANDA	3,742,000	1,579,000	1,677,000	579,000	252,980
SOMALIA	0	0	0	16,666,000	0
SRI LANKA	5,689,000	5,731,000	21,170,000	63,832,000	46,374,800
SUDAN	400,000	100,000	89,000	0	0
UGANDA	4,363,000	14,694,000	20,197,000	8,510,000	0

IMET   International Military Education and Training
FMF   Foreign Military Financing
DCS   Direct Commercial Sales
FMS   Foreign Military Sales
EDA   Excess Defense Articles

Appendix 2

British Evacuation Scheme.

The following document was found in the Northampton Record Office and relates to a previously unknown plan to compulsorily evacuate people from the town in the event of an invasion. It is undated, but from the content one can assume that is was distributed in June 1940.

COMPULSORY EVACUATION. PLAN B.

NOTICE TO HOUSEHOLDERS.

The Government has already drawn attention to the danger of invasion and advised all who can to leave the town now. There are still many here who could have gone, in particular there are still a number of school children for whom billets have been offered under the Evacuation Scheme.

It is by no means certain that, if invasion takes place, it will be possible to operate the plans which have been made for compulsory evacuation; but the Government have determined that in these plans the first place shall be given to the children. Arrangements will therefore be made which will enable the Government, if military operations permit, to order the compulsory evacuation of children between the ages of five and fourteen years in advance of the evacuation of other persons who are not required to remain to defend the town.

For this purpose, all children between those ages now in the town must be registered. Mothers of school children, children under five with their mothers or other women undertaking to look after them, and school children over fourteen years of age, will be allowed to go with the children if they are registered at the same time.

Children between five and fourteen must be registered during the week ending 28th June at the nearest school or registration centre shown on the posters which will be exhibited at schools and elsewhere in the town. At the end of the week, the registers will be closed and will not be reopened.

It will be an offence under the Defence Regulations:-

To fail to register a child between five and fourteen years of age who is in the town when registration begins; or

Bring a child between those ages into the town after registration has begun without informing the local authorities; or

To retain a child between these ages in the town after their evacuation has been ordered.

A person convicted of an offence under the Defence Regulations is liable to a fine or imprisonment or both.

Mothers who wish to go with their children should register themselves and any of their children who are under five at the same place as their school children. Other children under five should be registered at the nearest registration centre with their mothers or other women who will look after them: and school children over fourteen may also be registered. No mothers of children under five or over fourteen will be registered who are not in the town when registration starts.

After the evacuation of children has been carried out, the Government might find it necessary to order the evacuation of all other persons who are not required to remain. Evacuation would then be very difficult and anyone who can make private arrangements to move in advance should do so.

Appendix 3

ED/10/236. List of Camp School Sites as at the 26th of June 1939 (sub file number G672/3)

County	Evacuated Area	Site
	LONDON (15)	
Bedfordshire		Heath and Reach
Berkshire		Cockpole Green
Buckinghamshire		Horsleys Green
		Penley Hollies, nr Stokenchurch
		Moor End
		Finnamore Wood
Hertfordshire		Nettleden
Oxfordshire		Kennylands
		Bishopswood Farm, Peppard
		Uxmore Farm, nr Henley
Surrey		Merstham
		Tilford
		Sayers Croft, Ewhurst
		Elmbridge, Cranleigh

Sussex		Coopers Farm, Itchingfield
		Wren Warren, Hartfield
	BIRMINGHAM (3)	
Staffordshire		Pipe Wood, Rugeley
		Shooting Butts, nr Rugeley
Worcestershire		Warton's Park Estate, Bewdley
	MANCHESTER AND LIVERPOOL (6)	
Cheshire		Somerford Hall
		Marton Newchurch.
Denbighshire		Colomendy Hall (1)
		Ditto (2)
Lancashire		Moreton Hall, Whalley
	LEEDS & BRADFORD (3)	
Yorkshire. W.R.		Pateley Bridge
		Linton
		Grassington
	NEWCASTLE (2)	
Northumberland		Dukeshouse Wood, Hexham
		Bellingham
	SHEFFIELD (1)	
Derbyshire		Woolley Bridge or Kelstedge
	HULL (1)	
Yorkshire. E.R		Etton
	PORTSMOUTH (1)	
Hampshire		Laverstock. Wisewell

Index

Also by Tempus:

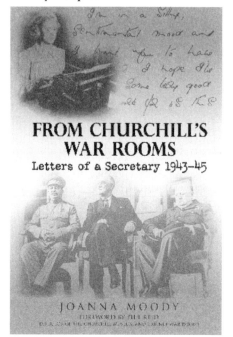

From Churchill's War Rooms
Letters of a Secretary 1943-45
Joanna Moody

978 07524 4074 3

The period 1943–45 saw some of the most important events of the Second World War, and few were fully aware of the decisions that were to affect the outcome of a global conflict.

Yet a young wartime secretary, Olive Christopher, spent this remarkable time working in Churchill's famous Cabinet War Rooms, where she was one of a small inner circle, party to the political secrets of those crucial final years. Working for long hours in an underground bunker opposite St James's Park, Olive wrote a series of letters to her fiancé, a major in the armed forces and posted abroad. Filled with incredible details about the glamorous lifestyle and travel Olive enjoyed because of the seriousness of her job, these letters form an astonishing record of how an ordinary girl could become privy to the most secret aspects of the Second World War.

Published for the first time, this illuminating and poignant correspondence offers a rare insight into the workings of the Cabinet War Rooms towards the end of the Second World War, and documents the rich wartime experiences of a woman with exclusive access to the closed world of Churchill's inner circle.

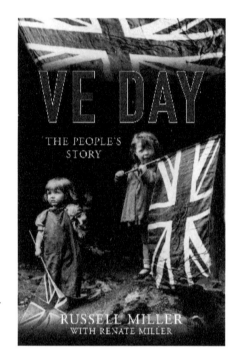

VE Day
The People's Story
Russell Miller with Renate Miller

978 07524 4312 6

This inspiring book draws from first-hand interviews, diaries and memoirs of those involved in the VE Day celebrations in 1945. It paints an enthralling picture of a day that marked the end of the war in Europe and the beginning of a new era.

VE Day affected millions of people in countless ways. This books records a sample of those views, from both Britain and abroad, from civilians and service men and women, from the famous and not-so-famous, in order to provide a moving story and a valuable social picture of the times. Mixed with humour as well as tragedy, rejoicing as well as sadness, regrets of the past and hopes for the future, *VE Day: The People's Story* is an inspiring record of one of the great turning points in history.

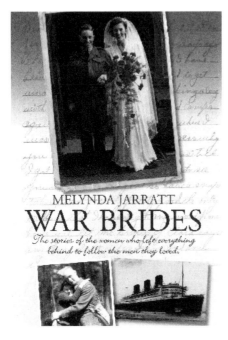

War Brides
Melynda Jarratt

978 07524 4309 6

'Overpaid, over-sexed and over here' was the verdict of many British civilians on American and Canadian soldiers serving in Britain in the Second World War. Yet for thousands of young girls, the influx of handsome military men meant flirting – and falling in love. The result was over 48,000 marriages to Canadian soldiers alone, and a mass emigration of British women to northern America and across the globe in the 1940s.

Historian Melynda Jarratt has painstakingly captured the incredible stories of young women – some say brave, some say foolish – who left their families and homes to move to a country thousands of miles away with a man they barely knew. Yet the ensuing decades brought happiness to many, and surviving women share their tales of love, family and starting again.

For some brides, the outcome was a very different story, and the darker side of the crossings reveals astonishing accounts of infidelity, domestic violence, poverty, alcoholism and divorce. This incredible new history draws on original archival documents, personal correspondence, and key first-hand accounts to tell the amazing story of the War Brides in their own words – and shows the love, passion, tragedy and spirit of adventure that thousands of British women experienced in a turbulent time.

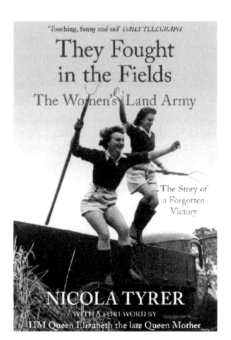

'Touching, funny and sad' *DAILY TELEGRAPH*

They Fought in the Fields

The Women's Land Army

The Story of a Forgotten Victory

NICOLA TYRER

WITH A FOREWORD BY
HM Queen Elizabeth the late Queen Mother

The Fought in the Fields
The Women's Land Army
Nicola Tyrer

978 07524 4313 3

The Women's Land Army was the forgotten triumph of the Second World War. While troops fought on the front line, a battalion of young women joined up to take their place as agricultural workers. Despite the urban backgrounds of many of the recruits, they learnt how to tend the land, repair machinery, rear farm animals and much more. These fearless girls formed a vital workforce, without which the nation would have starved. No farm job was too hard, too dangerous or too unpleasant. Back-breaking hoeing and thinning, thatching hay ricks, managing angry bulls and rat-killing – they did it all.

Hard-working they undoubtedly were, and often ruthlessly exploited by unscrupulous employers, but these were girls imbued with the optimism and energy of youth. Over the course of the war land girls built themselves a reputation for exuberance and sociability, happy to walk 9 miles to a dance after a hard day in the fields. At the outset their efforts had met with hostility and derision from the ultra-conservative farming community, unused to the presence of women on the land – many were unmercifully teased. But these dogged and cheerful women won the hearts of the nation and when the Land Army was finally disbanded in 1950, the biggest howl of protest came from the farmers.

With delightful photographs documenting the camaraderie of the Land Army and the real-life memories of those who joined, this nostalgic look at one of the real success stories of the Second World War will make modern women proud of what their grandmothers achieved in an era before our own.

If you are interested in purchasing other books published by Tempus,
or in case you have difficulty finding any Tempus books in your local bookshop,
you can also place orders directly through our website

www.tempus-publishing.com